ROMMEL'S NORTH AFRICA CAMPAIGN

German 88mm gun in anti-aircraft configuration. British inability to recognize its potential as an anti-tank weapon was typical of failures of intelligence and imagination in the early Desert War.

GREAT CAMPAIGNS SERIES

GREAT CAMPAIGNS

ROMMEL'S NORTH AFRICA CAMPAIGN

September 1940- November 1942

Jack Greene
Alessandro Massignani

COMBINED BOOKS
Pennsylvania

PUBLISHER'S NOTE

Combined Books, Inc., is dedicated to publishing books of distinction in history and military history. We are proud of the quality of writing and the quantity of information found in our books. Our books are manufactured with style and durability and are printed on acid-free paper. We like to think of our books as soldiers: not infantry grunts, but well dressed and well equipped avant garde. Our logo reflects our commitment to the modern and yet historic art of bookmaking.

We call ourselves Combined Books because we view the publishing enterprise as a "combined" effort of authors, publishers and readers. And we promise to bridge the gap between us—a gap which is all too seldom closed in contemporary publishing.

We would like to hear from our readers and invite you to write to us at our offices in Pennsylvania with your reactions, queries, comments, even complaints. All of your correspondence will be answered directly by a member of the Editorial Board or by the author.

We encourage all of our readers to purchase our books from their local booksellers, and we hope that you let us know of booksellers in your area that might be interested in carrying our books. If you are unable to find a book in your area, please write to us.

For information, address: COMBINED BOOKS, INC.
151 East 10th Avenue
Conshohocken, PA 19428

Copyright© 1994 by Jack Greene and Alessandro Massignani
Maps by Beth Queman

Library of Congress Cataloging-in-Publication Data
Greene, Jack.
  Rommel's North Africa campaign: September 1940-November 1942 /
Jack Greene, Alessandro Massignani. — Combined Books ed.
    p.   cm. — (Great Campaigns)
  Includes bibliographical references and index.
  ISBN 0-938289-34-9
    1. Rommel, Erwin, 1891-1944. 2. World War, 1939-1945—Campaigns—
Africa, North. I. Massignani, Alessandro. II. Title. III. Series.
  D766.82.G67 1994
  940.54'23—dc20   94-10346
                                                                  CIP

Combined Books Edition   1 2 3 4 5

First published in the USA in 1994 by Combined Books, Inc. and distributed in North America by Stackpole Books, Inc., 5067 Ritter Road, Mechanicsburg, PA 17055

Printed in the United States of America

Contents

Maps

Sidebars

Preface to the Series

*J*onathan Swift termed war "that mad game the world so loves to play." He had a point. Universally condemned, it has nevertheless been almost as universally practiced. For good or ill, war has played a significant role in the shaping of history. Indeed, there is hardly a human institution which has not in some fashion been influenced and molded by war, even as it helped shape and mold war in turn. Yet the study of war has been as remarkably neglected as its practice commonplace. With a few outstanding exceptions, the history of wars and of military operations has until quite recently been largely the province of the inspired patriot or the regimental polemist. Only in our times have serious, detailed and objective accounts come to be considered the norm in the treatment of military history and related matters.

Yet there still remains a gap in the literature, for there are two types of military history. One type is written from a very serious, highly technical, professional perspective and presupposes that the reader is deeply familiar with the background, technology and general situation. The other is perhaps less dry, but merely lightly reviews the events with the intention of informing and entertaining the layperson. The qualitative gap between the last two is vast. Moreover, there are professionals in both the military and academia whose credentials are limited to particular moments in the long, sad history of war, and there are interested readers who have more than a passing understanding of the field; and then there is the concerned citizen, interested in

7

understanding the military phenomena in an age of unusual violence and unprecedented armaments. It is to bridge the gap between the two types of military history, and to reach the professional and the serious amateur and the concerned citizen alike, that this series, GREAT CAMPAIGNS, is designed. Each volume in GREAT CAMPAIGNS is thus not merely an account of a particular military operation, but is a unique reference to the theory and practice of war in the period in question.

The GREAT CAMPAIGNS series is a distinctive contribution to the study of war and of military history, which will remain of value for many years to come.

"To the Fallen"

We had two goals in writing this work. Our primary goal was to offer a general narrative of the warfare in the Western Desert of North Africa and to analyze the decisive elements of the 1941-42 campaign and the impact of General Rommel. We wanted to present the campaign in a fresh new light, not as a simple rehash of an oft told story. We have illustrated our narrative with stories from eyewitnesses to the fighting in North Africa that both entertain and clarify what happened. These eyewitness accounts come from participants on both sides of the conflict. We have been fortunate to interview many veterans of the campaign and their contribution greatly enhances our work. Although the North Africa campaign is a subject in need of a multi-volume effort, we have focused on the key events and aspects that help to clarify what occurred, especially where they might have been recorded incorrectly in older works.

And that is the second key to this volume. Very few histories have made use of Italian source material. English and German sources seldom consult Italian works (though the Italian histories usually include English and German source material). This shortchanges Italy's war effort. For example, the successful use by Italy of German built 88mm anti-tank (AT) guns and Italian built 90mm AT guns is virtually unknown in English language histories of the war, nor is their vital role at the battle of Gazala recognized. We have carefully examined the Italian sources in light of the more readily available English and German resources, and while they do not always agree, we have tried to give a balanced account that reflects modern research.

We considered the nomenclature "Italo-German," which is after the Italian fashion and reflects the largest Axis contributor to the war in North Africa, before adopting the use of "Axis" in the text. This is why we refer to the "Commonwealth" as opposed to "British" troops, as it was a contribution by *all* the Allies, led by the United Kingdom, that ultimately brought about the Allied victory in Africa.

Dr. Richard Blanco read much of the manuscript and offered helpful and beneficial comments in maintaining our "forward progress." We would also like to thank Professors Lucio Ceva and Andrea Curami, Antonio Sema, Dr. James J. Sadkovich, Vance von Borries, Dr. Brian R. Sullivan, Harry Rowland, Richard Carczynski, and Herr Walter Spitaler, Dr. Klaus Hubbuch (a former DAK NCO), Herr Otto Heidrick, Rosa Queman and Bill Hoggard. Beth Queman worked on the maps and also read the text, both of which were a great aid. David Isby made valuable suggestions at several stages in the development of the project. Portions of this book first appeared in several articles in *COMMAND* Magazine, and are used with the kind permission of the publishers. As always, we take full responsibility for any errors.

NOTES ON THE TEXT: the British called their tank units "armoured divisions" and we have adopted the term "armored division." "Laager" originated as a South African term for a defensive night camp and was changed by the British to "leaguer." We use the former.

—Jack Greene, Baywood Park, California
—Alessandro Massignani, Valdagno, Vicenza

CHAPTER 1

Italy's Parallel War

*Italy belongs to the second category of states [semi-independent].
It is bathed by a landlocked sea that communicates with the
oceans through the Suez Canal, an artificial link easily blocked
even by improvised means, and through the straits of Gibraltar,
dominated by the cannons of Great Britain.... The bars of this
prison are Corsica, Tunis, Malta, Cyprus; the sentinels of this
prison are Gibraltar and Suez....Italian policy can have only one
watchword—to march to the ocean. Which ocean? To the Indian
Ocean, joining Libya with Ethiopia through the Sudan or the Atlantic, through French North Africa...in either the first or the second hypotheses we shall meet Franco-British opposition.*
    —Benito Mussolini

The first thing to understand about World War II in North
Africa is that this was primarily Italy's war.

Mussolini inspired Italy with a Mediterranean mission which
echoed back to the days of the Roman Empire. Italy was to fight
a parallel war, a struggle in which Italy would gain her place as
a world empire, alongside and parallel with Germany's European war. Yet it was in the opening moments of this parallel war
that Italy's war machine would be derailed with a series of
disasters from which she would never fully recover. Italy's entry
into the war is often misunderstood. With the outbreak of war in
September of 1939, Benito Mussolini, *Il Duce* of Italy, desired to
honor the Pact of Steel formed with Hitler's Germany, but Italy
was unprepared to fight at that time. Mussolini had told Hitler
that his nation would not be ready for war until the early part of

1943, as by then her navy would have additional new ships, her army would be well on the way to being re-equipped, and her air force would have many new warplanes. Mussolini mistakenly thought he could first fight France in a separate war, and then dispose of Great Britain in alliance with Hitler in the mid to late 1940s, after thoroughly modernizing Italy's military. Italy expended large sums of money on armament programs in the 1935-39 years, but it was poorly spent in many ways, and much of what was produced went to the Navy and the Air Force, then for the Ethiopian War, and later to aid General Franco and the Nationalists in the Spanish Civil War. In all of this, the Italian army was at the end of the line. When in 1940 Mussolini did bring Italy into World War II, he felt that it would be a short war.

Italians were not prepared for a long struggle. There was a lack of the typical wartime propaganda about "Total War" and the need for national sacrifice. As German Field Marshal Albert Kesselring remarked, "There was insufficient propaganda for the war and its aims."

Nor was Mussolini blind to his army's weakness. A major artillery re-equipment program had begun, and the creation of a mechanized and motorized Army of the Po had occurred, which operated under the doctrine of the *Guerra di Rapido Corso*, or War of Rapid Course, which was to a degree similar in concept to the *Blitzkrieg* doctrine developed by the German military. The Italian concept foresaw quick movement by infantry troops in trucks, who would dismount and exploit any successful breech in the enemy line. But this Army of the Po depended on trucks and the L3 "tank" (a tiny two man tankette armed only with machine guns), and not upon tracked vehicles and the powerfully gunned and armored tanks for the desert which would be vital for victory. A German observer of the embryonic, muddled, and mismanaged Italian 1939 maneuvers had said that the Italian Army of the Po's *Guerra di Rapido Corso* was in "children's shoes." Mussolini still felt that even with this weak army, Italy could not stand idle while Germany, Italy's brother in arms, fought the Allies and reaped the laurels of victory.

There were several fundamental problems that would be detrimental to Italy's campaign in North Africa in 1940. First, the military thought that chemical warfare would be conducted.

L3 tank in Italy (Luigi Castaman)

Italy had successfully used these weapons in Ethiopia, had considered using them in the Spanish Civil War, and the military thought the use of the weapons would make up, in part, for Italy's other military deficiencies, but chemical warfare was never employed. Secondly, the war in Africa was viewed as a colonial war—and this was interpreted by many in Europe, as well as in Italy, as a type of warfare different and secondary from the typical European version of war. As a result of this thinking, colonial military experiences were glossed over, and little modern military equipment was shipped to a secondary theater such as Africa. Additionally, Italian strategic doctrine foresaw the importance of war in the Alps, which made up most of Italy's continental borders. Thus the rapid fall of France would leave Italy with an idle but well trained and large Alpine mountain army which would be of little use in North Africa, though later of value in Greece and Yugoslavia.

Additionally, Italy's best equipment, especially armor, was inferior. Her most numerous main tank, the L3 (L = Light), was obsolete by 1940, nor had it been replaced in any sizable numbers by Italy's newer and larger, but still inferior, medium tanks. Italian medium tanks used rivets and not welding, tended to break down frequently, and initially went to Africa without radios. Always underpowered, the M13 series was armed with a 47mm gun (which was roughly equivalent to the British 2-pounder AT gun) and would be Italy's main AT gun for the entire war.

Part of this tank situation was due to lack of money, and also due to a monopoly on tank manufacturing by the giant industrial manufacturers, Fiat and Ansaldo, which perpetuated industrial inefficiencies and outright corruption. Interestingly enough, Marshal Ugo Cavallero, who was head of *Comando Supremo* (Italian Supreme Command) from December 1940 to February 1943, had been president of Ansaldo. He had been forced to resign in 1933 when Ansaldo tried to deliver repaired armor plates, defective collectors for boilers, and faulty naval guns for four warships under construction. Cavallero may have been unaware of this subterfuge, but his reputation was stained from that episode on. Cavallero was a physically unimposing man, but was thought to possess both "military capacity" and a "dynamic personality."

Italy's officer corps had many problems. Headed by an Alpine oriented and conservative Marshal Pietro Badoglio, victor in Ethiopia, Italy had a rigid seniority system for her officers. This rigid seniority system did not allow for the rapid promotion of deserving officers, and tended to retain poor officers in high command. In addition when a high officer failed in the field, he was given a new assignment instead of being retired or cashiered and was often sent to another theater. Witness General Italo Gariboldi, who simply exchanged command in Africa for Russia when he fell out with General Erwin Rommel in 1941. While many of Italy's technically educated officers joined the motorized units or the artillery (which throughout the war distinguished itself with a largely World War I collection of weapons), the rest of her army suffered because most officers were poorly educated, and did not "rub elbows" with the troops. The officers ate separately (and better if in the rear, though usually not better at the front), worked apart from their men, and were elderly at the highest level. Severe budget cuts had occurred in the officer corps in the 1920's which limited the overall number of officers, especially at the captain/major level. Thus, in wartime, the officer corps was forced to rely on the reserve officer who was, as a rule, very uneducated.

This deficiency might have been alleviated by a competent NCO class, but instead, there were insufficient NCO's and many were from the southern portion of Italy where the population was less healthy and poorly educated. Finally, for financial reasons, Italy was notorious in the 1920's and 1930's for inadequate military training and this failure would affect the conduct of her war.

Nor was the Italian enlisted man the finest in Europe. Unbelievable as it sounds, approximately 50% of the incoming troopers from the peasant stock in 1940 did not know their left from their right, and part of their initial training involved learning the difference! When compared to, say, an Australian recruit who often came from the country and was a good shot with a large rifle, one can appreciate Italy's military deficiencies. The Italian trooper would be given leave out of Africa once every 30 months, while the German soldier could count on going home every 12 months. The Commonwealth Tommy was regularly given leave to Cairo or his unit was moved to a quiet station. This would affect his morale and capability as the war drew on.

Finally, Mussolini was not as powerful as his fellow dictator. *Il Duce* was really one of two heads of state. The King of Italy, Victor Emmanuel III, still viewed himself as Warlord of Italy, and the Italian army was very loyal to the Royal House, hence the *Regia Esercito*, or Royal Army. Fascism, though longer in power than Nazism, had not transformed Italian society as the Nazis had done. More importantly, *Il Duce* erroneously saw himself as a great and capable warlord. While one can argue about the competency of Churchill or Hitler, there is little to praise about Mussolini's ability—he was a military failure.

Libyan horse drawn artillery in action, employing the 75/27 (Ufficio Storico).

The Libyan and Egyptian Stage

From the harsh experience of these bitter days we must conclude that in this theater of war a single armored division is more powerful than a whole army.

—Marshal Rudolfo Graziani

There were two Italian colonies in Libya: Cyrenaica in the east and Tripolitania in the west. The geography of both is quite alike and a similar terrain is stamped on Egypt. There is a thin coastal strip that rises up from the ocean. There are mountains between Derna and Benghazi in Cyrenaica, and mountains behind Tripoli. Beyond that is the plateau of the Sahara desert. From April to June there are ghiblis, or hot desert winds. Temperatures get as high as 138 degrees Fahrenheit in the high summer. It does get cold in the winter, and rains can be sudden and heavy from October to April.

The population of Libya was about 800,000 native people and 110,000 Italians. Many of the latter had emigrated to Libya in 1938 and 1939 in an orchestrated mass resettlement. (Ironically the last of the Italians would be forced to leave in 1970 by Omar Khadafi.) Tripoli was by far the largest city, with Benghazi the second. The majority of the people lived on 3% of the land. The hinterland was strictly for the Senussi tribes, desert explorers, and small military bases often linked only by aircraft or motor transport. The Italians did maintain a small camel corps, as did the Egyptian army. On the frontier with Egypt was "the Wire," a series of three barbed wire fences, which stretched for miles and had been built by Marshal Rudolfo Graziani in 1931-32 during the Senussi War. The Wire had been built to cut off communications of the Senussi tribesmen in Libya, led by the legendary Omar El Mukhtar, with their brethren in Egypt during their revolt against Italian colonial rule. Most of the fighting would take place between El Mechili in the desert southeast of Benghazi and the Egyptian border.

The most significant feature of this battlefield was that troops, equipment, supplies, and water had to be brought vast distances to where they were to be used. Going hand in hand with this was the absence of land features, which often necessitated celestial navigation for military movements. Most of the battlefield was hard, flat, covered with gravel, and with little vegetation. In some areas there were low spots, wadis (ravines or gullies which would be filled with torrents of water in sudden cloudbursts and become totally impassible), and cliffs and more wadis where the escarpment loomed up and the land dropped down to the ocean. This escarpment feature would channel much of the action, in places limiting north-south motorized movement. The terrain was pierced at a few points, but it made a vital feature of Halfaya Pass (also called Hellfire), a choke point for motor transport. Sand in the deep Sahara or in small coastal patches acts as an obstacle, especially for wheeled, as opposed to tracked, vehicles. Virtually all of the Italian trucks were two-wheel drive, a further limitation for off-road capability. Running the length of Libya was the recently completed asphalted Via Balbia, named for an ancient Roman governor. The road was paved in Egypt until it reached Sidi El Barrani, but would be paved to the Libyan border in 1940 when Italy advanced to Sidi El Barrani. Two-wheel vehicles could be driven in the non-sand areas, but they caused clouds of dust which would invariably attract the attention of the enemy. As the war progressed, formation driving of vehicles became common. Vehicles would be driven both abreast and in columns, hundreds of feet apart. This reduced the

Italian 75/27 1911 in the towed version in action (Ufficio Storico).

Austrian 100/17 howitzer, captured piece much employed by the Italians in World War II (Alessandro Massignani).

dust and also confused the enemy as to strength. Finally, it has been said that the desert was a tactician's paradise, and a quartermaster's hell.

In setting the stage for the later arrival of the Germans, it is useful to look at what the Italians fielded. The paper strength of an Italian metropolitan infantry division was two regiments of three battalions each of infantry, a machine gun battalion, and three battalions of artillery with a total of twenty-four 75/27mm field guns and twelve 100/17mm howitzers. A total of 11,000 men were in a division, with about 400 trucks and tractors, though after 1941 most infantry divisions usually numbered about 7,000 men in the field. With the exception of the German mountain division, Italy was the only great power to field a two-regiment division. This formation grew out of war experiences with Ethiopia, where a pair of two-regiment divisions operated successfully, moving quickly on that theater's poor road net, while deploying full divisional level artillery. Such a unit could have advantages in the rough terrain of Italy's mountainous European borders. The concept of this so-called "binary" division was that one division would fix an enemy division in place, allowing a second binary division to hit the fixed enemy unit in the flank. Part of the weakness of this organization was that the Italian infantry division in North Africa was never at full strength.

First inspections of the Italian troops in Libya revealed shortcomings involving "slovenly uniforms, mess halls, latrines, to inadequate medical supervision of local prostitutes." The poor training of the Italian troops in 1940 was such that Marshal Italo Balbo, Libyan commander at the start of the war, stated that he would have "to paint his plane red" to avoid being hit by friendly fire. Part of this was due to the lack of first rate Italian troops in the theater.

There is a theory that most of the combat in World War II was performed by the "elite" units, while the "regular" units simply did not measure up to the same degree. While some regular units like the United States 1st Infantry Division (The Big Red One), would have this elite status, it usually applied to the paratroops, armor, and similar units. The Italian army's successes and failures in World War II reflect this theory quite well.

The Italian elite was composed of seasoned units, such as the *Bersaglieri* (sharpshooters, comparable to the Jaegers in the earlier European monarchial armies), *Alpini* or mountain, armor, artillery, and paratroop units. In the 1940 fighting in Egypt and Libya, not one of the twelve regiments of *Bersaglieri* were initially present, though they would be some of the first reinforcements to be rushed over from Italy. Later, the *Folgore* paratroop division, really a brigade strength unit when assigned to Africa, would become famous during the fighting at El Alamein. Many units of Italy's army would fight well in the course of the war, even with inferior weapons, and, in some cases, poor leadership, but most of Italy's military successes in World War II are associated with these better units.

Ironically, the Italian navy was informed before the war that resupplying the African colonies was not their strategic duty—the combined Franco-British fleet was too strong. But with the fall of France, suddenly the navy had a new mission to supply Africa, a mission which it performed well over the next three years, failing only for short key periods. At the start of the war there was some minor naval support for land operations, but it was less effective compared to the British use of naval power to aid land operations.

Italy's *Regia Aeronautica*, or Air Force, deployed the *5th Squadra* in North Africa. Italian warplanes tended to be under gunned compared to German or Commonwealth aircraft, though usually quite maneuverable and reasonably fast. Her bombers carried small bombloads and were never numerous. The Italians did not maintain their aircraft at the same operational level as did the Commonwealth, and they lacked spare parts. It should be noted that their fighters lacked radios until well into the war. Facing Italy in North Africa was a formidable multi-national enemy.

The Commonwealth Position

It was rare for a British officer clearly to understand the independent status of the young nations, common for them to refer to the Dominions as colonies and to think of them as such...
—Australian Official History

The Commonwealth theater stretched from Kenya to Iraq to Turkey and to Libya. Now facing the Axis alone, the British Empire could still field tremendous strength. Troops came from all corners of the Empire. Nor must we forget the small contingents of Greeks, Poles, Czechs, Jews, and Free French who all enlisted in the cause of freedom in this theater.

Most of the infantry formations were made up of troops of the Empire, while the armor and specialist units, especially in the early part of the war, were British. Not only would British generals command the higher formations for most of the war, but they tended to get the new equipment first, which created resentment.

The need was great for help from the Empire. Britain required over 25,000 troops in Palestine just to keep the Arabs and the Jews from killing each other. An endemic civil war had been in progress there through most of the 30's, and the Grand Mufti of Jerusalem, the Moslem spiritual leader of Palestine, strongly leaned to the Fascist cause. The British government, until Churchill came to power, had adopted a policy of reconciling the Arabs to British rule, since there was no need to reconcile the Jews living in Palestine to British rule—obviously the Jews would not want a German victory, hence the British had to only curry favor with the Arabs. The pro-Axis attitude of Arabs was prevalent throughout the Arab world, fueled by the fact that the French and British controlled the Middle East, while the Germans and the Italians did not. The Arabs desired the complete independence they had not yet achieved. Axis policy called for talking about fighting "England" and not what the Middle East would look like after the war—to avoid having Arabs realize that they would be trading one colonial power for another.

The Egyptian government, on whose lands many battles would be fought on and over, was also sympathetic to the Axis

21

as they felt that an Axis victory would secure their complete independence. So throughout the war there was some clandestine intelligence cooperation between the Axis and members of the Egyptian government. Still, it should be noted, the Egyptian army did maintain order in Egypt and the Sudan, and later in the Middle East where Egyptian units would garrison Iraq (the Gulf War was not the first time in modern history when the Egyptian army served in that area of the world). Additionally, the AA batteries of Alexandria, Cairo, and Suez were Egyptian manned throughout the war. At the start of the war one Egyptian officer named Anwar Sadat, the later president and strongman of Egypt, was serving at Mersa Matruh, before he was sent with his unit further to the rear. He was part of a group of dissident Egyptian officers who were led by Abdul Gamal Nasser, also destined to rule Egypt after the war. One of their complaints at this time was that the British still ultimately controlled Egypt, even forcing them to buy military equipment at higher prices before the war from Great Britain, instead of, in one particular case, from Czechoslovakia. Their cause was also fueled by a "Pan-Arab" goal of uniting all Arabs, though this was but a pipe dream. Because of these pro-Axis undercurrents, Great Britain in the course of the war would force certain changes in the Egyptian government and military.

There were several strategic keys to the Middle East. Not only at stake was the Suez Canal, which was a link between the Eastern Mediterranean and India, but the oil fields of Iran, Iraq, and the Persian Gulf states which were vital; ultimately there was a possible linkup with Imperial Japan. In terms of oil, Iran was the largest area producer, producing in 1940 8.6 million tons, while Iraq produced 2.5 million tons in the same year. This was only 4.8% of world output, but if possessed by Germany and Italy, it would have supplied their war machine with enough to keep their economies running. As to the possible strategic linkup with Japan either in India or via the Indian Ocean, the ramifications of this might have forced Churchill out of power and possibly Great Britain out of the war.

To anchor her defense in Egypt, the Empire had the 7th Armored division, which became famous as the "Desert Rats." Made up of two brigades of tanks, and a brigade of motorized

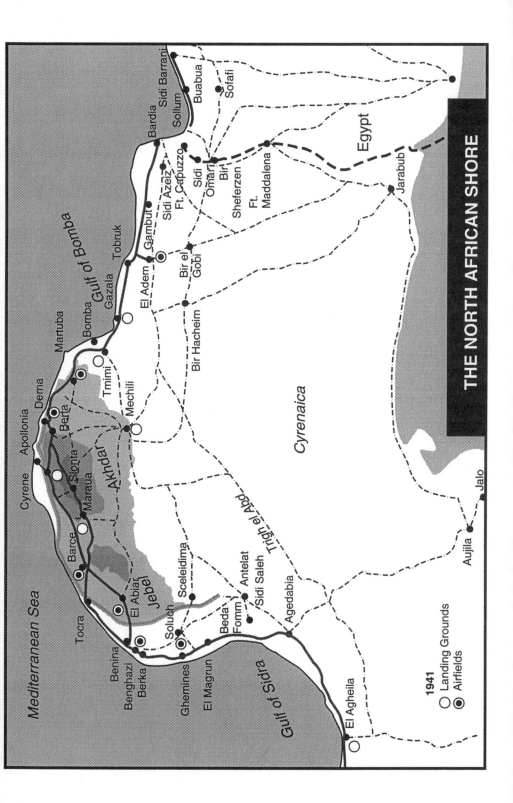

THE NORTH AFRICAN SHORE

1941
○ Landing Grounds
◉ Airfields

Mediterranean Sea

Egypt

Cyrenaica

Gulf of Sidra

Gulf of Bomba

Jebel Akhdar

Sidi Barrani
Sollum
Buabua
Sofafi
Bardia
Ft. Capuzzo
Sidi Azeiz
Sidi Omar
Bir Sheferzen
Ft. Maddalena
Gambut
Tobruk
Gazala
Bomba
Martuba
Derna
Apollonia
Cyrene
Barce
Siorta
Maraua
El Abiar
Tocra
Benina
Benghazi
Berka
Ghemines
El Magrun
Soluch
Sceleidima
Antelat
Sidi Saleh
Beda Fomm
Agedabia
El Agheila
Jarabub
Jalo
Aujila
Aujila
El Adem
Bir el Gobi
Bir Hacheim
Trigh el Abd
Mechili
Tmimi
Berta

infantry, the 7th had been trained by the legendary Major General Percy "Hobo" Hobart. Not even mentioned in the British Official History of the war in North Africa, he had been dispatched after the Munich Crisis in 1938 to build an armored division. Unfortunately, he rubbed some senior, and stuffy, British officers the wrong way—the then British commander for Egypt remarked upon his arrival, "I don't know what you've come here for and I don't want you anyway!" Yet he was the officer who built the 7th and created the atmosphere of success that would bring victory in 1940 against Italy and continue the fight until the end against the Axis powers. Hobart was relieved at the start of the war and sent home because of his abrasive nature, and yet was cheered by his men as they lined the road on his way out of Egypt.

The British light tanks were just armed with machine guns. The medium tanks carried a 2-pounder AT gun, which fired only solid shots (and uncapped to boot—it would not be until the introduction of the American 37mm AT gun on the Stuart tank that the British had capped ammunition), and, unlike the Italian 47mm, lacked a High Explosive (HE) round.

The Commonwealth also had the "I" or Infantry tanks, initially being the Matilda and later the Valentine tanks. These slow and heavily armored tanks were effectively impervious to the standard Italian and smaller German AT piece. The Matilda was the single most important weapon against Italy in 1940 that could not be answered until the Germans supplied their superior AT weapons.

The overall Commonwealth commander in the Middle East was Lt. General Archibald Wavell. He had fought in Palestine in World War I under General Allenby (later writing an account of the campaign), and was familiar with the theater. He realized from the start the problems he would have to deal with and his lack of adequate resources for all his tasks. His overall goals were to secure Egypt and Suez; then clear the Red Sea and liberate the *Africa Orientale Italiana* or A.O.I. (Italian East Africa, which included Somalia and Ethiopia), restoring the Emperor Haile Selassie to his throne; clear the North African shore; pacify the Eastern Mediterranean; and, finally, prepare for an attack into southeast Europe. Wavell was one of the most intellectual of

British generals and supported unorthodox concepts. He had met Orde Wingate and Harry Fox-Davies before the war. The former went on to fight with the Ethiopian Emperor in the *A.O.I.* and the latter formed the Long Range Desert Group which would operate deep in the desert in the course of the war, both with Wavell's blessing.

In the fight against the Italians, the commander of the Western Desert Force was the physically small Lt. General Richard O'Connor. He had been pulled back to command in Egypt by the time Rommel arrived, in part due to the Allied commitment to Greece which involved scraping together an army and shipping it off on short notice. O'Connor was an excellent and inspiring leader and one who has never received the full recognition that he deserves. Lt. General Philip Neame, new to the theater, had arrived to replace him in Libya.

The typical British infantry division of the day consisted of three brigades of three battalions each, a machine gun battalion and three regiments of artillery, usually each of twenty-four 25-pounder field guns. Also attached would be a regiment of 2-pounder AT guns. A British infantry division would usually have about 13,600 men, while the Australian and New Zealand divisions would be about 20-25% stronger. The first corps was formed in January of 1941 (the XIII), while the first army was created on 24 September of 1941 (the 8th). A British armored division had 9,600 men. So, it is always good to recall that a Commonwealth division would be larger and would have a great deal more artillery and AT weapons than an Italian division. They would often have a divisional cavalry unit assigned, which would be a partly motorized and mechanized battalion, sometimes including light tanks, which the Italian infantry division lacked until later in the war.

Early on, the British began organizing a tactical unit called the "jock column." This was named for Lieutenant Colonel—later Major General—"Jock" Campbell who died after Operation Crusader in an auto mishap. These jock columns were small formation columns made up of infantry, armor and artillery, but were too weak for the most part to be compared with the German battlegroup. They did offer an opportunity, however, to go "swanning" about as an independent command. Campbell

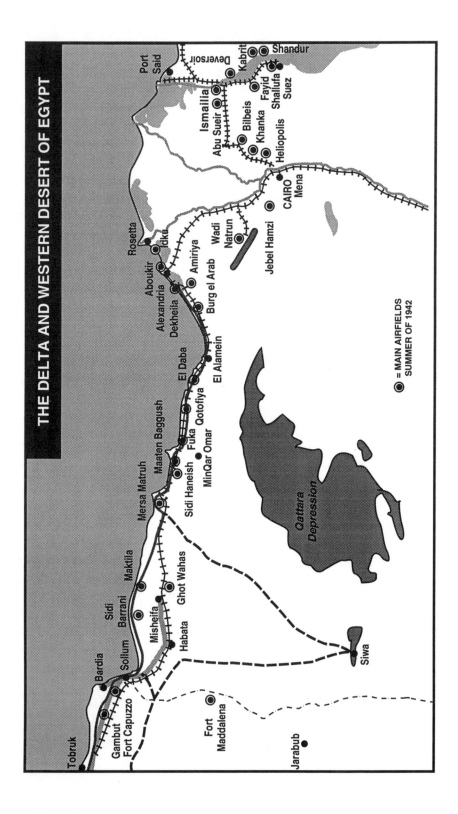

THE DELTA AND WESTERN DESERT OF EGYPT

Tobruk
Bardia
Gambut
Fort Capuzzo
Sollum
Sidi Barrani
Maktila
Misheifa
Habata
Ghot Wahas

Fort Maddalena
Jarabub
Siwa

Qattara Depression

Mersa Matruh
Maaten Baggush
Sidi Haneish
Fuka
MinQar Omar
Qotofiya
El Daba
El Alamein
Dekheila
Alexandria
Aboukir
Amiriya
Burg el Arab
Idku
Rosetta

Wadi Natrun
Jebel Hamzi
CAIRO
Mena
Heliopolis
Khanka
Bilbeis
Abu Sueir
Ismailia
Port Said
Deversoir
Kabrit
Shandur
Fayid
Shallufa
Suez

⊙ = MAIN AIRFIELDS
SUMMER OF 1942

said that a jock column could do any thing with two exceptions. "They could not capture ground from the enemy or deny ground to the enemy." He also stated on another occasion that, "as soon as we get the enemy where we want him, we must drop dispersed columns and concentrate every available gun." These controversial columns were used from the summer of 1940 until the arrival of Montgomery.

The British navy, with her Allies, would suffer losses throughout the war and never halt Italy's effort to supply Libya. But the Royal Navy did affect the land war in many direct ways, especially in the early part of the war. Through naval gunfire support from battleships, cruisers, and destroyers, to naval resupply operations to Tobruk, the White Ensign made a positive contribution to the Allied cause. With the arrival of the *Luftwaffe* with its deadly anti-shipping capability, and later with naval strength being siphoned off to fight Japan, the Allied navies had less of a direct impact on the war. Yet a new role developed which would always be there for the rest of the war—the possibility of an amphibious landing in the Axis rear. The Axis would constantly have troops, usually at divisional strength, deployed in the rear to combat this threat. This card was only played once, in the abortive raid on Tobruk on 13/14 September 1942.

The Commonwealth situation in the air was shaky, but the British did have the effective Hurricane fighter in the Middle East, and a trans-Africa air route (the so called "Takoradi air route") was inaugurated early to allow for shipment of airplanes across Africa and down the Nile to Egypt, thus eliminating the need to ship these planes by sea. The Commonwealth air units fared well not only against the Italian air force, but against the best of the *Luftwaffe*, the superior Me-109 fighter.

The role of Intelligence would increase as the war rolled on. Both sides operated agents, but the most important tactical information was derived by radio listening units operated by the Commonwealth and Axis forces near the front lines. Strategically, both sides had their methods of obtaining information, but the British use of ULTRA was vital. ULTRA was a means by which the radio signals of the various Axis armed services could be read, with differing results throughout the war, but as the war continued it would be easier and easier to read and act on Axis radio traffic to and from North Africa and Europe. Ultimately the effect of ULTRA would be decisive.

O'Connor's Offensive

Frightened, dazed, or desperate Italians erupted from tents and slit trenches, some to surrender supinely, others to leap gallantly into battle, hurling grenades or blazing machine guns in futile belabour of the impregnable intruders.

—Lt. Col. G. R. Stevens of the 4th Indian Division

The battlefield was "infested by a mechanized army against which I have no adequate means."

—General Gallina at Sidi El Barrani

The campaign in North Africa opened with some minor border skirmishes and the steady reinforcement of both sides throughout the summer. The Italians, under Marshal Graziani, at the urging of Mussolini and Badoglio, advanced into Egypt to Sidi El Barrani where the Italian army halted. There Graziani busied the army by extending the Via Balbia, building forts, water facilities, and planned for a further advance in December against Mersa Matruh.

Hitler sent General Ritter von Thoma as an observer to the battlefield in early November, in part growing out of a German offer in September of two armored divisions to fight in Africa. Additionally, Hitler began to prepare the *3rd Panzer* division for transfer to Africa. But von Thoma was not encouraged. Von Thoma came back feeling that Italian leadership was not up to snuff (he thought Graziani was poor as CinC), and the logistics, climate, and terrain were difficult. He did state that if German forces were committed, that it should be four divisions. More would be too difficult to support, and less than that could not complete the task—this was a remarkable prediction that was probably accurate.

Some Germans saw support for a Mediterranean policy as a way to bring Britain to her knees. Both Admiral Erich Raeder of the *Kriegsmarine* (German Navy) and General Alfred Jodl sup-

Italian truck mounted 65/17mm infantry guns; often used for assaults and recon (Ufficio Storico).

ported this policy, yet, General Franz Halder, Chief of Staff of the German High Command (*Oberkommando Der Wehrmacht* or *OKW*), remarked on the Italian advance, "Italy's economic dependence and lack of organizational ability hinder a decisive Italian effort." Hitler felt that the Mediterranean was secondary and would not have a decisive effect on bringing Britain to her knees. Marshal Badoglio hoped that the desolation of the desert would reinforce this feeling too, as the Italian army did not want Germans in *their* sphere. Equipment yes, but not with the troops. Thus, in a meeting between Mussolini and Hitler on 4 October 1940, Mussolini did admit that he might need heavy tanks, trucks, and divebombers to continue the third phase of the advance from Mersa Matruh to the Delta, but for now he did not want any German divisions. The ready to go *3rd Panzer*, even in desert camouflage paint, was assigned elsewhere.

After von Thoma's visit, Graziani gave some thought to concentrating vehicles and tanks into a division. But the most he ever implemented was a motorized force which, in part, was created due to the successful skirmishing of the British armored cars. This *raggruppamento*, akin to a reinforced regiment, or a special grouping of units at regimental strength or greater, became the *Maletti* group.

Additionally, there was a key tactical error that the Italians committed. The troops were disposed in a series of armed camps, but they were not mutually supporting and there was not a strong mobile force that could be relied upon to halt any troops that might push through the gaps.

General O'Connor organized an assault on the Italians, built around the Matilda tank, which would bring about a brilliant victory. Fighting alongside the 7th Armored division was the 4th Indian division. The 4th represented the unbloodied cream of the Army of India that had been trained for years, and many of its units had served on the northwest frontier of India. British Guards units were available here too, while the comparable Italian formation remained in Italy. The armor was well trained, and they had a heavy tank, the Matilda, which the Italians, like the Germans at Arras in 1940, could not face, and like the Germans at Arras, could only run from. All of these troops had been trained through the interwar period as a tough professional core group, and even with the war expansion under way had not yet been diluted. Under one of the best British commanders of World War II, the ingredients were there for an Italian disaster, and so it transpired.

From 9 December until 7 February, the Commonwealth advanced from Sidi El Barrani to Beda Fomm in a brilliant campaign. The 4th Indian was relieved part way by the 6th Australian Infantry division. Aussies were adept in World War I at trench warfare and would prove it again here in World War II, first in capturing Bardia and Tobruk from the Italians and later in defense of Tobruk against the Axis.

A destroyed L3 tank (Ufficio Storico).

The dawn of 7 February 1941 witnessed one last attempt by the Italians to break through to freedom at Beda Fomm, where O'Connor had trapped the Italian army by striking across the desert with the 7th Armored division, while the Australians advanced along the coast road. Four tanks actually succeeded, with a handful of troops in about thirty trucks, but the spirit was broken and by 0900 the battle was over. Marshal Graziani had returned to Italy in disgrace, General Tellera commanding the Italians on the field lay mortally wounded, and 25,000 Italians were prisoners, with 100 tanks, 200 artillery pieces, and 1,500 trucks destroyed or captured. The Australian Official History would say, "After the fighting had ended the desert looked like a film producer's conception of a battlefield. For ten miles the stony floor was littered with hundreds of Lancia and Fiat trucks, many overturned and splintered by shell fire, and with dozens of dark green tanks with crews dead inside them. There were lines of abandoned field guns with ammunition boxes scattered round." General O'Connor would report to Wavell, "Fox killed in the open." It had been close, but it was a brilliant victory.

So ended the first campaign, now to escalate to a war against the Axis instead of just Italy. Italy suffered 130,000 prisoners, lost 180 medium tanks, over 200 of the L3's, as well as 1200 artillery and mortar pieces.

Additionally, the *Regia Aeronautica* had suffered severe losses. This strategic attrition of material must not be overlooked, because with the poor production of industry, Italians could replace losses, but never get ahead. Many Italian divisions in Italy would never be fully equipped and thus not fully useful— even in relatively quiet areas on garrison duty. Psychologically the impact of this blow, along with the surprise night torpedoing of several battleships at anchor, combined to convince Italians that this war would not end in 1940 with an Axis victory. Both Italy and Germany were sending reinforcements, and one of the keys was the leader of the German force, General Erwin Rommel.

Italy's War Goals

Fascist Italy had her war goals. In 1940 she envisioned that the future extension of the Italian Empire would come at the expense of the French and British empires. France would give her Corsica, Tunisia (with border modifications into Algeria), Djibouti, and a land extension into Chad from Libya. In Europe, France would give up territory extending to the river Var on the Italian border with France. From the British Empire would come Malta, Perim, Socotra, and British Somaliland. Aden would go to Yemen, Cyprus to Greece (the dictator of Greece, Metaxas, was viewed as a friend). Egypt would be a dependency, while the Sudan would be the Italo-Egyptian Sudan. The League of Nation mandates in the Middle East would be independent in name but dependent on Italy. It was proposed to divide up Switzerland, with the Italian speaking portion joining Italy. The British and the French empires were not to be destroyed, at least not yet. Instead, the German and Italian Empires were to be established, with the Italian one being cut out of the hide of the peoples of the Mediterranean.

If these goals could be obtained, British and French power in the Mediterranean would be throttled and Italy would have her outlet to the Indian Ocean. A settlement program of Italian peasants into these new territories would have been accelerated with the successful conclusion of the war. The army in Italian East Africa would eventually number 1,000,000 men, complete with an armaments industry, and an increasing Italian population. It is clear that an Axis victory in World War II would have extended the life of colonialism in Africa much longer, and made independence for the native African states much bloodier.

A.O.I.

Africa Orientale Italiana was the name given to the new Italian Empire in Africa that was decreed on 1 June 1936. Approximately 12 million people lived in an immense area of 666,000 square miles divided into six provinces. The population in Ethiopia was constantly in a smoldering level of revolt from 1936 until the final liberation of Ethiopia by the Emperor Haile Selassie, which was largely accomplished with the aid of the Allied armies. Hot, dry, and devoid of forests throughout much of the land, it was a primitive area in which to fight.

While the *A.O.I.* was a new Italian possession, the roads had been much improved in those few short years, and one of the best divisions of the Italian army was based there—the *Granatieri di Savoia* (Grenadiers of Savoy). Often misrepresented as a stronger unit than it was, the *Savoia* was a standard Italian division with some artillery added to it in the course of fighting. In addition to this unit there was an ad hoc *Africa* Division, several *Blackshirt* battalions (which often were used to maintain order in the rear areas), a scratch company of Germans, and a few tanks including 24 M11's rushed down on the eve of war. A total of 255,950 men were mustered in the *A.O.I.*, of which 181,895 were black troops. Yet, even though the terrain was mountainous only one Alpine battalion fought there. The *Alpini* division sent there in the 1935-36 war fought excellently and one must wonder what might have been accomplished if more such quality forces had been stationed there at the start of the conflict.

Mussolini envisioned an army of 500,000 troops (eventually to grow to 1,000,000), an armaments industry, and emigrants from Italy starting farms throughout the Horn. This vision was not to be achieved, and, instead, the *A.O.I.* was to find itself early in the war surrounded by enemies, cut off from home, and lacking supplies.

In the first few months of the war the viceroy, Amedeo di Savoia, Duca di Aosta (Duke of Aosta), was ordered to stand and defend, but he still launched three small offensives. He overran British Somaliland, which was the only British colony to fall to either the Italians or the Germans in World War II. Defended by a token British force, it still fought well. The Italians advanced into Kenya and the Sudan and occupied some key border towns and momentarily gave a scare to the British in Egypt who feared an advance up the Nile.

By early 1941 the Commonwealth was ready to attack the *A.O.I.* Wav-ell wanted to eliminate the Italian threat so that the adjacent Red Sea would not be considered a war zone. This meant that the neutral United States could not send merchant ships there until the Italian presence was eliminated. To achieve this Wavell planned a three pronged attack. From the North would come the fine 4th and later the 5th Indian divisions. From Kenya would come the 1st South African division which was essentially motorized and had many South African built armored cars. Assisting them were the 11th and 12th African Divisions which were largely black units. Made up of units from throughout Africa, these two divisions performed well, but were not used outside of this campaign as the British felt that black units should not fight in the main, i.e., white, theaters. The third prong was the forces of the Emperor of Ethiopia, which included Lieutenant Colonel Orde Wingate who would be one of the most eccentric and capable British commanders produced in the war. He was instrumental in organizing this so-called "Gideon Force" which numbered about two battalions of Sudanese troops and poorly trained Ethiopians.

The first action opened with the advance of the 4th Indian division, just recently shipped down from successful action at Sidi El Barrani. The Sudan border was cleared, and the *A.O.I.* entered, but the 4th stalled at Keren, a mountainous pass where both Italian colonial brigades as well as the *Savoia* halted the British advance. Many have said that the heavy fighting here was only equalled by the fighting at Monte Cassino in Italy. Peter Cochrane who fought there remarked that "for my money [Keren] was a more hellish affair than Cassino for the attacking force," while another British veteran of the battle said, "Physically, by World War II standards, it was sheer hell." Furious fighting would continue here for weeks, eventually seeing the 5th Indian arrive to finally break the position, but by then, the rest of the *A.O.I.* position was falling apart.

The collapse began in early February with a rapid Commonwealth advance, under the command of Lt. General A.G. Cunningham. He was the brother of Admiral Cunningham, commander of the British naval forces in the Eastern Mediterranean for much of the war. Cunningham motorized much of the 1st South African division and simply rolled over successive Italian positions, defeating them in detail. He first occupied Italian Somaliland, and then, in conjunction with a small amphibious landing from Aden he liberated British Somaliland, then pushed into the highlands of Ethiopia. Facing minimal opposition, he captured Addis Ababa, capital of the *A.O.I.*, on 6 April 1941. Cunningham had defeated the superior Italian forces in detail and established a reputation which led to his command of the newly formed 8th Army. This was

the death blow to the Duca di Aosta, who retired on Amba Alagi with his main force, where he made a final stand, surrendering on 16 May 1941.

Gideon had also advanced into the highlands, far to the west in the interior, and applied a great deal of pressure for such a small force. Wingate perfected the technique of small, sharp night attacks, and this increased the pressure on the Italians and their Ethiopian allies. Winning some success in the hinterland, the fall of Addis Ababa allowed the emperor to begin thinking in terms of completing the liberation of all his county. So it came to pass that on 5 May 1941, five years to the day after the Italians entered Addis Ababa, the emperor re-entered his capital.

While the fighting continued until 27 November 1941, with the final surrender of the last Italian force, the Red Sea had been open to American shipping for months, and the threat to Kenya and the Sudan had been removed. Cunningham would go on to Libya, where he would lose his reputation while handling a much larger mechanized force. The Duca di Aosta would die in a Kenya prisoner of war camp in 1942, mourned by many on both sides, as he was both a gentleman and a leader.

Bersaglieri

Six *Bersaglieri* regiments fought in North Africa, plus minor units at the company level, especially after El Alamein, or unique units like the *8th Bersaglieri Armored battalion*,

mounted on armored cars and captured vehicles.

Italy entered the Second World War with 12 *Bersaglieri* regiments which were employed on all fronts, and of these, half served in North Africa. They were the *5th, 7th, 8th, 9th, 10th,* and *12th regiments.* This is a confirmation of the importance to Italy of the war in North Africa. At the outbreak of the war there were no *Bersaglieri* regiments in Africa. Like the mobile units, they were concentrated in the homeland.

The *Bersaglieri* corps was founded on 18 July 1836 as light infantry of the Sardinian Army and fought not only in the *Risorgimentowars,* but also in the Crimean War against the Russians. They took part in the First World War and then, due to financial reasons, many units were disbanded and even the traditional 12 regiments were considered for elimination. Only four regiments were under the colors in 1920, the other eight being limited to one battalion each. When Armando Diaz, the former Army Chief of Staff in the First World War, introduced his army reform (sometimes known as "Mussolini Reforms"), in 1923, the 12 regiments each consisted of two battalions, six regiments being on foot and six operating with bicycles. In Diaz' view they should operate "as bicycle units for the *celeri* divisions, and as pool for the formation of assault units."

Although by 1940 the Army Chief of Staff General Alberto Pariani was planning a war in North Africa, the mobile units remained in the Po valley as part of the Army of the Po.

Part of the Army of the Po consisted of *Celeri* divisions. Two *Celeri* divisions were first built in 1930 and a third was later added. These units of mixed cavalry and *Bersaglieri* were a legacy of the battle of Vittorio Veneto in 1918, where such units

pursued the retreating enemy. The reality of this new war would make the different speeds of cavalry and bicycle lead to the death of the *Celere* type division.

Also starting the war in the Army of the Po were three *Bersaglieri* regiments in Italy's three armored divisions: *5th (Centauro), 8th (Ariete),* and *12th (Littorio).* In the two existing motorized divisions there were the *7th (Trento)* and *9th (Trieste)* regiments. All these units later fought in North Africa.

At other times the *Bersaglieri* regiments operated at the army corps level, as was the case of the *10th* regiment when it arrived in Africa in 1940 and was employed as a "fire brigade," as were other *Bersaglieri* regiments during the war with Greece because they were confident, well trained, and effective soldiers. Another example of corps level employment was in 1942, when the *7th* and *9th* regiments were taken from *Trento* and *Trieste* divisions and assigned to *X* and *XXI Corps.*

At the beginning of the war the *Bersaglieri* were formed with three battalions. In the motorized and armored units each regiment had one motorcycle and two trucked battalions, and also a 47/32 anti-tank gun company; in the *Celere* division the three battalions were put on trucks and were supported by one anti-tank company and one motorcycle company.

A practical example of their TO&E is the *8th regiment* landing in Africa with 73 officers, 1,800 NCOs and *Bersaglieri,* 126 vehicles and 60 motorcycles, 32 machine guns, 70 light machine guns, 1,770 rifles, and 15 RF 3C radios. It consisted of two motorized battalions *(V & XII)* and one motorcycle *(III)*battalion, and the *132nd anti-tank company* 47/32 (with 8 pieces). During the transfer in Africa another anti-tank company was added, the *142nd*.

Unfortunately TO&E changes of the Italian Army in the Second World War are not well documented, nor do the recent works of the Ufficio Storico ("Official Story" or histories published by the Italian Government) do much to remedy this situation. But something is known of the North African campaign's new organizations which developed. For example the "AS '42" organization, applied to the Italian divisions starting with January 1942, called for more anti-tank and anti - aircraft weapons. Due to shortages, this enhanced formation with less manpower was realized only in part.

From January 1942 the *Bersaglieri* regiments in Africa *(7th, 8th, & 9th)*, had to reorganize to two motorized battalions and one support heavy weapons battalion, while the motorcycle companies were eliminated. Taking the *8th* as an example again, it was formed with the following: *V* and *XII battalions*, one regimental headquarters company of one signal and one services platoon; one 81mm mortar company with nine pieces. The *V* and *XII battalions* each had: three official companies (two was usual and if possible the third) each with four platoons, one fusiliers platoon with six light machine guns, one machine gun platoon with four machine guns, one platoon with three anti-tank/anti-air 20mm guns or 3 Solothurn anti-tank rifles, one platoon with three anti-tank 47/32; the *III anti-tank weapons battalion* was forming in Italy with three anti-tank 47/32 company for a total of

five platoons. While the *8th* would remain with the *Ariete,* the other two regiments left their divisions in order to be assigned to army corps.

The number of 47/32mm anti-tank guns, while still a poor weapon, reflected evolution mirrored in German formations at that time. The German *90th Light division* had added many of the ex-Russian 76.2mm guns which operated as both an anti-tank weapon as well as giving supporting fire to the infantry. In the *164th Light Afrika division* to arrive from Crete, the Germans had a mix of three anti-tank rifles and six 75mm or 76.2mm guns with each company. This general upgunning and reduction in manpower was an attempt to respond to the desert war with its heavy demand on supplies, hence the desire to reduce manpower, but increase firepower because of the heavy use of armored fighting vehicles.

It is very difficult to state a recruiting rule for the Italian Army, especially in the Second World War. For the *Bersaglieri* a common rule demanded good physical condition and medium height. Examining the losses of the 8th *Bersaglieri* regiment published by General Vicini it is possible to state that this unit, based in peacetime near Verona in Northern Italy, was composed of 35% from Lombardy and 20% from Venezia while only 10% came from Sicily. It is true that almost all the regions of Italy were represented at some minimum level.

Bersaglieri were armed with a carbine version of the '91 model rifle of the infantry units. This was very accurate but the 6.5 mm was a little less powerful than that of other major belligerents, except for Japan.

Hand grenades were the same as those of the infantry—poor—and were: the Breda 35, OTO, or Srcm. They were known collectively as "Red Devil Grenades" by Allied forces as they had a dull red color. They gained the "devil" moniker due to defective fuses which might work *after* being disturbed when thought to be dead.

These mobile units revealed the weakness of the Italian economy and war industry. In 1939 Italy had 290,000 registered cars (one for every 112 people) and this in part due to higher costs of fuel than in other countries, produced fewer people capable of driving or knowledgeable as mechanics, and thus suitable for mobile units. However, the *Bersaglieri* did enjoy good quality (like the *Alpini)* NCOs, which was rare in the Italian Army.

Operations in North Africa of *Bersaglieri* units began with the last phase of the O'Connor offensive, when the *10th Bersaglieri* regiment arrived on the front. It never really saw action as it was surprised and destroyed on its trucks along the trail near Beda Fomm, the first major unit ambushed on 5 February 1941 by British tanks which had crossed the desert to surprise the retreating Italian army. This loss was due to the rapid advance of the 7th Armored division and the lack of proper security measures.

With the arrival of the *Ariete* armored division and *Trento* motorized division, another two regiments arrived. These units, although with the same arms and means, were better trained and better officered, and not depressed by the retreat of General Graziani's army before General O'Connor's ad-

vance, and took part in the first limited offensive of Rommel in Cyrenaica. Although their role is not well known, these regiments participated in the entire campaign.

Additionally, the *9th regiment* arrived in Africa on 26 August, 1941. The *9th Bersaglieri* had *XXVIII* and *XXX* battalions, the *XXX motorcycle battalion,* and the *XL Heavy Weapons battalion* and was attached to the *Trieste* motorized division. Its fine performance was displayed on 26 and 27 November 1941 at Belhamed, while the 8th participated in the fighting at Bir el Gubi and Point 175.

During the *Venezia* operation launched by Rommel on 24 May 1942, the *7th Bersaglieri* was under command of *XXI Corps*, the *9th* being assigned to *X Corps*. The *Littorio* armored division arrived in Africa at this time with the *12th Bersaglieri* regiment.

The *5th regiment* was sent to Africa with the *Centauro* armored division in November 1942 with *XIV* and *XXII battalions* in Tripolitania and *XXIV battalion* in Tunisia after the Torch operation. In January 1943 all three battalions were in Tunisia but were employed by the Germans often as separate units. It took part with the *XIV battalion* in Rommel's operation against the II US Corps and fought at Kasserine Pass. Later, in March 1943, the regiment was employed at El Guettar. At that time the *7th regiment* rebuilt the *XII battalion* (which was destroyed at El Alamein) and fought also at El Guettar with the *Centauro* division. The *7th* was disbanded on 26 April 1943. After El Alamein the *8th* veterans were employed in the *Giovani Fascist* division with three battalions reformed, as the *X, XI* and *LVII.*

38

Finally, the rebuilt *10th Bersaglieri* regiment arrived in Tunisia with *XXXIV, XVI* and *LXIII battalions*, at Bizerte and was deployed as bridgehead protection, later assigned to the von Manteuffel division. A recent biography of General von Manteuffel states that "our *Bersaglieri regiment* was almost completely destroyed. It resisted until the bitter end."

This regiment was also employed in the successful counterattack against the Allied landing operation at Douar Chemti. It ended the campaign with the *5th*, when they counted between 500 and 800 rifles each.

It can be said that the *Bersaglieri* regiments in the North African campaign had given much and received little in terms of historical attention. The quality of the Italian Army varied much from top to bottom and the *Bersaglieri* enjoyed a good standard of conduct, if the long fatigue of continuous employment is taken into account. Along as motorized troops—operating like armored infantry —they were able to learn desert warfare very quickly.

The Blackshirts
by Antonio Sema

At the beginning of 1923 the government of Mussolini decided to disband all existing party military formations in Italy, disarming in this manner all of his adversaries. At the same time the *Milizia Volontaria per la Sicurezza Nazionale* (militia volunteers for national security) or *MVSN* was founded, and to this organization flocked men, aged 17 to 50 years old, from the fascist action squads.

The *MVSN* answered to the orders of the government head (not of the king) and its duties were maintaining public order. Additionally, in September 1923, three legions of *MVSN* took part in counterinsurgency operations in Libya, deploying about 2,500 militia. During the government crisis following Giacomo Matteotti's murder in 1924, the *MVSN* was partially mobilized (six legions) to give Mussolini a physical weapon as he fought to remain in power. At the time the *MVSN* had available 50,000 rifles and 400 machine guns, but at the height of the crisis it received an additional 100,000 rifles from the army. When the crisis was overcome, with a net increase in power of Mussolini, the *MVSN* was recognized as *forza armate dello stato* (armed force of the state), remaining always under the *Duce's* orders but, since it was placed among the other armed forces, also obliged by oath to the king.

Later the *MVSN* was granted the duties of handling "premilitary" service. This was a kind of compulsory military training for the Italian youth; for example in 1931-32 over a million young men participated in the premilitary training of the *MVSN*.

The basic unit of the *MVSN* was the Legion, which was like a depot unit or cadre unit, and was able to mobilize all its men in about 24 hours. To this end, the Legion was formed by a group of officers and militia who were residents of the same city or in areas near the headquarters of the Legion. Of these organizations, between 120 and 140 were formed, depending on the time period under consideration.

Over the years of the regime new duties were assigned to the *MVSN*. In 1927 the *Milizia DAT* or "Militia for the Territorial Air Defense" was created; in 1930 the *Ispettorato DICAT* or "Territorial Air Defense" was founded, and in 1934 it was the "Militia Dacos," or *Milizia artiglieria da costa* (coastal artillery).

In 1939 the names changed, and thus *DICAT* became *MACA (Milizia artigliera contraerea)* and *DACOS* became *MILMART (Milizia Artiglieria Marittima)*. They were enormous organizations. In June 1940, *MACA* had 2,900 officers and 75,000 militia equipped with 4,286 Saint Etienne model machine guns, 116 Breda 1935 model 20/65 machine guns, 94 Skoda 5/27 and 90 Skoda 77/28 from the First World War, as well as 232 Vickers 76/45 guns and 480 Ansaldo 76/40 guns of more recent production. In total the *MACA* deployed 22 Legions with 218 batteries, of which six were in North Africa and six in East Africa. At the same date the *MILMART* had 1,000 officers, 2,000 NCOs and 30,000 militia. In the North African theater some navy pieces were employed as long range anti-tank artillery in December 1941 and one battery was attached to the *Ariete* and made famous from the action in the defeat of the 22nd Armored brigade at Bir el Gobi.

Similar to these units were other special militias with police duties, always recruited on a territorial basis.

It should be remembered that there were rail, forest, roads, harbor, communication, and border police, or militia style units in Italy. In a few years the militia had become an armed force with many duties and of great size. In 1930 militia had 23,000 NCOS, over 22,000 *capisquadra* (squad leaders), over 350,000 Blackshirt troopers and 250,000 rifles of the 91 model, 16,000 Beretta pistols, 700 Fiat-Revelli 1914 model machine guns, ten mountain guns and eleven armored Lancia RO and Fiat 15 model cars.

The Military Dimension of the Militia

Born to fulfill internal order duties, the *MVSN* saw their responsibilities progressively increased. This was to give the militia a new identity when Fascism had eliminated every form of opposition in Italy. But the *MVSN* did not remain too long a time in the cumbersome role as an expensive duplicate of the police apparatus of the fascist state. Apart from the execution of the premilitary training courses, the militia soon assumed an effective military role that before was hindered by the jealous army. It was soon foreseen that the men of the militia should be mobilized at the same time as the army and absorbed in the regular units of *Regio Esercito* and *Regia Marina Militare*. However, in this context, in 1928 it was decided that at the moment of mobilization the men of *Camicie Nere* (Blackshirts) and *Dicat* battalions would not be absorbed by armed forces.

The *CCNN* men were volunteers, members of the Fascist party (*PNF* or *Partito Nazionale Fascista*) between 27 and 36 years old, who had to obligate themselves to serve in the *CCNN* for 10 years at least. For the first time in 1928 two battalions of these new *CCNN* units participated officially in army maneuvers.

Each *CCNN* battalion included three companies each with six light machine guns. The militia were armed with rifles, hand grenades and daggers, with the dagger taking on a symbolic role for the *party*. A battalion was composed of 20 officers, 650 NCOs and militia, 52 horses and/or mules, two trucks and 18 light machine guns. Each company had three rifle platoons. Each platoon was composed of two rifle squads and one light machine gun squad. All the rifles of the *CCNN* were equipped with a grenade launcher *(tromboncino)*.

According to existing plans, each Army division had a *CCNN* battalion. In reality, only half of the existing divisions received one. On paper the *CCNN* battalion was supposed to emulate the *Arditi* (highly trained assault troops of the First World War), but in reality they were light infantry not particularly well trained, but (it was supposed) enthusiastic and aggressive, destined to operate in offensive support of the frontline units.

In the case of the war with Ethiopia, however, the *CCNN* battalions were regrouped in *ad hoc* divisional units, particularly fit for the regime for propaganda use. During the Ethiopian campaign seven of these units were built. Five *CCNN (23 marzo, 28 ottobre, 21 aprile, 3 gennaio* and *1 febbraio,* all important dates of fascist history) divisions had the same TO&E organization:

Three *CCNN* **Legions:**

1) each of two battalions, one machine gun company and one 65/17 battery
2) one machine gun battalion
3) two replacement battalions
4) an artillery battalion of three 65/17 companies, Engineers and service—all the support units coming from the army.

The *CCNN* division *Tevere* instead had four legions and eight battalions, but without the machine gun company and the support batteries, while the *Cirene* had eight Legions and 16 battalions with four batteries. There was even the *9th reserve CCNN* division. Out of a total of 167,000 *CCNN's*, 115,000 were sent to the *AOI* and fought well.

Only in the Uaerieu Pass battle did they suffer a bitter setback, losing on one single occasion 19 officers and 245 militia. At the end of the operation several *CCNN* units remained in East Africa with counterguerrilla and patrolling duties in the colony, fighting until the Commonwealth conquest of Ethiopia and the return of the Emperor Haile Selassie of Ethiopia to his throne.

The positive colonial results enforced the prestige of the *MVSN*. In 1936 it could deploy 132 legions, each of them having two battalions available. Of these, one was active, composed of 21- to 36-year-old militia, the other territorial (from 40- to 55-year-olds), with their replacement battalions and other support units.

But the failure in the Spanish Civil War stopped plans for further expansion of the militia. With the Franco falangists fought about 29,000 *CCNN*, regrouped in 36 "Banderas" (similar to battalions) and 11 banderas groups.

But only two of these were independent while the other nine were regrouped in hastily improvised and hurried manner in three "volunteer divisions," which resulted in their totally lacking in services and artillery and were put under command of old army generals. After the defeat at Guadalajara, caused by the collapse of the CCNN, they were reorganized (in 1937) into two divisions: *Fiamme Nere* (Black flames) and *23 marzo*, this last being later merged with the *Littorio CCNN* division in 1938. Another *CCNN* division, the *9th*, was built in Italy as a reserve, or depot, for Spain. It has been argued that the Italian contribution to Franco's war effort, both in terms of troops and in war supplies, was key to his final victory in the Spanish Civil War.

Experience of the Second World War

Taking into account the increasing difficulties in the international scene, four *CCNN* divisions, the so called "libiche" (Libyan) were deployed in North Africa with the names: *23 marzo, 28 ottobre, 21 aprile* and *3 gennaio*. Mobilized in September 1939, they were regrouped immediately in two *CCNN* corps, the *XXII CCNN corps* and *XXIII CCNN corps*, under command of Generals Umberto Somma and Mario Berti respectively. Mario Berti would later command the Italian army defeated at Sidi Barrani in December of 1940 at the start of General O'Connor's offensive.

In a short time however the *21 aprile* division was disbanded in order to reinforce the other three divisions and to replace elements of the infantry division *Catanzaro* sent to Africa. The *Cantanzaro* would fill itself out with Italians already in Africa by late fall of 1940. At the outset the four *CCNN* divisions included eight legions for a total of 24 *CCNN* battalions and four machine gun battalions, while the army supplied the engineers, services and artillery units. At the end of 1940 the *MVSN* had become a bulky and complex organization, able to deploy 312,000 men. Of these, 112,000 were in 194 active battalions (24 Libyan battalions, eight colonial battalions, 10 frontier battalions, 108 assault and mountain battalions, 39 replacement battalions, four Libyan machine gun battalions and one machine gun battalion). Additionally there were:

64,000 men in 135 territorial battalions,

85,000 men in the *MACA*

25,000 in the *MILMART* and

26,000 in *AOI*, for a total of 30 battalions.

The *CCNN* units in Libya were overrun during the British offensive in December-January 1940-1941 and were not reformed.

Other *CCNN* units, starting in 1941 were emblazoned with the name "M" battalion (M for Mussolini); they were those *CCNN* units that had distinguished themselves in combat. Thus, later in the war, even on the mainland, there were several units with the designation "M."

According to most scholars, the performance of the *CCNN* units during the Second World War was generally always inferior to the equivalent German units, with the only exception being the *CCNN* units sent to Russia. In partial mitigation of this judgment, it should be remembered that equipment and training of the *CCNN* units, along with their cadres, was on the average inferior to that of German units.

CHAPTER 2

Rommel & the German Army Arrive

The lunacy about it all is that on the one hand the Italians are screaming blue murder and painting their shortages of arms and equipment in the blackest terms, and on the other hand they are so jealous and infantile that they find the idea of using German soldiers and German materials quite repugnant. Mussolini would probably like it most if the German troops would fight in Italian uniforms there, and our aircraft flew with the Italian Fasces on their wings!
—Adolph Hitler

A commander must accustom his staff to a high tempo from the outset and continually keep them up to it. If he allows himself to be satisfied with norms, or anything less than an all-out effort, he gives up the race from the starting-post and will sooner or later be taught a bitter lesson by his faster-moving enemy and be forced to jettison all his fixed ideas.
—Erwin Rommel from *The Rommel Papers*

North Africa proved to be the world stage for Lieutenant General Erwin Rommel.

Germany entered the war in Africa to keep Italy in the war, to protect her southern European flank, and especially to protect the Rumanian oil fields. Hitler was worried that if Italy lost

Rommel in a staff car being briefed on the situation (Klaus Hub-buch).

Tripoli, the last outpost of her African Empire, that her heart would be out of the war and Mussolini and fascism could fall. Hitler decided to send a *Sperrverband*, or "blocking formation." So the war in Africa would remain Italy's war but now Germany was there to supply just enough troops and equipment to block the Commonwealth advance in Africa while the war would be decided, in Hitler's view, on the steppes of Russia.

Italy recognized that the Parallel War was over. One of the early adherents of fascism, Marshal Emilio de Bono, had stated in December of 1940, "We, as Italians, have lost the war. The Axis will have to win it." And here was the rub. Hitler had no real concept of what a Mediterranean strategy offered in terms of possible victory as his fevered vision of the War in the East dominated his thinking, and he did not realize until too late that through the Mediterranean, the Allies could re-enter Europe.

When Hitler later poured troops into Tunisia in 1942-43 to try to stave off the fall of North Africa to the Allies, he was still afraid that the loss of Africa would take Italy out of the war. Instead, he simply filled the Allied "bag" with prisoners. If he had used a portion of those troops, equipment, and supplies in 1941, or even possibly 1942, the outcome of the war would have been quite different. The fall of Egypt and the Middle East might have brought about a linkup with Japan in the Indian Ocean, and would have kept Italy in the war, giving the potential for termendous amounts of oil and other resources for the Axis, and resulted in the cutting off of the Persian corridor of supplies by the Allies to the Soviet Union. All of these plums were in the grasp of a leader who could see the advantage of a Mediterranean strategy and with much less of an investment of armies than was made on the Russian steppes.

One of Hitler's vital errors—and Mussolini pointed this out time and time again—was the need for supplies to enter North Africa through Tunisia. The distance from Italy was much shorter via Tunis and Bizerte, which would reduce shipping losses, and the port capacity in Tunisia was much higher than in Libya. But Hitler was afraid to offend the Vichy French government, and so it would be too late for the Axis when they finally entered Tunisia.

Rommel

Personally chosen by Hitler to be sent to Africa, Rommel was never a member of the Nazi party, but was viewed as a protege of Hitler's. An optimistic man, he was loved by the common trooper, but not by the officers. He had an excellent grasp of the desert environment which lacked regular features, such as towns, etc....He had a fine understanding of the *Panzer* division and was certainly air minded, knowing that the *Luftwaffe* could act like mobile artillery. Never commanding from the rear, he was up front and in the thick of the fighting, often times under artillery fire, directing operations quickly and decisively. He had the uncanny ability to not be shot or captured, though with

Italian manned German built 88mm AT/AA gun (Ufficio Storico).

many close calls— once he entered a British hospital field station by mistake! He walked through the hospital, and got back to his lines.

Rommel took on celebrity status as the war progressed, even writing his wife once that "World press opinion of me has greatly improved." Commonwealth soldiers would say on a particularly good maneuver that it was "a Rommel." General Auckinleck in 1942 had to issue a message that stated we were not fighting "Rommel" but the enemy and went on to say "I am therefore begging you to dispel the idea in every way you can that Rommel is anything but an ordinary German general, and a pretty unpleasant one at that, as we know from the mouths of his own officers." His special status was a theme that surfaced time and time again during this campaign.

One reason why Rommel appeared brilliant was due to the poorer quality of the Commonwealth forces. The desert was a learning experience for the Commonwealth armies who faced Rommel with a revitalized Axis army. While there were many exceptional Commonwealth troops, the top Commonwealth leadership, after the capture of General O'Connor, was poor. The poor quality of many British officers was remarkable and this helped make Rommel look good. The Italian historian Emilio Faldella has said that "the myth of Rommel was created by the English, who preferred to justify their defeats with the presence

German Mk III tank, probably taken while in depot; note the cover on the tracks (Ufficio Storico).

in the enemy camp of an exceptional general, rather than recognize the superior quality of the combatants, German and Italian."

And Rommel was not perfect. Possibly the greatest error he made was not following his orders. Rommel was unaware of the coming war with the Soviet Union, but his actions would become a drain on Germany over the next two years and would take Hitler's attention away from the "true war," which from an ideological and political point of view was against the Soviet Empire. However, one result of his disobeying orders was that it made Rommel a German national war hero.

Another of Rommel's failures was to not understand the full combined use of land, sea, and air. For example he never made use of the small paratroop and amphibious capability that he had as early as 1941. Another error he committed was his tendency to not concentrate his forces. Several times in the campaign Rommel strung out units over a great distance, and this inability to concentrate his strength kept him from victory. The fact that he never attended General Staff school may have been the cause of his inability to work closely with the Quartermaster, which in this campaign was paramount. Marshal Kesselring, who later commanded the Mediterranean Theater for the Germans, felt that Rommel was too hot tempered, and never learned to work well with his Italian allies. So we can say he was a brilliant tactician, an inspiration to the troops, but strategically limited, and never received all the support that he wanted or needed in this vital theater of war.

Rommel's tools of war at hand were varied. The primary weapon was the 9,300-man *5th Leicht* (Light) *Panzer* division, under General Johannes Streich, a divisional unit type which was later eliminated from the German Table of Organization and Equipment (TO&E). It had a little less in the TO&E department than the conventional *Panzer* division. The *5th Leicht Panzer* had 27 armored cars, some classic VW bugs utilized as early "dune buggies," and some motorcycle troops in a reconnaissance (recce) battalion; two *PanzerJaeger* (tank hunting) battalions armed with 37mm and 50mm AT guns; a field artillery battalion; an anti-aircraft battalion with the deadly dual purpose 88mm gun; some engineers; and two machine gun battalions, all of which were motorized. Arriving on 24 April was the *3rd* company of the *Intelligence Unit 56* (later known as the *621st Radio Intercept Company*) under *Oberleutnant* Alfred Seebohm, which was primarily a tool for radio reconnaissance. This unit, which operated close to the front would be key, until its capture in 1942, for supplying Rommel with important tactical information on Commonwealth plans and strengths. It would be his "most reliable source of intelligence."

In terms of tanks the TO&E called for two battalions of 70 light and 80 medium tanks. At the end of March the Germans had about 55 light and 130 medium tanks in Africa. The light tanks, the Pz I (*Panzerkampfwagen* or armored war wagon or tank, hereafter "Pz") and Pz II were of little value, but the medium Pz III and IV were the main battle tanks for Rommel throughout this campaign. The Pz III's had been uparmored since the fighting in France, and most of the initial arrivals received extra 30mm face-hardened plates to protect the vulnerable points on their hulls and part of their turrets. They were armed with the short 50mm AT gun, which could penetrate 60mm armor at 400 yards. The Pz IV's, which were usually present in a 1 to 2 ratio

Italian truck mounted 90mm AT/AA guns (Ufficio Storico).

to the Pz III (though a ratio that would quickly fall off to 1 to 3 or more), were also being uparmored, and were armed with a short 75mm gun. While primarily used against enemy infantry and AT guns, they could damage a tank at 3,000 yards by blowing off a track, and it could penetrate about 45mm of armor at 600 yards. After the first tank arrival from Europe, all later tanks came with the improved armor plating already attached.

The Germans initially used a 37mm AT gun which was not effective against Commonwealth tanks like the Matilda. But by Operation Battleaxe, Rommel had fifty-four 50mm AT and thirteen 88mm AT guns out of 155 German AT guns total. The 50mm AT gun had a slightly better penetration ability than the one mounted on the tank, but the Germans also had a variety of ammunition which was helpful. The German AT shell had an HE capability in an armor piercing shell, and later was capped for improved penetration. Later a small issue of *Panzergranate 40*, a tungsten-core shot, was issued, which was superb for penetration at medium ranges. Thus, the 50mm with the *Panzergranate 40* could penetrate a Matilda at 500 yards, while an 88 could do the same at 2,000 yards! The Italians developed an effective hollow charge round called the "EP" (*effetto pronto* or prompt effect) for their 47mm and 90mm AT guns. The advantage of the German system was that their tanks were better armored than either the Italian or Commonwealth tanks, which were still married to conventional armor plate and not face-hardened plate. The Germans also had a greater variety of shells, firing from their better guns. Finally, the Germans were capable of recovering and repairing damaged tanks with mobile equipment. The Italians and Commonwealth were still both learning this technique by mid-1941, so that for most of the year their damaged but repairable tanks did not return to combat at a rate comparable to the German ones.

It is interesting to note that by the time of Operation Crusader, captured samples of the *Panzergranate* 40, a Pz IV, a 50mm AT gun and other equipment had been sent to Great Britain for examination. However, even with an example at hand, the Pz IV's armor was *still thought* to be conventional as opposed to face-hardened armor. It was not until March 1942 that this fact was discovered, but a start had been made in learning Germany's secrets.

The current British armored cars were armed at best with an AT rifle and a machine gun. The Germans now introduced an armored car to the desert that a diarist of the King's Dragoon Guards commented on. "These 8-wheeled armored cars are faster, more heavily armed with a 37mm gun (in reality it was a 20mm gun) and more heavily armored than our armored cars. Their cross-country performance is immeasurably superior to ours over rough-going." This feature gave the Germans an advantage at the scouting.

It was clearly not merely tanks and other equipment that gave the German *Panzer* division its advantage. The Germans had created a team of weapons and crews that acted together, which was usually led from the front by the divisional commander, a concept pioneered by Guderian, and certainly understood and emulated by Rommel. With motorized infantry, artillery, AT and AA guns, engineers, as well as the tanks, the *Panzer* division could call on whatever it needed as each objective came into view. Enemy tanks advancing—deploy AT guns; soft target ahead like trucks—artillery and tanks fire into them; obstacle

Rommel with a German artillery piece in background (Klaus Hubbuch).

ahead—bring the engineers forward. It was all done rapidly, illustrating the use of combined arms and mutual support. With *Blitzkrieg* tactics, which were derived from the World War I infiltration tactics of moving forward, bypassing strong points, and creating complete disruption in the enemy rear, this made a formidable weapon.

Italy, too, had not stood idly by. Her obsolescent equipment was still the same, and though Italy was busily shipping several divisions to the Albanian-Greek front, she did send two of her best formations to fight in Africa at the same time as the German troops began to arrive. The *Ariete* armored division was a trained formation under the outstanding leadership of General Ettore Baldassarre and, along with the *Trento* motorized divi-

A column of M13/40 medium tanks (Ufficio Storico).

sion, gave the Axis some additional punch. The *Ariete* had 7,000 men, 117 L3, and 46 M13 tanks by the end of March in Africa. Additionally, the five Italian infantry divisions already in North Africa, which had been drained of troops and equipment to fight with Graziani, were now being strengthened.

Additionally, the Germans formed the *Fliegerfuehrer Afrika* (Africa Air Command) which brought the Stuka and the Me-110 to Africa. Shortly thereafter the Me-109 would arrive, which would give the Axis the edge in the air. The Italians also sent additional planes to their *5th Squadra* stationed in Africa.

As reinforcements poured into Tripoli and headed to the front, *Comando Supremo* and the German leaders in Berlin called for a holding action while plans could be formulated for further action. The war in Greece needed to be resolved, and in the course of radio traffic, the British had discovered by the use of ULTRA that the Axis planned no early offensive. Additionally, Wavell thought that it would take 30 days for the Axis to get sufficient supplies up to the front, and the German troops would need to get acclimatized to the desert environment. Wavell informed Churchill that in Cyrenaica "the next month or two" would be a dangerous time, but Wavell felt comfortable in proceeding to conquer the *A.O.I.* and shipping troops to Greece to help fight in that war. But Rommel was not to follow orders.

The Axis Counteroffensive

Order, Counterorder, Disorder.

—von Moltke

As the dust from Beda Fomm settled, the British were busily reorganizing. The 7th Armored division, now an exhausted and depleted formation, was shipped back to Egypt, re-equipped, and was off to Greece, along with the 6th Australian, the 7th Australian, and the 2nd New Zealand divisions. The 2nd Armored division, under Major-General M.D. Gambier-Parry, was moving forward into Libya, but it was under strength and worn out (it had been moved forward without the benefit of tank moving equipment). The 2nd Armored was even equipping three squadrons with captured Italian M13 tanks (which quickly broke down), and was spread between Tobruk and the front line at Mersa El Brega. The 9th Australian division also moved forward minus one battalion still in Darwin, Australia, and two of its best brigades, traded for less well trained ones, on their way to Greece; but it was under the best Australian divisional commander, Major General L.J. "Iron Pants" Morshead (he earned the nickname from his troops for being a disciplinarian). Part of the 9th was guarding Benghazi. The Polish brigade was in Egypt with the forming British 6th Infantry division (later renamed the 70th), both lacking complete equipment. The 4th and 5th Indian divisions were in Eritrea and the Sudan, while in East Africa was the 1st South African division, and the 11th and the 12th African divisions (these latter two would see action in the *A.O.I.*, but because they were predominantly black troops they would not see action in North Africa).

So Wavell was going to hold in Libya, while he knocked out the *A.O.I.* and helped Greece. Additionally, a new commander, Lt. General Philip Neame, arrived in Libya to replace O'Connor.

It was a weak Commonwealth force facing the Axis in Libya in March 1941. Instead of six artillery regiments called for in the TO&E (assuming no corps artillery) there were but three, and instead of two or three AT battalions, there was only *one battery* of 2-pounders. To boot, one of the artillery regiments was armed with World War I 18-pounders. But problems ran deeper than this. There was a lot of prejudice among the high British officers towards the ANZAC (Australian New Zealand Army Corps) officers and troops. General Wilson called them "troublesome," Auchinleck never liked them, and even O'Connor blamed the Australian troops for drunken disorders and looting (to which there was some truth). It would not be until General Montgomery arrived that the ANZAC troops were truly understood and accepted by the "Union of British Generals" who ran this theater.

General Gariboldi, overall commander in Libya, did not want to attack until the end of May when the *15th Panzer* would also be present. He had 37,000 Italians with 9,300 Germans at the front and 7,000 trucks shuttling supplies from Tripoli to the front. He was concerned that if there were an Axis defeat, the *Italian* infantry would be left in the lurch, as the more mobile German forces could simply retreat. But Rommel ordered some probes of the British front, with Gariboldi's reluctant blessing.

Rommel was under Gariboldi's command, but if Rommel felt orders to him would endanger his command or were dishonorable, then he could appeal directly over his superior's head. Rommel did appeal from time to time, both officially and unofficially, as he was no stranger to backdoor communications. The Commonwealth had a similar situation as the Australian, New Zealand and to a degree South African troops could appeal to the Home Government, but Indian troops could not.

At dawn on 24 March the *recce* battalion of the *5th Leicht Panzer* attacked El Agheila and the Commonwealth units fell back to Mersa El Brega without a fight. This position was strong, but Rommel thought if he moved quickly he could outmaneuver the Commonwealth from it. Attacking up the Via Balbia next to the coast, with his German support troops on the 31st, Rommel captured the postion by 1 April, took 800 prisoners, and with the *5th Leicht Panzer* continuing to spearhead the advance, he pushed the *Ariete* armored and the *Brescia* infantry divisions forward onto the attack as the Commonwealth troops retreated in disorder. Agedabia fell on 2 April.

Rommel paused when General Gariboldi sent this message: "From information I have received I deduce that your advance continues. This is contrary to my orders. I ask you to wait for me before continuing the advance." But Gariboldi was in the rear and Rommel was at the front and his field intelligence notified him of the continuing disarray and withdrawal of British troops. How could he, in good conscience, allow the Commonwealth troops to escape?

The loss of Agedabia forced the British 2nd Armored division to retreat into the desert to El Mechili, but it was forced up into the Jebel Akhbar, because the British felt they could not muster enough strength and speed to reach El Mechili in the face of the Axis advance. Major General Gambier-Parry of the 2nd Armored calculated that the 2nd's tanks were mechanically so unreliable that one tank would break down in every 10 miles of movement. In the retreat from Agedabia, the 2nd would virtually self-destruct with little actual fighting, though much of the personnel would make Tobruk and would later ship out to the rear. As a unit it would never reform.

The fall of Agedabia also brought Wavell up to Tobruk from Egypt, and General O'Connor was ordered to join General Neame to see if he could help. This order would shortly lead to an Allied tragedy.

The pause after the fall of Agedabia was not well used, as orders and counterorders flowed across the Commonwealth's front. One diarist wrote that "Columns crossed and recrossed, and tanks, armored cars, anti-aircraft and field guns and other vehicles were all mixed up together." By the end of 3 April, Wavell had ordered a general withdrawal.

Rommel ordered the advance to continue in four columns. One column that pushed along the coast road was made up of

47/32 AT gun mounted en portee (courtesy Lucio Ceva & Andrea Curami).

the recce battalion of the *5th Leicht Panzer*, and a battalion each of the *Bologna* and *Brescia* infantry divisions, with some artillery from the *Brescia*. Meanwhile, elements of the *5th Leicht Panzer* and *Ariete* (arranged in two very spread out columns) pushed across the bulge toward El Mechili and ultimately to Tobruk. Two columns were bound for El Mechili and victory, while a new fourth column, spinning off from the advance on Mechili, would achieve a special success.

This new fourth column under Lieutenant Colonel Ponath, in command of the *8th Machine gun* battalion, had been ordered to cut off the Via Balbia near Derna. He raced across the desert arriving there on the evening of the 6th. It would be this force, consisting initially of approximately 10 trucks, that would virtually behead the Commonwealth force retreating toward Tobruk. General O'Connor was sleeping in the back of a truck, with Lieutenant-Colonel Combe and General Neame in the front seat, on their way to Tobruk after a command conference up in the Jebel Akhbar, when they were stopped by a German sentry. Ponath had captured the current field commander of the Commonwealth force, as well as their greatest previous commander, and by 8 April about 900 other additional prisoners. On the evening of the 6th, another small, largely Italian, unit attacked an RAF post at Acroma, which was on the outskirts of Tobruk. A look at the map shows that while the Commonwealth tried to make a hold at El Mechili, the Axis, though not yet in strength, were far in the Allied rear.

The 9th Australian had begun to withdraw from Benghazi to Tobruk in any sort of vehicle obtainable—in one case employing a broken down flatbed truck pulled by a working truck. Their rearguard in the Jebel Akhbar, east of Benghazi, pulled back toward Tobruk, covering the retreat. The 9th made three stands between Benghazi and Tmimi before finally retreating into Tobruk. While the Ponath force captured some forces and leaders, the retreat by the 9th was successful and most of the 9th Australian and remnants of the 2nd Armored succeeded in reaching Tobruk.

The 2nd Armored division originally had been ordered to El Mechili, but only the headquarters unit and General Gambier-Parry made it to El Mechili. It is important to note that the British and Axis *both expected* the bulk of the 2nd Armored division to arrive at El Mechili, but it never did. The attrition of retreat destroyed the unit, and Gambier-Parry would end up in the bag.

In the desert, there were small mixed Axis units everywhere. Rommel flew from unit to unit in the desert, forcing the pace to get his men to El Mechili and victory. At one point he saw a stopped unit. "If you don't move again at once, I'll come down—Rommel." was the message dropped from the plane. Soon the unit was moving forward.

With the success at El Mechili, the Axis pushed on and came up against the fortress of Tobruk, which through the summer of 1941 would gain its niche in history. Still, Rommel was so unhappy with General Streich's perceived lack of drive that he put Major General Prittwitz, who had just arrived at the front, in command of the *15th Panzer* division.

It was at this point that Rommel was presented with one of three captured command vehicles, his "Mammut" (Mammoth). It was described by a German war reporter, Fritz Lucke, as "an armored box as big as a bus, on giant balloon tires as big and fat as the undercarriage wheels of a Junkers plane. The walls are

Rommel's "Mammoth" command vehicle (Klaus Hubbuch).

windowless and painted in blue-gray camouflage tints. Only the driver and his co-driver have windshields, protected behind armored visors." This vehicle would soon become a common sight on the front.

O'Connor had been asked what key abilities made a great captain, and he answered that a top commander had to be able to carry out a retreat. This retreat had been an Allied failure and both O'Connor and Neame were now prisoners. The next act of this drama was about to begin.

Tobruk

His greatest stroke of all was executed in the adversity. By (garri-soning) Tobruk he forced the Germans on to the defensive and probably saved Egypt. By holding Tobruk and aggressive action on the Egyptian front he gained five months stability for the for-mation of the 8th Army.
    —Wavell's biographer John Connell

We must attack Tobruk with everything we have, immediately when your Panzers have taken up their positions, and before Tommy has time to dig in.
    —Rommel

The stand at Tobruk in April of 1941 was crucial in saving the Middle East for the Allies. The stand here by the Australians kept the Axis from sweeping on against a depleted enemy. As Wavell told the acting commander of Tobruk, Australian Lieutenant General John Laverack, "There is nothing between you and Cairo." Certainly no large armor force existed to face the Axis. Tobruk lay like a fort on a flank (its garrison ready to sally forth if Rommel advanced too far into Egypt). It was a supply point, and by blocking the Via Balbia forced traffic around it on a 50 mile circuit over rough roads and trails, which existed until the bypass was built that summer and fall. It also forced a static battle on the Axis instead of a mobile one, and the latter was what they were best at. Other reasons for keeping Tobruk were to reduce the air threat to Alexandria and (contrary to Hitler's decision) to help keep Tripoli for the Italians—the political effect on Egypt would be bad if it were lost.

For the Axis, to acquire Tobruk for future supply was vital. Rommel at one point said, "Remarkably, some of my commanders kept wanting to pause so as to take on ammunition, fill up with gasoline and overhaul their vehicles, even when an immediate thrust by us would have had superb chances." General Streich's reply to this criticism was "That was always the salient point, that there just wasn't any gasoline for Rommel's pipe-dreams. And that wasn't the fault of 'some of' his commanders, but of Rommel himself." The two German *Panzer* divisions

British prisoners about to head for Europe in an Italian convoy (Ufficio Storico).

needed 24,000 tons of supplies each month, while for a future offensive they needed an additional 20,000 tons. The *Luftwaffe* required 9,000 tons a month. Italian troops and civilians used 63,000 tons. Tripoli, many miles to the rear, could easily handle only 45,000 tons a month, and Benghazi less. Rommel needed Tobruk.

The dash across the desert lifted Axis spirits in a quiet period of the war, and as Allied prisoners were being shipped from Libya to Europe, Rommel had become a star. If Tobruk fell quickly, he planned to push on to Mersa Matruh and Siwa Oasis—the same Siwa which housed the oracle that Alexander the Great visited to learn his fate—and from there the Axis would be poised to seize the Delta and all of Egypt.

The Aussies had four brigades (the 18th of the 7th Australian division, 20th, 24th, and 26th of the 9th Australian division) at their disposal, though the 24th had only two battalions, instead of the usual three. Also present was the 18th Indian Cavalry, formerly of the 3rd Motor brigade, which had not been sent forward to be destroyed at El Mechili. The Australian organic

A destroyed British tank (Luigi Castaman).

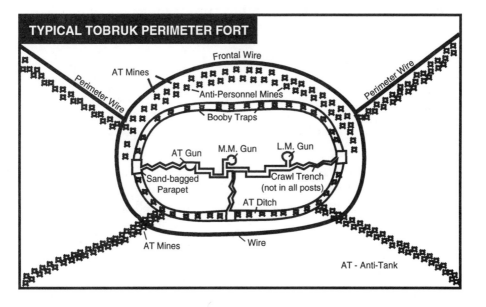

artillery was not present, but there were two British 25-pounder artillery regiments and one with twelve 18-pounders and twelve 4.5 inch howitzers; two AT regiments (each minus a battery), rounded out with an AA brigade around the harbor consisting of 16 heavy and 59 light AA guns (much of it formerly Italian). Additionally, many of the captured Italian field guns were formed into "bush" artillery and deployed along the front. A weak 3rd Armored brigade was formed consisting of a regiment of armored cars, 26 cruiser tanks, 15 light tanks, and four Matilda tanks. Non-combatants and some of the flotsam from destroyed Allied combat units (along with the remaining Italian and some German prisoners) were sent back to Egypt as shipping became available. The Royal Navy's Inshore Squadron operated from Tobruk with a variety of small craft and was responsible for running in supplies and replacements, and transporting out wounded and excess personnel.

The position at Tobruk was strengthened from the original Italian fortress. General Neame ordered in March, before his capture, improvements including the completion of the AT ditch, laying of mines, and work on both the inner and outer defensive lines.

Both Laverack and Morshead had decided upon an offensive-defensive plan, and there would be no retreat. The Australian stand at Tobruk was based on their World War I experiences. In that war, the Aussies had a commanding presence on the Western Front in 1918, in part due to their aggressive night patrolling. Night combat was one of the few forms of combat at which the Germans were unskilled. So the Aussies would regularly send out night patrols which established an ascendency over the front lines, though they carried a cost—losses. Rommel said in the summer of '41 that "The Australian troops are fighting magnificently and their training is far superior to ours, Tobruk can not be taken by force, given our present means." German Major Bellerstedt said that "The Australian is unquestionably superior to the German soldier: 1) In the use of individual weapons, especially as snipers. 2) In the use of ground camouflage. 3) In his gift of observation. 4) In using every means of taking us by surprise." Lieutenant Schorm of the *Deutsches Afrika Korps (DAK)* wrote in his journal that "Our opponents are Englishmen and Australians. Not trained attacking troops, but men with nerves and toughness. Tireless, taking punishment with obstinacy, wonderful in defense...the Australians are extraordinarily tough fighters."

Three initial attacks were made in mid-April to break the fortress. The first assault was made with Rommel thinking the Commonwealth were evacuating and not fighting at Tobruk. This would be a costly error.

The first assault made on 11 and 12 April was almost a probe. It was only then that Rommel discovered that the ships in the harbor were not there to evacuate the Aussies! In this German repulse Major General Prittwitz was killed.

The second assault was led by the *5th Leicht Panzer* regiment which penetrated the first Australian line on 13/14 April. But the Australians had planned for this. Their artillery delivered concentrated fire, often over the sights and at ranges as close as 600 yards, on the spearhead of the *5th Leicht Panzer* after it passed through the first Australian line. This first line was not defeated, but it quietly waited for the German infantry of the *8th Machine gun* battalion to follow, and slammed into them as they came forward. The Commonwealth followed up with a tank counterattack on the German tanks, which combined with the artillery fire was too much for the Germans. Surprised, and not in a mobile battle, the Germans were no match in this style of fighting. The *8th* suffered 75% losses, including 250 captured, and the *5th Leicht Panzer* lost 16 out of 38 tanks. Allied losses were less than 100 men. It was at this point that General Laverack was relieved and sent back to Egypt, since Tobruk was garrisoned by essentially one division, and he was a Corps commander. Later he would command the Australians in the attack on Vichy Syria, while Lieutenant General Noel Beresford-Peirse was given command of the Western Desert Force, which included the garrison in Tobruk.

The next attack was on 16/17 April and was led by the *Trento* and *Ariete*, and they suffered their first setback. One battalion in particular (lacking any AT guns) of the newly arriving *Trento* was mauled on the 16th. This was caused by an artillery barrage which scattered the Italian battalion and then shifted fire onto the Italian rear, keeping them from retreating. Then Australian troops and Bren carriers advanced and captured much of the battalion. The *Ariete* arrived with only a dozen L3's and seven M13's, and acting sluggishly watched as the *Trento*'s prisoners marched away into the Australian prisoner pen. The Italians suffered 24 dead, 112 wounded, and 436 prisoners, while Australian losses were negligible.

Rommel confronted General Baldassarre, the *Ariete*'s commander, about the poor performance of the tanks, and asked for an attack the following day. Four M13's and seven L3's, all with volunteer officers (as this mission was viewed as hopeless), attacked the Australian position in an unsupported assault. German troops finally arrived as the Italians were retreating from Australian artillery fire—and the German AT guns knocked out two Italian tanks!

An analysis of these actions is revealing. Both assaults were conducted with a lack of artillery preparation, though the *Luftwaffe* lent some support in the German attack of 13/14 April. The Germans launched a co-ordinated assault, with objectives that were known to the officers and men; the Italian battalion was unsure of its objectives at the time of the assault and thought they would have tank support, which was not forthcoming. The few tanks that the *Ariete* could field were present on the 16th, but not up with the infantry of the *Trento* (*Ariete* fielded so few tanks due to the wastage of the advance from Agedabia to Tobruk and their tanks were mechanically unreliable). Rommel wrote of the Italian attack, "It was now finally clear that there was no hope of doing anything against the enemy defenses with the forces we had, largely because of the poor state of training and useless equipment of the Italian troops. I decided to break off the attack until the arrival of more troops." Yet it must be noted that both the Germans and the Italians lost their respective actions. German Colonel Olbrich (soon to be relieved and sent home) felt that part of the reason was due to what the Germans were told before the battle. He wrote that, "The information distributed before the action told us that the enemy was about to withdraw, his artillery was weak and his morale had become very low....The (German) regiment had not the slightest idea of the well-designed and constructed defenses...." So we can conclude that both of the Axis partners lost; the Italians were not as well equipped or as well trained as the Germans. The Australians in a prepared defensive position were tough.

On 24 April Rommel radioed that the situation was not good, that "Italian troops (were) unreliable," the *5th Leicht Panzer* needed to be expanded into a full *Panzer* division and the arrival of the *15th Panzer* had to be accelerated. Two days later leading elements of the *15th* were airlifted into Benghazi. The arrival of this division would affect Commonwealth plans.

These initial assaults in April had been beaten back, with Germany suffering her first defeat in Africa. General Halder, never a Rommel admirer, dispatched General Friedrich von Paulus, the Quartermaster General of the German army, later commander at Stalingrad, to Africa to observe the situation. Halder said von Paulus was "perhaps the only man with sufficient personal influence to head off this soldier gone stark mad." Von Paulus concluded that logistics were key to this theater and that the Axis were in a dangerous position lying between a fortress and a growing mobile British force. But before this could be developed, von Paulus was asked by Rommel to help on the next assault on Tobruk scheduled just a few days after he arrived in Africa.

The next attack between 30 April and 4 May 1941 was defeated in part due to the increased strength of the defenses at Tobruk, including the use of mines, and greater defense in depth. Additionally, Morshead made excellent use of reserves, including his tanks. The German and Italian divisions made a lodgment; the Aussies counterattacked but could not force them out. But the Axis could not break in further. Losses for the Germans were 125 dead, 402 wounded and 131 missing; and for the Italians were 155 dead, 347 wounded and 238 missing. The Commonwealth losses were 59 dead, 355 wounded, and 383 missing. Rommel, after this episode, decided that his *Panzer* General Streich was correct in advocating an attack against Tobruk to the east, close to where the Commonwealth made the breakin in January of 1941, but he relieved Streich, due to continuing friction, with General Johannes von Ravenstein, who took over on 31 May.

After this action, von Paulus recommended that the supply

lines be improved, and the first step involved the improvement of the facilities at Tripoli and Benghazi for receiving supplies, and AA protection. After supplies were built up, the next step was to increase the number of vehicles available to the Axis forces. To place this in context, there were 164,000 German and Italian troops in North Africa that summer, along with 8,800 Italian and 7,000 German vehicles demanding fuel, and even 3,500 horses and 1,500 asses belonging to the military. Civilian and military requirements called for 30 shiploads a month to arrive in North Africa, preferably as close to the front as possible. General Halder commented that "By overstepping his orders, Rommel has brought about a situation for which our present supply capabilities are insufficient." All of these preparations took place with the backdrop of the planned attack against the Soviet Union and the Balkans campaign.

During the rest of the summer and fall, with the Axis air forces dominating the sky, there was constant skirmishing, patrolling, and losses around the perimeter of Tobruk. Overall, the honors went to the Commonwealth. Eventually the Australian command—and government in Canberra—insisted that the Australians be evacuated from Tobruk; this was carried out in a series of convoys so that all Australians could fight together. Not quite all were hauled out by the time of Crusader. They were replaced by the Polish Carpathian brigade, a Czech battalion, and the British 70th Division. The old 3rd Armored brigade was folded into the new 32nd Army Tank brigade organized in Tobruk and strengthened with both Matilda, or "I", tanks and cruisers. The process resulted in about 47,000 men being evacuated with the loss of 34 warships and merchant ships and 33 more damaged (many of them being quite small).

Brevity & Battleaxe

It doesn't look so hot but nothing can be done against it. It will prove the undoing of the Mk. II (Matilda).

> —Captured British officer when shown an 88mm AT gun after Brevity

On 25-26 April, Axis units of the newly formed *Herff Group*

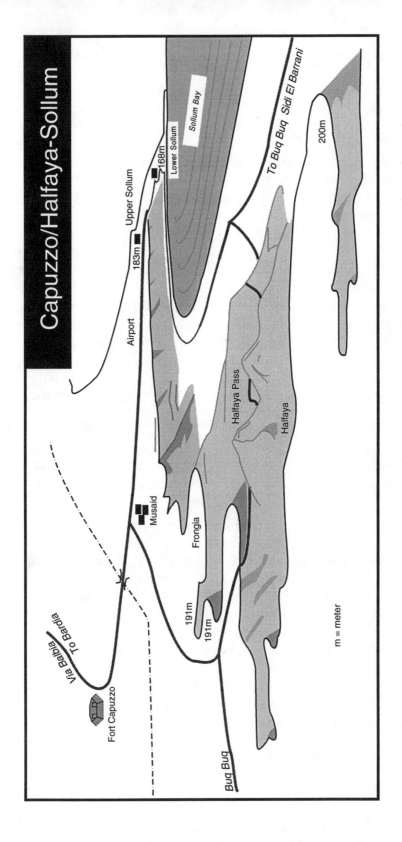

Capuzzo/Halfaya-Sollum

Fort Capuzzo

Via Balbia
To Bardia

Buq Buq

Musaid

Frongia

191m

191m

Airport

183m

Upper Sollum

168m

Lower Sollum

Sollum Bay

Halfaya Pass

Halfaya

To Buq Buq Sidi El Barrani

200m

m = meter

pushed the Commonwealth away from Fort Capuzzo and seized Halfaya Pass. Portions of the *Herff* group then took up defensive position with a mixed Axis force consisting of the *8th Bersaglieri* and a platoon of *Arditi*, with the Italians under Colonel Montemurro, and a smaller group of Germans under Colonel Herff, with some 88mm guns for defense. The *Arditi* were hand picked men formed from existing units (unlike the World War I practice of creating a separate special corps of *Arditi*). The main garrisons were at Sollum, Halfaya, Musaid, Fort Capuzzo, and Points 206 and 208, with a local reserve, including some armor, at Bardia, which altogether numbered some 6,000 men. There had not been enough time or supplies to place minefields and barbed wire, so fortifications consisted of the rocky positions and some old walls. It was this obstacle that Wavell intended first to crush and then push on Tobruk. In April Wavell reported,

> I have just received disquieting intelligence. I was expecting another German Colonial (Light *Panzer*) division, which disembarked at Tripoli early this month, to appear in the fighting line about the end of the month. Certain units have already been identified. I have just been informed that (the) latest evidence indicates this is not a colonial but an armored division. If so, the situation is indeed serious, since an armored division contains over 400 tanks of which 138 are medium. If the enemy can arrange supply it will take a lot stopping.

Part of Wavell's problem was that he overestimated what was in a German *Panzer* division based on what was fielded in the French campaign; since then the TO&E had been reduced. So he felt he must strike and strike with strength. This also had to be done against the background of the retreat from Greece involving several Commonwealth divisions and the German air assault on Crete. Additionally, the Middle East was starting to heat up in Iraq and Vichy Syria.

The first Commonwealth attack against Rommel was due in part to the impact of ULTRA. With the dispatch of the German *15th Panzer* to Libya, ULTRA alerted the British to this fact, hence the Commonwealth offensive. Additionally, ULTRA had intercepted von Paulus' report to Germany stating that the Axis forces needed to reorganize and re-equip. Knowing the failure of the Axis before Tobruk, and wanting to strike a blow before the *15th Panzer* arrived, Wavell ordered an attack. In retrospect it seems absurd to think such a small Commonwealth force could break its way against two Axis armored divisions, even if understrength, and the *Trento* division.

Knowing the *15th Panzer* was on its way, triggered the sending of the Tiger convoy of reinforcments to Egypt, running it directly through the Mediterranean. But the decision to launch Operation Brevity before the Tiger convoy tanks arrived at the front was due to the ULTRA intelligence. ULTRA, at this time, was primarily of value in deciphering messages and reports such as von Paulus sent, and determining the Axis order of battle. Once a battle commenced, ULTRA was, at this stage of the war, far too slow to influence events decisively, and Axis field intelligence was superior to the Commonwealth tactical intelligence capability. Additionally the British were still learning the capability of the German equipment. For example, it was only after Brevity that the Commonwealth began to realize the Germans were using the 88mm AA gun as an AT gun. Intelligence reports knew of this from the French campaign, but the Commonwealth forces in North Africa had yet to learn this!

Still, Wavell was receiving a welcome addition. Not only did the Royal Navy bombard Benghazi with a cruiser force on 7 May, and by destroyers on 11 May, but the convoy, with the loss of only one of the five fast transports, landed 43 Hurricane fighters, 135 Matildas, 82 Cruisers, and 21 puny Mark VI tanks. The equipment would not be ready for Brevity, but would be for Battleaxe, so Wavell could use all that he had on hand.

Now, with Churchill's urging, Wavell was going to attempt to push the larger Axis force back to Derna and relieve the sally port of Tobruk. The Commonwealth erroneously still thought their Matilda tanks could roll over the Axis opposition. Brevity would prove this wrong. Additionally, the physically large 88mm AT guns could be well camouflaged. By designing a firing position that stayed close to the ground (within three feet was the rule of thumb), a position could be hidden due to haze created by the heat of the desert. So an approaching enemy might have to get in closer than 150 yards before really seeing the enemy's positions, and at that range they would be a very vulnerable target.

In Operation Brevity the British advanced with three small groups. One thrust was on the coast, primarily made up of infantry. Its goal was to block the Axis forces and then capture the lower portion of Halfaya Pass and Sollum. The second group, made up of the 24 Matildas and the motorized 22nd Guards Group (its transport stolen from the 4th Indian division), was to advance along the top of the escarpment and seize the top of Halfaya Pass. The third group, under Brigadier W.H.E. "Strafer" Gott was to take a weak "7th Armored Brigade Group" and advance west, destroying any enemy forces encountered. General Beresford-Peirse had overall command and was in the rear.

The operation began on 15 May. The British enjoyed some initial success, and captured Halfaya Pass and Fort Capuzzo. In this action, after Germans in a nearby position had retreated, the *Bersaglieri* remained. When the *Bersaglieri* realized, at 400 yards, that their 47mm AT guns were worthless against the Matilda's hull, they shifted targets to the Matilda's tracks and undercarriages when they came up crossing the low stone walls and rocks of the position. Seven Matildas were knocked out in this fashion.

The Commonwealth was forced to retreat when Rommel realized how weak the enemy force was and prepared a counterattack, using the Bardia reserve and a battalion of the *8th Panzer* regiment. Gott, too, realized the same thing and ordered a retreat just in time, in spite of orders from General Beresford-Peirse to hold. Gott retained Halfaya but abandoned all other positions captured. The Italians lost 395, while the Germans lost 258 men and a few tanks. Commonwealth losses were over 160 men and some tanks. Rommel recommended the Iron Cross First Class for Colonel Montemurro for his conduct in the action. The Italian official war historian Mario Montanari gives several reasons why the Italians defeated the enemy in this action, in contrast to the Battle of Sidi El Barrani in 1940. He states that the Italians fighting here were better trained, had superior officers, showed a higher level of *esprit de corps*, and had some victories (such as El Mechili) under their belt. Furthermore, they had the German example to follow, and they had confidence in German tanks and in Rommel.

Motorcycle mounted **Bersaglieri** *in the desert; note the distance between bikes, maintained for dust control* (Ufficio Storico).

The Germans, under Colonel Herff, developed an attack on Halfaya Pass on 26 May, and by the 27th forced the British out of the position. The British suffered 173 casualties in this failed defense.

For Battleaxe the Axis defense had undergone some changes. Halfaya was held by 400 Italian and 500 German troops with artillery consisting of five 88's, four Italian 100/17mm's, and a battery of French built 155mm guns. Also present was Captain Wilhelm Bach of the first battalion, *104th Rifle* regiment, a former pastor. Bach would become a legend here for his very pious and inspiring attitude and being very capable in his defense of Halfaya.

Additional garrisons were, again, at Sollum, Musaid, Fort Capuzzo, Points 206 and 208, with a local reserve at Bardia. During this action a *raggruppamento* of about 2,000 men under Colonel Montemurro made up of *Bersaglieri* and elements of the *Ariete* would guard against a sortie from Tobruk. Montemurro would return to Italy on 20 September, due to his poor health, and Rommel would say at his farewell, "The German soldier

71

astonished the world, but the Bersaglieri astonished the German soldier."

Axis intelligence was well prepared for the Commonwealth attack. Their radio intercept intelligence units had been reading the Commonwealth radio mail for this operation and kept Rommel well informed throughout this action.

Operation Battleaxe began on 15 June under the command of General Beresford-Peirse, who was sixty miles in the rear, and employed the 7th Armored and 4th Indian divisions (now fully returned from the *A.O.I.* and refitted), and the 22nd Guards brigade. The plan called for the Indians, backed by Matilda tanks, to seize Halfaya Pass, while the 7th Armored "Desert Rats," also supported by the Matildas, would swing around on the south side of the escarpment and cut off the coastal garrisons and then fight an armor battle. The Commonwealth had about 200 tanks total. Wavell thought he was facing 300 German tanks, with 200 before Tobruk, and 100 forward near Bardia and Sollum. His goal was to defeat the German tanks in detail. In reality, the *15th Panzer* had only 85 tanks and the *5th Leicht Panzer* had only 100.

The battle at Halfaya Pass was so bitter that it would be renamed Hellfire Pass. The attacking British tank commander reported "they are tearing my tanks to bits." The Matilda tank could not stand up to the German 88m AT gun, but after fierce fighting, a lodgment was made by the Guards and Indian infantry. It was here the German 88's and Italian 100/17mm's under Major Pardi, combined with newly laid minefields, inflicted heavy losses on the British and helped retain the pass for the Axis. The motorized infantry of the *62nd* regiment of the *Trento* was at Halfaya Pass and at one point they knocked out seven of ten attacking Matildas with the 47mm AT guns and one truck mounted 105/28mm Italian naval gun.

It was in the armor action to the west that one of the new German oasis companies first saw combat. Point 208, an old Arab graveyard, was a fortified position for the *1st Oasis Company*. Lightly armed with machine guns and AT rifles, with no man over the age of 30, the company had four 88mm guns attached, a small Italian contingent, and some 37mm AT guns. Eventually numbering five companies, they would be effectively wiped out during Operation Crusader and deactivated in April of 1942. They received one of the first attacks in the battle and held, inflicting tank losses on the advancing Commonwealth. The Axis retention of Halfaya Pass meant the Commonwealth forces could not link up and could not push in the Axis defenses.

An armor action developed on 16 June, and the Germans had some anxious moments. But their superior weapons and training gave them a great advantage in open combat. As both the *5th Leicht* and *15th Panzer* advanced toward the coast on the British left flank during Battleaxe, Rommel sent a message by plane to the defenders at Halfaya Pass. It read, "Our counterattack now making fine progress from the west. Enemy forced onto the defensive. Victory depends on your holding the Halfaya Pass and the coastal plain." The defenders answered this call and held, helping to secure the victory Rommel helped to inspire. By the evening of 17 June, Wavell had arrived at the front and agreed with various commanders there that it was time to withdraw. Total Axis losses in the operation were 592 Italians and 685 Germans, while the Commonwealth suffered 969 casualties. Tank losses, after damaged ones were repaired, were 12 for the Germans and 91 for the Commonwealth (64 were Matildas). The advantage of controlling the battlefield at the end of an armored battle was really brought home here, as the Germans could easily recover their damaged tanks. A handful of Matildas made it into the German inventory and would continue to turn up from time to time throughout Operation Crusader.

The Commonwealth tried to control the air in this action, and suffered the loss of 36 planes. Air Marshal Tedder learned from this action the need to have tighter cooperation between the air and land forces, and though his plan would not see fruition for many more months, a start in tighter coordinating of Allied land/air operations was under way.

The Italians paused to study the situation and planned to improve their strength in North Africa by 100,000 men, 14,000 vehicles, including two additional armored divisions, and increasing the artillery complement of all their frontline units by an additional 850 artillery pieces. This included the introduction

90mm guns in action (Ufficio Storico).

of their 90/53mm AA/AT gun, a truck mounted weapon that was quite similiar in combat to the German 88, but would not arrive until after Crusader. It suffered from being a high profile weapon and, it was a poor off-road weapon as it was not mounted on a four wheel drive truck. Earlier, Germany had supplied some 88's to the Italians and an Italian battalion of them would fight as AA guns in the coming battle. Also planned was the assignment of small numbers (approximately 15) of the obsolete L3 light tanks, usually mounting flamethrowers, to the Italian infantry divisions.

While a fine plan on paper, the reality would be that only a small part of the Italian program could be implemented. At least the Italian infantry divisions now had enough artillery in numbers, if not quality, to match an equivalent sized Commonwealth formation. Italy had also moved the *Giovani Fascisti* (Young Fascists) of two battalions to North Africa. The equivalent to older Hitler Youth members, they were nicknamed "Mussolini's Boys." These young men would fight well in the coming battle. Additionally, the *Trieste* motorized division had

Rommel conferring with General Bastico (Klaus Hubbuch).

arrived in August and elements of the *Littorio* armored division also arrived.

They had the right ideas, but a lack of resources to implement them, especially in light of losses about to be incurred in Operation Crusader, as well as wastage in Russia, where Italy was sending an expeditionary force in the "Crusade against Bolshevism." Finally, ULTRA, joined with the advantages of planes, ships, and submarines operating from Malta, and the technical advantages of radar, combined to hurt the supply lines between Europe and North Africa to a degree which resulted in large Axis losses and periodic halting of convoy sailings. All this would keep their plans from becoming reality.

On 12 July an Axis command change took place. General Gariboldi returned to Italy and later went on to the Russian Front. His replacement took over on 19 July and was General Ettore Bastico, a friend of Mussolini, who had served in Ethiopia and Spain. He had recently been commander of the garrison in the Dodecanese islands in the Aegean. Bastico was placed in command of *Comando Superiore Africa Settentrionale* (Superior North African Command). His chief of staff, General Gastone

Gambara, was a Fascist hero in the Spanish Civil War and friend to Mussolini's son-in-law Count Ciano, the foreign minister of Italy. Bastico was expected to give Rommel less rein than Gariboldi. Gambara was also given command of a special independent corps, the *Corpo D'Armata di Manovra* (Army Corps of Maneuver), made up of the *Ariete* and *Trieste* divisions, and the Italian *Raggruppamento Esplorante* or *RECAM* reconnaissance group. Rommel hated not having this Italian unit under his command. Rommel referred to Bastico, who was known to be "difficult, autocratic, and violent," as "Bombastico," and both Bastico and Gambara as "shits."

Comando Supremo's Ugo Cavallero insisted that one commander be named to command both the Italian and German units in the frontline and that the commander be Rommel, even though he was both a German and low in seniority. This may have been done by Cavallero to make the command situation in Africa more efficient, and in part due to his dislike of Bastico. Cavallero also believed strongly in cooperation with Germany and may have been in part motivated by this. Bastico kept direct command through Gambara of the *Corpo D'Armata di Manovra*, but Rommel now commanded all other troops, Italian and German, on the frontline and theoretically reported to Bastico.

Another factor now came into play, one which the Italians resented as a growing intrusion into their theater. Earlier the German High Command had sent additional staff elements, under Major-General Alfred Gause, an engineer, as Chief of Staff to Rommel. Part of Berlin's reason for establishing a staff level command was to bridle Rommel with a larger command structure. After meeting and being impressed by Rommel during Battleaxe, Gause had his entire staff placed at Rommel's disposal and worked well with him over the coming months! Now with Rommel's victories, both in Brevity and Battleaxe, and the news reports being disseminated, his stock rose even higher. Hitler wanted to promote Rommel to be a full *Panzer* general after the victory at Battleaxe, but this created resentment among the German generals, including Halder, as well as with many Italian generals. It was finally decided to make Rommel a commander of a *Panzer gruppe* (Armor group) with his com-

Rommel in the desert (Bundesarchiv, courtesy of *Moments in History*).

mand including the Italian *XXI Infantry Corps* and all German units, effective 15 August 1941.

As Rommel made his meteoric rise, some of his fellow officers became jealous. Colonel von Herff, the man who recaptured Halfaya after Brevity, said that Rommel gave "erratic leadership" and made "grotesque decisions." Rommel's habit of court-martialing an officer for failure caused General Streich to complain that "This has not been the way in the German army before." The South African Official History summarized the situation well. It stated that,

> Rommel had arrived in Africa six months earlier in charge of an enlarged light division, placed at the disposal of the local Italian Headquarters to stiffen up their anti-tank defence. He was now safely established as the commander of a large army, with powers which, by alternately ignoring his Italian chief and treating with studied insolence, he had made into a virtually independent jurisdiction.

This command arrangement was certainly difficult and would create problems in the coming battle.

German strength also increased with the formation of an infantry division, the *90th Light* or z.b.V. (Special Services) *Afrika* division which was formed from pooling various units together. Part of it was made up of ex-French Foreign Legionnaires. At this time it consisted of only two regiments with five infantry battalions and it would be a nonmotorized unit for Crusader. Not until July 1942 would it have three regiments of two battalions each.

The *5th Leicht Panzer* was reconstituted as the *21st Panzer* on 1 August 1941. With virtually no German tanks arriving between July 1941 and 19 December 1941, there were generally only repaired damaged ones to add to the force. Due to these shortages, both *Panzer* divisions would only have three companies of tanks instead of the usual four until 1942. This would be the *Deutsches Afrika Korps* or *D.A.K.* and was under the command of Lieutenant General Ludwig Cruewell.

Preparations were still going forward for the assault on Tobruk. Rommel visited Europe for a vacation. Suffering from jaundice, he was in Italy with his wife near the start of Operation Crusader. He planned for the invasion of Egypt to begin as early as February 1942, unless Bizerta in Tunisia could be used for supplies, a situation which would further ease his logistical problem.

Churchill's loss of faith in Wavell and the two defeats in North Africa, combined with Wavell's foot dragging over Iraq and Vichy Syria, brought about a change of command. General Claude Auchinleck was given command on 5 July 1941. He was to wait, in spite of Churchill's urging, until November when the 8th Army, activated on 24 September, was strong enough to attempt a further relief of Tobruk. Auchinleck was not going to rush forward, which was what Churchill wanted and pressured him to do, until he was at proper strength. According to Winston Churchill, "General Auchinleck's four and a half months delay in engaging the enemy was alike a mistake and a misfortune." Churchill held this view for three reasons. First, Germany was fully engaged in her war with Russia, and an Allied offensive in Africa would help Russia; secondly, due to ULTRA revelations which Auchinleck was not as well informed about as Churchill, Winston knew that the Axis supply situation was at best poor and possibly precarious. Finally, Churchill was a very aggressive leader.

Auchinleck received reinforcements from the Empire and Allied nations. By July 1941, 5,000 tons of supplies per day were being unloaded at Egyptian ports. New aircraft reinforcements were arriving on the Takoradi Air Route using airfields in both Commonwealth and Free French territories, like Chad. The first South African units arrived for duty in North Africa now that the *A.O.I.* campaign was over. The Commonwealth troops that had served in Greece had been refitted and brought up to effective strength. These new forces meant the Western Desert Force was about to become the 8th Army.

Something had to be done to relieve the pressure on Tobruk. As Operation Crusader loomed, the unrest in the Allied camp created by the string of Axis victories in 1941, culminating with the fall of Greece and Crete, and the actions in Iraq and Syria, had created an atmosphere in the Middle East that the Australians called the "Muddle East!"

Sideshows

There is no more murderous wolf for the Arabs and no deadlier foe of Islam than Britain....If you give some attention to the location of countries and continents, and if you understand the strategic significance of the British wars, you will then see that the Arabs have no future unless the British Empire comes to an end.

> —Colonel Salah ad-Din as-Sabbagh,
> most prominent leader of the
> Golden Square

Two small campaigns of interest were fought in 1941. The first concerns the nationalistic and militaristic government of Iraq mesmerized with the vision of creating a greater Mesopotamian kingdom that would include Syria and possibly Palestine, in the form of an Arab federation and as an expression of "Pan-Arab" sentiments. This would give Iraq an outlet to the Mediterranean and create a powerful country. With the success of the Axis in the spring of 1941, it seemed to some of her lead-

ers, primarily in her army, that their hour had arrived. Combined with a Vichy ruled Syria on her flank, and vague promises of aid from the Axis, Iraq decided it was time to eliminate British residual rule in Iraq, symbolized by two British controlled airbases. The policy that was adopted was in co-ordination with the Grand Mufti of Jerusalem.

Into this came the Free French under de Gaulle. In his early attempts to rally the French Union to the Cross of Lorraine and the Free French, de Gaulle had come to look at Syria as a prize. As one would expect in the Middle East, there were many wheels within wheels turning in this political arena involving Turkish neutrality, Arabs, Jews, Free French (and who was to lead them), the Commonwealth, Vichy France, and more!

It was in Iraq that this first came to a head. Early in April there was a coup against the pro-British regent led by Iraq's army and the "Golden

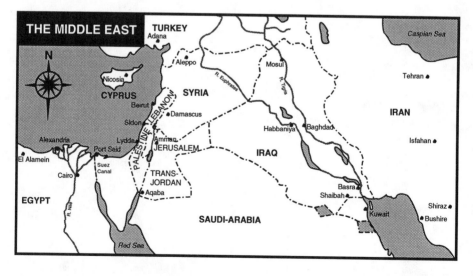

Square" faction within it. The British tried to negotiate with this new government but Churchill adopted a relatively hard line, introducing Indian troops under treaty right into the Basra area, where one of the two British airbases was located. By the end of April the Iraq government felt strong enough to refuse the introduction of additional Commonwealth troops into Iraq and moved a force on 30 April outside the other British airbase near Baghdad at Habbaniya. On 2 May, the British government countered, and authorized a re-emptive airstrike with some third rate aircraft against this Iraqi position. Hostilities had commenced.

While the Iraqi government thought they would receive Axis support, and Mussolini wanted to help, as did the German Foreign Minister Joachim von Ribbentrop, Hitler was too preoccupied with the upcoming war with Russia and gave scant attention to this sideshow. After the disasters that had struck the military machine of Italy, Mussolini was in no position to offer any substantial help and so Iraq was largely on her own. Germany did authorize the *Abwehr*, or Secret Service, to plan some sabotage on the oil pipelines in the region and military supplies were to be flown to Iraq. One problem that arose is that since the Iraqi army of four divisions numbering 50,000 was armed with British equipment, the Germans could not supply ammunition to them!

The French government in Syria and Vichy, for political reasons, wanted to curry favor with Germany at this time and so when they were approached by Germany to help Iraq by supplying war materiel and landing rights for Axis aircraft,

they agreed. Germany and Vichy France kept this secret from the Italians! By the second week in May there were 24 German He-111's and Me-110's in Iraq while numerous Ju-52's had arrived with supplies, while French war materiel was arriving in Mosul, Iraq. By the end of May Italy had supplied some equipment and a squadron of Cr-42's. But this was not enough in the way of help for Iraq. The Golden Square was emboldened at this point to think that Iraq could hold out for three months against the Commonwealth forces and that by then Axis support would be substantial, so they sought no compromise. It is ironic to note that this Iraqi government approached Saudi Arabia, the most independent of all Arab states, for support against the British, but the government of King Saud argued strongly for Iraq and Britain to end the fighting.

The reality of the Iraqi position was to be much harsher. The Iraqi army proved to be a weak reed. First Wavell, after much protesting to London and asking for a compromise with Iraq, scrapped together a small column called "Habforce" in TransJordan which headed off towards Iraq from the west to relieve Habbaniya. Habforce units included the famous "Arab Legion" trained by Major John Bagot Glubb, or "Glubb Pasha," which would later become the Jordan Arab Army. Meanwhile the Indian strength gathering at Basra grew in numbers and strength.

Habforce pushed across the desert quickly, though it did have to deal with one small mutiny of Arab troops who felt they had no quarrel with fellow Arabs, brushed aside feeble Iraqi resistence, cut off Baghdad from Mosul and linked up with Habbaniya on 18 May. By the end of the month, the Iraqi government had either fled to the north or over the border into Iran. On 1 June 1940 the Commonwealth troops had entered Baghdad and the former government was restored—after some riots on 2-3 June in the Jewish section of Baghdad which resulted in over 150 Jewish dead. By the end of the war all four leaders of the Golden Square had been caught and executed.

Field Marshal Wilhelm Keitel gave Cavallero his evaluation of these events later, writing, "The Iraqi government attacked too soon. Support was not made ready in advance. Germany and Italy were determined to make effective help available, [but] this failed on account of too rapid a collapse of the Iraqi will to resist and difficulties in transporting troops, weapons and supplies." One key factor was the swiftness with which Churchill acted in nipping this affair in the bud.

Arab reaction to the revolt was muted, though in Egypt the dissident Arab military officers wanted to "make Egypt a second Iraq," but Aziz al-Misri who led the dissident officers at this time felt that the time was not right and that they must wait until the Axis army penetrated into Egypt. So these officers, including Nasser and Sadat, would wait.

The Allied invasion of Syria and Lebanon, the Vichy French mandate, was to be a much different situation. Again, Wavell resisted efforts to mount this effort, and it was one more nail in his coffin as commander of this theater. The Free French predicted little resistence, but this was not to prove true.

The Allied forces entered Vichy-controlled Syria (which included Lebanon) on 8 June 1941. Facing them was the *Armee de Levant* which numbered about 33,250 French regulars. They were organized into 20 battalions of French, 11 of local native troops, 9,000 men in cavalry units, and some tanks and artillery. The tanks numbered 90 R35's and 56 FT17's, the former being quite good because they were armed with a 37mm gun and had 45mm of frontal armor. While some of the native troops simply disappeared, the tough French Foreign Legion and other professionals would valiantly resist the Allies (but never the Axis, a theme that would recur throughout the war). The Vichy French also supported this with light naval forces there in several skirmishes off the coast including one bombardment of Australian positions from French destroyers.

The Allied forces consisted of a two-brigade 7th Australian division, six Free French battalions, a brigade of the 4th Indian (trained in mountain warfare), and some miscellaneous forces that included horsemen of the British 1st Cavalry division, commandos, and some Jewish units including one with Moshe Dayan, later the Israeli defense minister. It would subsequently be reinforced with Habforce, the Arab Legion, a Czech battalion, some tanks, and other dribs and drabs that were scrapped up from wherever they could be found.

The Australians pushed up the coast and attacked the first night with the intent to move quickly forward and capture Beirut. Checked at the end of the first day they knew they faced a determined enemy and "it was evident that [the Vichy] intended to fight hard and that there would be no swift occupation of Beirut by a force which had only to brush aside token resistance." It would be hard going as the Aussies slowly advanced up the coast toward Beirut.

Fierce fighting also took place in the drive on Damascus, including Vichy French tank counterattacks which tried to cut the Allied supply lines and did force the surrender, with the help of the tanks, of the 1st Royal Fusiliers battalion on 16 June. The Allied force did capture Damascus on 21 June, though the hills around it were not to be cleared of Vichy troops before the armistice.

Vichy tried to reinforce its garrison from France by moving several battalions to Greece for sea transport from there, but it was too little too late, while German aid did not materialize with the war with Russia about to begin. The Vichy troops fought as hard as they did because they were well trained professional soldiers and they wanted to show that their army was ". . .ready to sacrifice itself in a struggle against Eng-

lish attacks, hopeless though it may be, because it believes that by this demonstration of loyalty to Germany it can improve the position of metropolitan France and the rest of the colonial empire for the duration of the armistice treaty and in the peace treaty." They had fought hard enough to force the Allies to bring up additional forces and fighting would last until 12 July when the French commander surrendered.

Allied losses were about 3,300 and the Free French lost 1,300. Vichy losses were about 6,000 of which 1,000 were dead. This action created much bitterness in various circles in France and may have been unnecessary, but it did secure the flank north of Egypt and made a good impression on neutral Turkey.

The Vichy French troops had a choice of returning to France or a possession like North Africa, or becoming Free French. Out of 37,736 offered this choice, only 5,668 joined the Free French. Some of these surrendering units went on to fight the Allies again in Vichy North Africa in 1942. Two Australian divisions would be occupying Syria for the remainder of the year, along with other forces.

Rommel and One Translator's View

Walter Spitaler, born in 1918, an inhabitant of the South Tyrol (a part of Italy dominated by German-speaking inhabitants), opted for returning to Germany when Mussolini and Hitler made a special agreement concerning the German people of this Italian region, and ended up serving

in both armies. Later he acted for a short period of time as a translator for General Rommel.

Spitaler completed his service in the Italian army in December of 1939 where he served in the *Trento* division. The *Trento* motorized division had men from all of Italy serving in it but the majority hailed from the Trento and Bolzano regions of northern Italy. He was immediately recalled to service with the German army after Christmas of 1939 and by the time he arrived in Africa was a sergeant.

Spitaler's opinion of the NCO class was that while the Italian army had some very good NCO's, there "were also many bad people, who remained in the army but were not fit for command." The German NCO was quite good, but as the war went on the "quality of the German NCO became poorer."

Spitaler was one of the first advance members of the *Wehrmacht* to arrive in Italy and was one of the first to serve in Africa. Spitaler served the first two weeks in Africa as Rommel's interpreter before being replaced by a *Sonderfuehrer*, a special semi-civilian rank which was similiar to an administrative rank of captain.

Spitaler confirms much about Rommel that we know. Toward officers, Rommel "was hard with all the officers (Italian or German) without exception . . . (and he) expected from the officers what he expected from himself. And if and when he found them in the rear...woe!...with NCO's and the soldiers he was friendly." Spitaler says that the soldiers gave "a hearty welcome to Rommel when he visited the troops on the frontline, including the *Bersaglieri*. He always brought something with him, for example the mail. He was undaunted under the artillery bombardments, while I heard from others that later in the war he feared the [enemy] fighters."

After the short period of translating, Spitaler remained close to Rommel and was authorized by him to purchase food from the Italian *Intendenza* or supply service. This was due in part to Rommel's liking pasta! Spitaler tells that "Rommel ate pasta when he was traveling out of the headquarters." Spitaler goes on to say that "when he was with the HQ he ate like the soldiers, including camel flesh the few times we were unfortunate to receive it. But when he was traveling, I was charged with purchasing for Rommel pasta, tomatoes, parmigiano cheese and olive oil."

He recalls one personal encounter when he had shaved his Italo Balbo style beard off. Rommel "asked me why I no longer had my beard. I answered that the lieutenant had ordered me to shave it off, and he replied 'You have my permission to have the beard.'" Spitaler remained with the *Panzermachrichten* (an administrative section) that was attached to *DAK* headquarters until being slightly wounded at El Alamein and was then shipped home.

El Mechili

Fought in the early part of the war, these two small battles are often ignored. The first action was an armor engagement on 24 January 1941, which, if it had been strategically handled differently by the Italians, might have avoided the defeat at Beda Fomm. The second action was during Rommel's remarkable advance on Tobruk, where, on 8 April 1941 the 3rd Indian Brigade was forced to surrender to the *12th Bersaglieri*.

During January, after the fall of Tobruk, the 6th Australian troops advanced to the edge of the Jebel Achdar, or Cyrenaica bulge, and had been halted at Derna. This check to the Australian advance at Derna was due to elements of the Italian *XX Corps,* numbering about 5,000 men made up a battalion of Libyan paratroops, *2nd* battalion *86th* regiment of the *Sabratha,* the *18th Libyan* battalion, an ad hoc battalion of the *Marmarica* and some Italian naval 102mm guns.

To the south of Derna was Gen-

eral Babini's *Brigata Corazzata Speciale,* or Special Armor Brigade at El Mechili. El Mechili was an old Turkish fort with water, located at the terminus of several desert trails. Outside the small fort was an airfield. Formed on 29 August, the *Babini Brigade* was originally more an administrative unit than a combat unit, and had two *raggruppamenti,* each of one medium and three light tank battalions. The first *raggruppamento* had been parceled out in penny packets and had been destroyed at Sidi El Barrani, Bardia, and Tobruk. This second one was made up of the *3rd* and *5th* battalions of medium tanks; it had a total of 57 of the new M13 tanks, and was formed on 25 November 1940 to face the 7th Armored. The three under-strength Italian Armor divisions re-

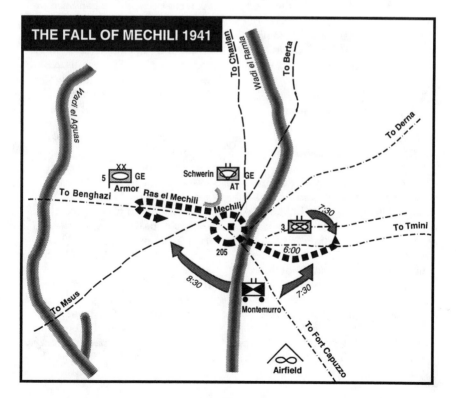

THE FALL OF MECHILI 1941

mained in Italy for a long planned invasion of Yugoslavia. The crews had little time to train with them, but the M13 was armed with a turret mounting a 47mm gun, the largest gun so far on an Italian tank. The *20th* battalion of twenty-five L3 tanks was also present. Supporting it was artillery of the *Raggruppamento Celere* of the *XX Army Corps* and the motorized *Piano* group or *Raggruppamento Motorizzato* which numbered 1,896 men. It was largely artillery with several companies of motorized machine guns. Italian intelligence, in one of its rare coups in this campaign, had discovered by radio traffic that the British 4th Armored brigade, supported by divisional artillery, was to attack on the 24th to seize El Mechili, so the Italians tried to set up an ambush.

Instead, the British got the drop on Babini's column, and began to fire on it as it was moving. Babini reacted by ordering his tanks to charge the British position; they were forced to withdraw with the loss of one cruiser and six light tanks. Babini lost eight M13's.

Chief of Staff General Giuseppe Tellera correctly decided that the British would now concentrate their 7th Armored division against Babini, and so, with Marshal Graziani's fear that the British fielded too many tanks against the Italians, ordered Babini's troops to withdraw from the Derna front on 25th. Tellera was probably correct in ordering a retreat. If he could not offer reinforcements to Babini, the 7th Armored Division would have overwhelmed Babini. O'Connor was "incensed" that the Italian armor was not destroyed and that it had escaped. The upshot of this was that

the British rested for almost two weeks and prepared to launch an attack across the desert to cut off the Italians at Beda Fomm, which would be the final curtain call of the Italian disasters in the winter of 1940-41.

The second battle of El Mechili was fought on 8 April 1941. Of the four mixed columns that Rommel had sent racing across the desert, three were to rendezvous at El Mechili, which was garrisoned by General Gambier-Parry with his 2nd Armored division headquarters, the regiment-sized 3rd Indian Motor Brigade, M Battery of the Royal Horse Artillery, and part of the 3rd Australian AT Regiment. The 3rd Indian Motor had no armor, no AT guns, was minus one battalion, lacked half of its radios and its primary weapons were rifles. But it had been expecting the arrival of the 2nd Armored division, which never arrived. Rommel had elements of his army arriving at El Mechili on 6 April and wanted to attack, which created a scene with General Streich (who Rommel accused of cowardice) but there were virtually no troops to attack with. Rommel did muster a small attack which he neglects to mention in his memoirs. On the following day, Rommel had to fly to various Axis columns and to guide them in to complete the encirclement of the Allies by the end of the 7th. Rommel ordered his troops to attack on the 8th. By then Gambier-Parry had ordered his troops to break out and retreat on Tobruk at first light.

North and northeast was the *Schwerin* battlegroup, east was the *Fabris* battlegroup (made up largely of the *3rd Bersaglieri Motorcycle* battalion of the $\bar{A}$*riete* and part of the so-called *Santamaria Reconnaissance Group).* It included two batteries, a company of 47mm AT guns, three sections of 20mm AA guns, some engineers, and a German radio team. The *5th Panzer* regiment HQ was to the west. Approaching was approximately two-thirds of Colonel Giuseppe Montemurro's *12th Bersaglieri* battalion of the *8th Bersaglieri* regiment, while behind it were the main German tanks, though they never arrived before the battle was decided. The Indians launched four probes about 0530, searching for a way out of the bag. One probe was blocked by the *3rd Bersaglieri* battalion in the south, another was repulsed by the *Schwerin,* and the third was repulsed by the *5th Panzer* HQ command unit. The fourth probe advanced between the *Montemurro* and the *Fabris* battle-

groups to hit the *Fabris* in the rear. This probe failed because of the Italian 75/27mm guns, and because of flank counterattacks of the *Montemurro* and *Fabris* battlegroups.

At this point *Montemurro* received orders to advance. While moving under fire with his *12th Regiment,* the retreating Indian column, after its encounter with the HQ of the *5th Panzer* regiment, came in sight. *Montemurro* quickly deployed and opened immediate fire with all available guns. General Gambier-Parry and the 3rd Indian Motor Brigade surrendered to *Montemurro,* as the HQ of the *5th Panzer* regiment arrived. A total of 1,200 POW's were taken, though some troops, including some brave Australians, did escape the bag. *Montemurro* and the *12th Bersaglieri* would go on from there to win further honors.

Barbary Corsairs

There is an interesting sidelight to Derna, the small port just west of Tobruk. This was the site where ". . . to the shores of Tripoli" from the U.S. Marine Corps hymn originated and went on to become an American legend. It was Derna that was stormed by a mixed force of Arabs and Christians under the command of ex-Consul William Eaton and Marine Lieutenant Presley O'Bannon whose namesake would see action in the Solomons as the destroyer *O'Bannon* in 1942.

During the 1801-1805 war with the Barbary Corsairs, it was decided that the brother of the current pasha

of Tripoli, Hamet Karamanli, should be supported in an attempt to regain his control of his castle at Derna. He had lost it in a revolt against his brother in a 1802-1804 rebellion. Previous to that, Hamet had been the pasha of Tripoli but had even earlier lost the throne to his brother.

In an incredible saga, a small motley army made up of a handful of Marines, some local Christians (largely Greeks) and Arabs, marched across the desert to the Gulf of Bomba where they met up with a small squadron of U.S. Navy ships. An attack was made on Derna and in a stirring action, highlighted with a charge led by the Marines, the castle was captured and the brother of the pasha was once again in control of Derna, that is, until a Tripoli army arrived. While under siege it was learned that peace had been concluded between the United States and Tripoli and so all the Christians and Hamet Karamanli and his suite were lifted off secretly from Derna by the U.S. naval squadron, though the locals were left to the tender mercies of the Tripoli army.

The Young Fascists Division

In 1938 the premilitary education training was taken from the *MVSN* and assigned to the *GIL* or *Gioventu Italiana del Littoria,* which regrouped young fascists between age 17 and 21, who were obliged to follow courses organized by the local *GIL* command.

From 25,000 of these young men were formed 25 battalions of *Giovani Fascisti* (Young Fascists), known as *GGFF.* At the outbreak of the war many people in the *GIL* tried to enlist as volunteers, convinced that the premilitary training already received was far beyond the required standard for war. On the other hand, much of the Italian public was far from enthusiastic for the conflict; and for this reason the *PNF* organized a rally called "March of the Youth" *(marcia della giovinezza),* which would start at Marenzano in Liguria and end at Padua in Veneto, marching through the entire Po Valley. It was to show the high enthusiastic adhesion of the youth to the war, influencing the popular attitude. This did not happen due to deficiencies in the general organization of the rally. The march aroused more than some doubts and much criticism. There were also polemics with the Army, since at some

point it was believed that Mussolini wanted to promote all the *GGFF's* membership to complement officers; to avoid this possibility, the senior officers of the Army obtained the disbanding of the *GGFF* and their later enlistment in the regular armed forces.

Only three *GGFF* battalions remained and were later reduced to two, mainly of university students. Although it was a very restrictive measure against the *GGFF,* it was possible to select the best elements among who were still available and enthusiastic. Waiting for an opportunity for employing them and with the settling of the unavoidable polemics between the Army and the *PNF,* it was possible to impart to the *GGFF* a meticulous training with particular attention to the best physical conditioning. The unit was then sent to Africa as a well trained and *elan* filled unit.

The *GGFF* arrived in North Africa at the end of July 1941 with a total of 69 officers and about 1,500 NCOs and volunteers.

After further intensive training they were issued better equipment. Besides the standard individual armament of rifle, hand grenades and dagger, the *GGFF* obtained also 27 automatic rifles (light machine guns), 9 machine guns, four 81mm mortars, four AT 47/32 guns and 15 Solothurn AT rifles. They had 24 Passaglia anti-tank bombs, ineffective devices which equipped the tank hunter squads, distributed one per platoon. The newly formed unit was called "Gruppo di battaglioni GGFF" and had available also an effective *autodrappello* (transport unit) at the headquarter level and one mobile repair unit, which guaranteed the unit's total independence. For this reason the GGFF were included in the *Raggruppamento Esplorante del Corpo d'armata di manovra (RECAM)*, later called *Raggruppamento esplorante corazzato*, or REC.

RECAM included:
1) HQ
 GGFF battalion group
 PAI *(Polizia Africa italiana)* battalion on motorcycle
 one artillery mobile group "Voloire" with
 three squadrons of 75mm guns on captured vehicles
 one 120mm squadron on Lancia 3RO trucks
 one C3 light tank company
 one M13/40 tank company (terribly understrength)
 one L6 tank platoon
 two armored cars

In the most famous fighting of the GGFF at Bir el Gubi the following units participated:
 HQ *Gruppo battaglioni GGFF*
 C3 tank company
 1st GGFF battalion with one mortar platoon and the gun company of the *8th Bersaglieri* regiment
 2nd GGFF battalion
 PA/radio unit

one 47/32mm AT platoon of *9th Bersaglieri* regiment
one machine gun platoon of the *8th Bersaglieri* regiment

In 1942 the GGFF battalion group was transformed into the GGFF regiment, because of the proposed building of a new armored division called GGFF of which only the one regiment was ever formed. It was one of four battalions with:
 2 rifle battalions (ex-GGFF battalions)
 1 AT battalion with 47/32 mm (ex GGFF)
 1 CCNN "M" battalion (X brigade)

The TO&E organization of the GGFF armored division was never realized in Tunisia and relied on units available:
 GGFF regiment
 8th Bersaglieri regiment (with elements of the *5th Centauro, 7th Trento* and *8th Ariete Bersaglieri* regiment)
 139th artillery regiment (ex-*132nd Ariete*)

The division lacked, however, tanks.

The entire history of the militarized Blackshirts of the Fascist regime of Mussolini strikes one as an unrealized dream. From the idea of *elan* filled party men led by aging and physically out of shape party leaders into battle, to the GGFF made up of University students with both intelligence and commitment to a bankrupt ideology fighting in the desert sands of North Africa, this interesting aspect of Italian history has been for too long not fully researched because of the dead hand of the past. A complete study of this aspect of the war, if possible, will only be written when Italy is not afraid to look fully at her past.

CHAPTER 3

The Approach of Crusader

Tell your Major Revetria he's much too nervous. Tell him not to worry—because the British aren't going to attack....

—Rommel's Intelligence officer Major Friedrich Mellenthin on 11 November to his opposite on General Bastico's staff

...the enemy attack will not be merely diversionary, but a heavy offensive aimed at forcing a final decision.

—General Bastico to Cavallero on the eve of Crusader

Rommel was ignoring the growing body of intelligence that suggested a British counterattack, and he was determined to finish off Tobruk—it had become an "obsession." To accomplish this he massed 461 pieces of Axis artillery, part being *Panzergruppe Artillerie 104* under the command of Major General Karl Boettcher. *Panzergruppe Artillerie 104* included nine 210mm howitzers, thirty-eight 150mm howitzers, and twelve 105mm, though the latter were used in a field role. Boettcher envisioned a three hour preparation bombardment of the defenses of Tobruk, and Rommel would order the assault to occur in the third week of November. This would be followed with the new *Afrika* division punching a hole in the Tobruk defenses and the *15th Panzer* exploiting through, with the *115th Rifle* regiment in their vehicles. General Enea Navarini's *XXI Corps* of Italian infantry would cover the left flank of the advance and launch a feint in the west. Troops thoroughly practiced attacking various types of trench and bunker complexes. Air photographs were

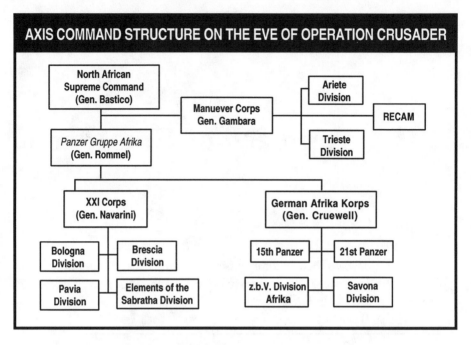

AXIS COMMAND STRUCTURE ON THE EVE OF OPERATION CRUSADER

- North African Supreme Command (Gen. Bastico)
  - Manuever Corps Gen. Gambara
    - Ariete Division
    - RECAM
    - Trieste Division
  - Panzer Gruppe Afrika (Gen. Rommel)
    - XXI Corps (Gen. Navarini)
      - Bologna Division
      - Brescia Division
      - Pavia Division
      - Elements of the Sabratha Division
    - German Afrika Korps (Gen. Cruewell)
      - 15th Panzer
      - 21st Panzer
      - z.b.V. Division Afrika
      - Savona Division

distributed down to six-man sections. All would be supported by the Axis air forces giving ground support, primarily Stukas and CR42's (the CR42 was an Italian biplane fighter converted to ground support duties, but could not carry a large bomb load like the Stuka).

Von Paulus had pointed out to Rommel the weakness of his Sollum front and this was further highlighted by the Commonwealth Brevity and Battleaxe operations. Realizing that this front needed to be strengthened, especially in light of his forthcoming assault against Tobruk, Rommel reinforced the Sollum front, a decision that would influence the forthcoming battle.

In the interim, Rommel conducted Operation Midsummer Night's Dream starting on 14 September, an excursion into Egypt looking for a British supply dump and an exercise to keep his forces sharp. He went in with part of the newly renamed *21st Panzer* under General von Ravenstein (formerly the *5th Leicht*, the change took place on 1 August). Von Ravenstein had his trucks and tanks drag brushwood to create clouds of dust to simulate a much larger force. While ULTRA and other intelligence sources did not reveal this move to the Commonwealth, it still hit empty air and was bombed by the RAF. Rommel took some light casualties (including his driver killed by an enemy fighter), but it reinforced his conviction that the Commonwealth was not planning any major advance.

One other important task was completed that hot summer in the desert—the building of the bypass road. This road was an extension of the Via Balbia around the perimeter of Tobruk, allowing for faster movement to the Wire and was called the *Strada del'Asse* or *Achsenstrasse*. The Commonwealth had not been idle either, and had advanced their Egyptian railhead to within 60 miles of the Wire. ULTRA did give the Commonwealth a solid understanding of the enemy order of battle. It gave the Axis 385 tanks, and if the Italian L tanks are not included, it was right on the mark. The fundamental problem for the Commonwealth was not realizing how effective German equipment was, especially the 88mm AT gun, against the Commonwealth tanks which Hitler was describing as late as June of 1942 as "tin." Additionally there was not a deep understanding of the German tactics, which the Italians were beginning to emulate more and more. For example, the Commonwealth thought that the Germans would set up an AT line (which the Commonwealth tanks might run into), while in reality the Germans brought their AT guns along with them at all times and operated them directly with their tanks. The capability of Axis armor was also downplayed. The 2nd Royal Gloucestershire Hussars regimental history tells of a British Intelligence officer who,

> had previously given us a talk on German and Italian tanks, and had said that the only tank that might bother us was the German Mk. IV, and that there were only twenty of them in North Africa. The German Mk. II and III and the Italian M.13 would, he assured us, present no difficulties. We almost felt sorry for the enemy.

The discounting of the Mk. III (Pz III) was due to the supposed inferior armor, which in reality was just the opposite. Nor must we underestimate German intelligence services which were quite efficient at the tactical level in these days, and Italian intelligence at the operational level which had been predicting a Commonwealth attack for some time.

20 November was the date to attack Tobruk. As the time

88mm gun showing high profile (Ufficio Storico).

approached there were disquieting reports, primarily Italian, which indicated an upcoming attack by the Commonwealth. The German command refused to believe it, and Rommel ignored information that indicated such an attack. On 18 November Gambara sent a message to *Comando Supremo*, "Intercepted enemy messages (radioed in the clear) make us suppose that there is an imminent enemy attack from the south on Sidi Omar and Bir El Gobi." Still, the frontier was shielded by German reconnaissance units, and General Gambara and the commander of the *Savona* division on the Wire, General Fedele de Giorgis, had the *Trieste, Ariete,* and *Savona* divisions on alert when the Commonwealth struck. The Commonwealth position was stronger than at any previous point and had recovered from the defeats of the spring and summer. General Auchinleck was in supreme command and is considered by many to be the best Allied General to fight Rommel. He certainly was the reason, due to his resolve, why the Commonwealth would win at Crusader; and it was due to his efforts that Rommel would later be stopped on the El Alamein line. But he was weak in certain key areas. He chose poor subordinates, possibly in part due to being in India for most of his life and not knowing who was who. Cunningham and Ritchie are examples of such choices, both of whom were in over their heads when it was rough going.

He also did not inspire his troops, and especially depressed the troops of the Empire, like the South Africans and Australians, by continuing the British policy of parcelling out the various formations in tiny packages. Not only was he a great advocate of the jock column, which did not fit into British doctrine, but it was not unusual to see a South African unit serving with an Indian unit and a British unit as an ad hoc brigade, or brigade group, and this was simply not good policy. Below Auchinleck's brigade group was a smaller one, the battle group, which was still larger than a jock column. A South African staff officer remarked that the difference between the two was "a Battle Group was a brigade which has twice been overrun by tanks."

The Commonwealth Plan

There remained, however, a marked difference between Auchinleck's and Churchill's views of the offensive. Churchill expected it to open 'a continuing path' leading, as a matter of course, to Tripolitania, and if possible to French North Africa or even Sicily. But Auchinleck was still inclined to see it in terms of security rather than gain.
—New Zealand Official History

By 18 November German tank strength was 70 Panzer II's, 130 Panzer III's, 35 Panzer IV's and a few captured Matildas. The Germans had thirty-five 88mm guns (12 on the Sollum front and the rest with the *Afrika Korps*—these numbers are often switched in sources), one hundred and one 50mm, two 75mm, and thirty-three 37mm AT guns. The British knew at the start of Operation Crusader that the German 37mm and 50mm AT guns could use a special shot that could penetrate their tanks at medium ranges; for example, 440 yards for the 50mm AT gun. They had not yet realized the great range of the 88mm gun, thinking that it was effective only at medium ranges—certainly not the 2,000 yards it was capable of. They had no idea of the

Italian L-tanks being transported by truck (Ufficio Storico).

number of German tanks which had extra armor added to their hulls, though it was essentially all the Pz III's and IV's, and they did not know it was face hardened—which meant that the 2-pounder AT gun could only penetrate at short range.

The Italian tank strength was concentrated mostly with the *Ariete*, which had one hundred thirty-seven M13 tanks and fifty-two L3 tanks. The *RECAM* of the Italian army had 39 L tanks, nine M13's and about 20 armored cars. *XXI Army Corps* had 51 L tanks distributed to it, though most of these L3's were configured as flamethrowers, a type of weapon particularly hated by infantrymen.

The Axis position had the Sollum frontier covered by two weak unattached German battalions, a battalion of German

Italian AB41 armored cars accompanied by motorcycle troops on the right (Ufficio Storico).

motorized infantry courtesy of the *DAK*, several *Oasis* companies, and the Italian *Savona* infantry division, reinforced with some artillery and miscellaneous units, all behind minefields (including mines designed for tanks) and fortifications. This was a much improved defensive position than what faced the Commonwealth during Brevity and Battleaxe.

Surrounding Tobruk was Navarini's *XXI Corps* made up, from west to east, of the *Brescia*, *Trento*, and *Bologna* divisions, with the *Pavia* nearby in reserve. Also present in the lines was the new German *Afrika* division. The *DAK* lay between Bardia and Tobruk near the Via Balbia, with the *15th Panzer* closest to Tobruk. The *Ariete* was moving forward to Bir El Gobi and the *Trieste* motorized division lay slightly in the rear near Bir Hacheim. In the open between Tobruk and the frontier were the two German *Recce* units, detached from their respective *Panzer* divisions, acting as a screen. They would be first to alert the Axis of the attacking Commonwealth.

The Commonwealth had improved its tank situation in three ways. First they had increased their overall numbers, as well as their capacity to repair damaged tanks, so that they had a substantial numerical advantage over the Axis. Also, they had many tanks now in reserve so that depleted formations could be brought up to strength in the course of the battle. The normal turn around time for repairing a tank was still high—three months. This was due to lack of mechanics, as well as transport to and from the front. Secondly, they had the first American built tank in the Middle East—the Stuart. It was called the "Honey" by the troops, a name coined when the first batch arrived in the Middle East and it was assigned for testing. Testing one of these was Major R. Crisp, a famous South African cricketer, who asked his driver, Whaley, what he thought of it and Whaley said, "It's a honey, sir." The Stuart was very reliable compared to British built tanks, and the 37mm gun it carried had an explosive shell as well as a solid shot. The only disadvantage it had was that it required frequent refueling due to its small fuel tanks.

The final advantage the British had was the new Crusader tank which was present in substantial numbers. It had 40mm frontal armor, which was better than the older cruiser style tanks, but mechanically it was still not very good and most of them ended up with the 22nd Armored brigade, which was a green unit fresh from Great Britain. Another problem with the British built cruiser tanks were that they tended to "brew up," or burn, easily, an unpopular feature with the crew!

Total Commonwealth tank strength under General Cunningham broke down as follows. The 7th Armored "Desert Rats" had 335 Crusaders and older cruisers and 165 Stuart tanks. The Stuarts were concentrated in the 4th Armored brigade. The 1st and 32nd Army Tank brigades had 213 I-tanks (Matildas and Valentines), two Crusaders, 33 older cruisers, and 25 light tanks. Commonwealth infantry divisions at this time usually had light tanks and Bren carriers in their divisional cavalry regiments (which were the equivalent of a battalion). At no time were these tanks concentrated, and later their force would be further diluted due to losses. Still, Auchinleck had tanks in reserve, while most Axis reinforcements would be sunk at sea and Axis convoy sailings were suspended for part of the battle.

The Commonwealth plan for Operation Crusader was initially quite straightforward but did not develop as planned at all. As a battle, it lasted much longer than anticipated and would leave both sides exhausted, the Axis in retreat, the Common-wealth in control of the battlefield and Tobruk relieved—a victory.

Auchinleck wanted to protect the Nile Valley and the remain-der of the Middle East, so he was not inclined to begin the offensive early. Churchill and others put pressure on him to undertake the advance so as to relieve Tobruk, which would take a lot of pressure off the Royal Navy which had to resupply the port, and bring them closer to Malta so the RAF could better support Malta's defense and operations against the Axis supply lines. Churchill wanted to throw the Axis out of Africa as quickly as possible, especially since Germany was deeply in-volved in the Soviet Union and the Soviet Union might fall—so he wanted to get on with it.

Several plans were considered before the adoption of a plan that called for the infantry and "I" tanks of XIII Corps to advance against the Sollum front, cut it off and reduce it if possible, and then advance along the escarpment to the west. XXX Corps, with three Armored brigades and the 1st South Africans (chosen due to their motorized experience in the fighting under Cunningham in the *A.O.I.* and made fully motor-ized for this battle by stealing trucks from other units), was given the task of guarding the left flank of XIII Corps and destroying the Axis armor. The expected reaction of the Axis armor was to deploy their tanks south of Fort Capuzzo. A tank battle would result in which the British armor units would destroy the Germans in a defensive battle. The Italian armor tended to be discounted in the Commonwealth equation. The Tobruk garrison would then sortie when ordered to linkup, most likely with the South Africans, after the British had defeated the German tanks. Out in the deep desert, a mixed "Oasis Force" was to capture Jalo Oasis.

Auchinleck first sent the 8th Army into an intensive training period. This affected all troops in his command, but was unevenly spread due to the arrival of new materiel and other factors. The result was the newly arrived 1st South African division actually delayed the offensive for a week as they had spent most of their time entrenching Mersa Matruh instead of

South African prisoners at the time of the fall of Tobruk (Ufficio Storico).

training, and the 22nd and 4th Armored brigades had not received enough practice with their new tanks.

The new players in the desert were the South Africans, known as "Springboks," and they were a rather unique breed. By 31 October 1941 there were nearly 60,000 South Africans in Egypt, which included two divisions, seven air force squadrons, "four armoured car regiments, and a large number of engineers" and laborers, many of whom were men of color. The 1st and 2nd South Africans were present for this battle, though the 2nd was only used at the end to clear the frontier posts and acted as a reserve for the first part of the battle. The 1st had the fewest number of troops of color of any fighting South African army unit to fight in the desert.

The South Africans did not field enough men to fight in the major units that they raised. So it became common for them to use only two of three brigades when they went into battle. This is why the 1st South African would fight during Crusader as a two brigade division. This situation was due in part to there being too many formations requiring troops (many new ones had been formed at the outbreak of the war), non-white troops were not allowed to fight, and many white South Africans, primarily the ones of Boer descent, did not want to volunteer to help the British Empire.

The white South Africans divided their men of color into two groups: natives and "coloured men" (i.e., mixed races) of the Cape Corps. The native troops were employed largely as orderlies, laborers, stretcher bearers, and truck drivers. The "coloured men" were used primarily as long distance drivers, eventually working on routes that stretched from Persia and Turkey, but also served at the front with native drivers. The racist philosophy of many of the South Africans resulted in one interesting incident after the surrender of the 2nd South African at Tobruk in 1942. Several South African officers approached Rommel and asked him if they could be kept in prisoner pens separate from their fellow black troops. Rommel asked if they had fought together in their army against the Axis, and since they had, he ordered that they be put in the same prisoner pen!

Before turning to the battle, the situation in Tobruk needs to be touched on. In Tobruk was the 70th British Infantry, the Polish Carpathian brigade, a battalion of Czech troops, the 32nd Army Tank brigade, and some miscellaneous units including some Australians who had not been evacuated yet.

The Polish unit was made up largely of men who had escaped their country after its fall in 1939, a very dedicated group. As one Australian said, they were,

> self-selected by initiative, sifted by adversity, culled of he weak-hearted by surmounted barriers and motivated by insatiable hatred of their nation's oppressors, the bank of eager, vengefull men who constituted the Carpathian Brigade were trained to a pitch that matched their ardour to fight.

They were placed opposite Italian units on the western side of the Tobruk frontlines which upset them, as they wanted to be opposite the hated Jerry.

Opening Round

The Germans never again massed such quantities of heavy tanks nor did they ever attack our armoured forces with such ferocity.
—General Gott's aide after the armor battles

The concentration of the Commonwealth forces was completed by 17 November. The preparation was well handled, many of the tanks even advancing with a "sunshade" which made them look like trucks from enemy aerial reconnaissance, though it was also helped by some heavy rains which kept many Axis aircraft grounded. At dawn on the 18th XXX Corps began to cross the frontier and by the end of the day was at its first day's objectives, though the British built cruisers had suffered numerous breakdowns. During the day XIII Corps closed up on the fortified Axis frontier. The fundamental problem with Cunningham's plan now began to reveal itself. The future actions of the British armor were predicated on the German armor moving forward to do battle. But Rommel did not react as expected. He continued to virtually ignore the Commonwealth advance, though his *Recce* units reported the Commonwealth advance, as he did not want to delay his assault on Tobruk. It was decided by General Gott, commander of the 7th Armored division, to advance further and take both Bir El Gobi and Sidi Rezegh.

Gott joined the advance of the 22nd Armored brigade, detailed to Bir El Gobi, and personally ordered the attack on a portion of the *Ariete* which was deploying into that position. His reasons have never been fully stated, but may have been seen as an opportunity to "blood" the newly arrived 22nd on what was thought to be a relatively weak unit, and to protect his left flank. The *Ariete*'s strength was overestimated by the attacking 22nd Armored brigade, as not all of the *Ariete* had arrived.

The battle opened with the *Ariete*'s artillery and the *Bersaglieri* deploying into three strongpoints, while a company of their tanks advanced to meet the approaching 22nd. In this, the *Ariete*'s tanks suffered a check and they fell back on their

Captured Italian truck mounted 102mm naval gun used during Operation Crusader; note British intelligence officer in the foreground (courtesy Lucio Ceva & Andrea Curami).

strongpoints. The *Ariete*'s tanks next deployed to the north of the three strongpoints and supported by a battalion of 105/28mm guns under Major Pasquali and the *Milmart* (Italian coast defense unit) of seven truck mounted naval 102mm guns with armor piercing shells designed to fire against ship's armor under Captain Priore. The latter weapon was a stopgap and was being used here as a heavy gun to stop Allied tanks.

At noon the 22nd Armored began the attack with the British tanks advancing in a large semicircle. The main thrust was centered on the middle strongpoint which was defended by *Bersaglieri*, 47/32 AT guns and artillery of the second battalion of the *132nd* artillery regiment. The Italian defense was well "organized and could effectively react" from defilade positions from which they could hit the 22nd's tanks at an angle.

The strongpoint on the Italian right was able to frustrate the 22nd Armored which moved across their front, suffering their fire in the process, to reinforce the attack on the center, which made little progress. On the Italian left, the *Bersaglieri* had just

Italian **Bersaglieri** *motorcycle troops mounted on Moto Guzzi's* (Ufficio Storico).

arrived and went into immediate combat in the open. Fortunately, they were supported by their artillery and AT guns which helped to restore the situation, but only temporarily. This British tank attack was described by Major Hastings as "the nearest thing to a cavalry charge with tanks seen during this war." By 1330 the Italian position on the left was beginning to crack and tanks of the 22nd were among the defenders. Some of the defenders surrendered, but with no one to receive their surrender (the 22nd had no sizeable amount of supporting infantry) they went back to their guns and the fight. This was a common occurrence in the course of the war in the desert.

By 1500 the 22nd was massing to continue the advance, having captured the Italian left position, but the stand by the *Bersaglieri* had allowed the tanks of the *Ariete* to form up behind them, supported by the guns of the *Milmart*. The British advanced with the sun in the eyes of the Italians, but the high profile truck mounted 102mm guns (mistaken for 88's) played havoc among the Crusader tanks, and it was an action at close enough range that even the Italian 47mm gun was effective.

Finally a battalion of the *Ariete* hit the flank and rear of the disordered 22nd, and forced it to retreat, which they achieved with their greater speed.

As Piscitelli Taeggi Oderisio wrote,

At 5:00 pm there was no more bullet whistle, no more shell burst. Here two tanks clashed with bows locked, they remained half suspended like rampant lions. Together they burned. One, two, three at a time, exploded machinegun rounds with short and sharp shots, like popping wood pieces in the fire box. Some feet away another tank had its turret thrown away and lying on one flank, as if a knife had cut off the head of an orange, smoking slowly from the damaged opening. And with the coming of dusk, more fires became visible. All around the fires were burning, and then sometimes would come an explosion with a big flaming outburst.

The Italians lost 34 tanks, eight 47mm AT guns, one 65mm gun, 15 dead, 80 wounded, and 82 missing. The Italians claimed that the British lost about 50 tanks and other support vehicles. (It is argued that the difference between the 25, claimed in the British Official History, and the 50 the Italians claim, represents the British tanks repaired after Operation Crusader was completely over in January). Three British accounts during and just after the action state that they either won the battle or the Italian unit was officered by Germans or, in one account, that Pz IV tanks fought alongside the M13's and German infantry were present! Germans were not present and Rommel was unaware of the action for hours. Correlli Barnett in his book *The Desert Generals* states the loss as 52 British tanks, while General Verney, divisional historian for the 7th Armored, gives the loss as 45 tanks.

In any event, the 22nd Armored was repulsed and suffered substantial losses at the start of the battle and left the *Ariete* in possession of the field. Italians feel that this combat improvement is due to elite units being sent to Africa, lessons learned, and the impact of the Germans in the theater. The weapons were generally the same but better used and some effort had been made to improve leadership. Interestingly enough, at the tactical unit level, there was a spirit of revenge against the Italian High Command and government for the disorganization, for both the lack of equipment and the poor quality of it, and for being forced to fight this "poor man's war" (the Germans were considered to be the billionaires of the war from the Italian point of view). "First win this war, then rendering of all accounts" was an element of the Italian spirit in November 1941.

Meanwhile, the rest of the 7th Armored division was successful in its advance. The 7th Armored brigade advanced on Sidi Rezegh's *Regia Aeronautica* landing ground. The 6th Royal Tank Regiment charged the field, accompanied by South African armored cars, and in the ensuing action planes were taking off, some exploding in mid-air, "but there were others which turned the tables by flying low and shooting up the attackers." Sidi Rezegh became a focal point in this battle because one of the three escarpments blocking the way to Tobruk diminishes here and the second escarpment can easily be ascended.

The 7th Support Group was hesitant to move forward to Sidi Rezegh with bad news coming in from Bir El Gobi. So even though the *Afrika* division, with little in the way of AT guns, was on the escarpment above Sidi Rezegh and worried about the British tanks below, the British armor would not move further until infantry support arrived.

Further east the 4th Armored brigade met up with *DAK*. General Cruewell had moved the *15th Panzer* to the escarpment near Gambut, overlooking the open desert to the south and stationed it near the *21st Panzer*. The reconnaissance forces of the 4th were having trouble pushing back the German *Recce* units and so reinforced it with the 3rd Royal Tank Regiment. Rommel would not release these two *Panzer* divisions for an attack but he did authorize a battle group, which he accompanied, to push back the Commonwealth reconnaissance forces, and so *Kampfgruppe Stephan* was formed, which advanced south toward Gabr Saleh and hit the remaining part of the 4th Armored brigade with its "honey" tanks. Forces were evenly matched. The ensuing two hour action saw 23 Stuarts put out of action (12 were repaired in three days' time) and the Germans lose three tanks, with four damaged. The British claimed as certain 19 German tanks destroyed.

The key point here is what the British were reporting and what were the true German losses were widely at variance with reality. This would continue throughout the battle and would contribute to a false picture of the battle being formed in the rear at 8th Army headquarters.

Cunningham decided that for 20 November actions the 1st South African division would watch Bir El Gobi, while the 4th Armored brigade held Gabr Saleh, the 22nd Armored recovered and supported the 4th Armored, and the remainder of the 7th Armored division closed up on Sidi Rezegh. Rommel, alarmed that his assault on Tobruk was being interfered with, ordered the *DAK* to destroy the attacking British armor. Cruewell planned to attack each British column, but aimed his first blow too far east trying to crush any British armor between the escarpment and the Sollum Front, and it fell not on the 4th Armor, but on empty air.

Rommel had finally awakened from his slumber, with the final wake up call coming from a BBC broadcast to Cairo which stated, "The 8th Army with about 75,000 men excellently armed and equipped, have started a general offensive in the Western Desert with the aim of destroying the German-Italian forces in Africa." The planned Axis assault on Tobruk was over.

Rommel ordered *DAK* to take back Sidi Rezegh, which would halt the attempted linkup with Tobruk. This move against an isolated and smaller Commonwealth force with the full weight of *DAK* armor, would be the high point for the Axis in this battle.

Other decisions had been taken which set in motion the next stage of the battle. General Gott had suggested to General Willoughby Norrie, XXX Corps commander, that maybe 21 November should be the time to launch the 70th Infantry into its breakout from Tobruk—after some discussion the codeword for sortie of the garrison, "Pop," was given. Now with the *DAK* centered near the frontier, and planning to attack the 4th Armored on the 21st (gleaned by the Commonwealth from poor German radio communications), the 7th Armored brigade, the 7th Support group, and the 5th Brigade of the South Africans would support this breakout, and the 4th Armored, reinforced by the 22nd Armored would defeat the *DAK*. Interestingly enough, the New Zealand 2nd Infantry division, reinforced with Valentine tanks from the 1st Army Tank brigade, was standing ready and volunteered to help, but the British Armor disdained their use and refused it. It was too early in the war for proper co-operation between the various arms of the Commonwealth army.

Surprisingly, only an indecisive armor action was fought between the *15th Panzer* and the 4th Armored early on 21 November, though the 4th was forced back. The 22nd Armored brigade was late in arriving, and the *21st Panzer* was also late due to slow refueling. Twenty-six Stuarts were damaged or destroyed in this action while German losses were negligible.

The situation by the afternoon of 21 November reminded one of a fancy multilayer European cake. The Tobruk garrison had punched a costly hole, 4,000 yards deep and 4,000 yards wide, with German and Italian troops lining the edge. Next was a layer of Axis troops facing to the south preventing a linkup by the 7th Support Group north of Sidi Rezegh airfield. Then facing south was the 7th Armored brigade vainly holding off the *DAK*, which in turn was conducting a rearguard action, to combat the approach of the 4th and 22nd Armored brigades. Additionally, XIII Corps had been authorized to begin swinging around the Sollum front and begin assaulting the extreme southern positions at Sidi Omar and Nuovo Sidi Omar. Finally, the 1st South African was sending its 5th brigade toward Sidi Rezegh while the 1st South African brigade lay posted in front of the *Ariete*. As the British Official History stated, "A complicated situation indeed, which, if suggested as the setting of a training exercise, must have been rejected for the reason that in real life these things simply could not happen!"

The morning of the 21st was greeted with a Commonwealth success on the escarpment above Sidi Rezegh. Four minutes of artillery preparation fire opened the morning and then the Support Group's King's Royal Rifle Corps charged the ridge under heavy Axis artillery fire. The 6th Royal Tank Regiment then followed up and supported the assault. The Bren Carrier platoons led the attack— with the infantry on foot charging the hill—and captured 700 German and Italian troops. A 400 man battalion, supported by the 6th Royal Tank Regiment, had achieved this with but 84 casualties.

The second escarpment had now been breeched. The 6th Royal Tank Regiment pushed on, unsupported, toward El Duda, which was a small hill on the bypass road and which would be the next goal in linking up with the Tobruk garrison. But Rommel was present and watching this all unfold. He ordered the *3rd Recce* battalion from the *21st Panzer* up, attaching four 88mm AT guns, which combined with the *3rd Recce*'s organic 37mm and 50mm AT guns had by the end of the day destroyed all the tanks of the 6th Royal Tank Regiment which had crossed the escarpment.

Meanwhile, as *DAK* advanced to the north, they kept a strong rearguard, holding off the advancing 4th and 22nd Armored brigades. Though nominally speedier than the German tanks, the 4th and 22nd never came to grips with the *DAK* that day, largely due to the brilliant training and interaction of the German arms, though both Commonwealth brigades were slowed down due to the need to refuel.

For the 7th Armored brigade of British armor and the 7th divisional Support Group, supported by eight 25-pounders, to hold off two German *Panzers* was impossible. But, as the armor commander said of the assault of the *DAK*, "I had to treat it as a diversion, because the attack toward Tobruk was the main operation and had to go through." The *15th Panzer* would report that "Our tanks carried on the engagement vigorously, siting the anti-tank forces to the flank, and the enemy tanks were forced back north." The armor action at this First Battle of Sidi Rezegh on the 21st ended in a German victory if based on losses alone, but the reality was somewhat different. The 7th Desert Rats were severely drained, but they had held off the *DAK* and, in some ways more importantly, exhausted the ammunition of the German *Panzers* with their defensive stand. The armor battle that Cunningham had begun was roaring along, but not the way he expected.

Also on 21 November the largely British garrison in Tobruk had sortied in the early morning in an attempt to clear the ridges around Tobruk and link up with the advancing relief force. Demonstrations took place along much of the defensive perimeter, while the main assault was made with two infantry brigades and the 32nd Army Tank brigade against the Axis infantry. During this action the British did quite well, though suffering tremendous losses (a battalion of the Black Watch alone lost 200 killed). The advance involved I-tanks of the 4th Royal Tanks as well as 28 assorted cruiser tanks and 21 light tanks of the 1st Royal Tank regiment, which suffered most of its losses due to minefields and hidden AT gun positions. The front was a series of strongpoints, and not continuous trench lines. One was the "Tugun" position held by the *Bologna* infantry division, anything but an elite Italian formation. The New Zealand Official History states, "The more elaborate attack on Tugun went in at 3 p.m. and gained perhaps half the position, together with 250 Italians and many light field guns; but the Italians in the western half could not be dislodged and the base of the break-out area remained on this account uncomfortably narrow." The Official History goes on to comment on the ". . . strong Italian opposition at Tugun" as part of the reason for the decision to halt the sortie at this time.

On 22 November, as the Desert Rats concentrated their drained units, a battle for the airfield raged with the *15th Panzer*. Part of the 7th Support Group was overrun in the battle and many British tanks were destroyed. General Gott ordered the 7th Support Group to retire on the 5th South African brigade which had finally arrived on the edge of the battle. The retreat from battle succeeded, but the *15th Panzer* had called for the *21st Panzer* to help, and this brought about a fresh disaster for the British at Sidi Rezegh.

The *21st Panzer*, just after dusk, overran the laagered 4th Armored brigade, literally overrunning the brigade headquarters and smashing the 8th Hussars. The 7th Armored division was now down to less than 100 tanks.

Cunningham was ignorant of the results of this action, as reports simply were not forthcoming after the exhausting day's action. But he arrived at the decision that the battle had taken another new turn and was becoming an infantry battle. To help this along he ordered the New Zealanders to begin their advance from the rear of the Sollum front with two of their three brigades, the 4th and 6th, along with their supporting Valentine tanks, toward Tobruk. The 5th New Zealand with the 28th Maori battalion, and New Zealand cavalry would stay on the frontier. This would set in motion, along with Rommel's action, the key for victory in Operation Crusader and the ultimate linkup and relief of Tobruk.

Sunday, 23 November, was *Totensonntag* or the Day of the Dead—German Memorial Day. It would be a day of dramatic events in the desert battle and would result in the utter destruction of the 5th South African brigade as a fighting unit. General Cruewell had decided to mass the armor of the *DAK*, along with the *Ariete*, and literally start from the north of the battlefield and sweep all before it to the escarpment at Sidi Rezegh.

First he had to concentrate his forces and push the *15th Panzer* off to the north to link up with the *Ariete*, now proceeding from Bir El Gobi. The *15th Panzer* scattered the 7th Support Group, which was in its way, and came upon the halted transport portion of the 5th South African, which it attacked. The ensuing action saw the soft targets of the transport suffering badly, but brave fighting of the artillery did hurt the *15th Panzer*. Just past noon the *Ariete* and the *15th* linked up and shortly thereafter the *5th Panzer* regiment of the *21st Panzer* joined them. By 3:00 p.m. they were ready to begin a grand sweep across the desert.

The blow was about to fall on the 5th South African brigade which was formed up in a defensive laager or box, backed by their field and AT artillery. A portion of the *Ariete* was on the Axis left (four companies of tanks, a battalion of the *8th Bersaglieri*, a battalion of 65mm guns *en portee*, mounted on trucks, and two batteries of heavier artillery), then came the *15th Panzer* and then the *5th Panzer* regiment on the right or east wing. Armor was in the front with the infantry behind in their trucks, only to debus when under gunfire. General Boettcher's artillery delivered softening up fire from the northern escarpment. It would end up being primarily a German battle as the *Ariete* with its far weaker and underpowered tanks started late hitting off to the northwest of the main South African position. The *15th Panzer* literally broke into the South African position, while the *5th Panzer* hit to the right of the position. The slowness of the Italian tanks uncovered the German left flank to the counterattacking 22nd Armored brigade, but a battery of 88mm guns helped stop them. The tanks of the *Ariete* arrived only in time for some mopping up, though the truck mounted 65mm guns, firing as they advanced, did overrun a battery of 25-poun-

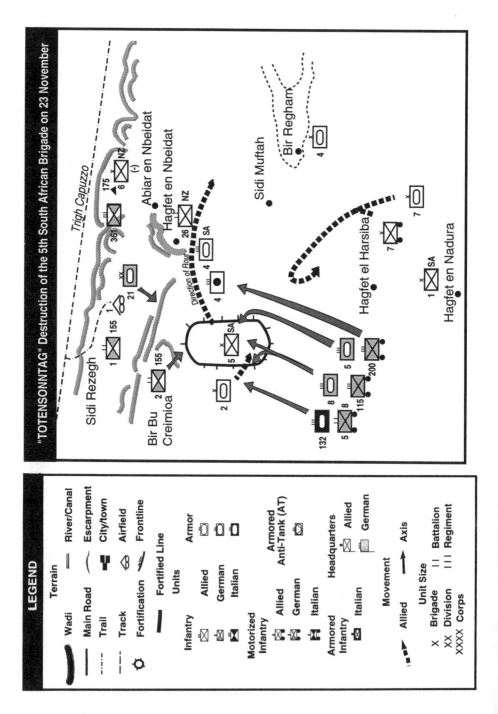

"TOTENSONNTAG" Destruction of the 5th South African Brigade on 23 November

ders. The Italian artillery commander Piscicelli recalled having an opportunity over the next few hours to examine first hand the excellent Commonwealth 25-pounders.

The Commonwealth artillery aquitted itself especially well, with the 25-pounders firing solid shot, which was effective from 600 yards and in against the German tanks. As a South African artillery officer reported, "At about 1515 approximately 200 enemy vehicles headed by tanks made an attack from the south-west, and the troop on my orders immediately engaged them over open sights." The German officers literally led from the front, and suffered terrible losses. Lieutenant-Colonel Zintel led his *115th Rifle* regiment "standing upright in his vehicle...(and) was one of the first to be killed...100 meters from the foremost enemy positions." Heinz Schmidt, aide-de-camp to Rommel had just transferred to the *115th Panzer* regiment and he wrote later,

> "Attack!" The order was passed swiftly. The regimental commander led, standing erect in his open car. The Major's car followed, with me right behind him. We headed straight for the enemy tanks. I glanced back. Behind me was a fan of our vehicles—a curious assortment of all types—spread out as far as the eye could see. There were armoured troop-carriers, cars of various kinds, caterpillars hauling mobile guns, heavy trucks with infantry, motorized anti-aircraft units. Thus we roared on toward the enemy "barricade."

Schmidt was wounded (slightly in the buttocks) along with the major (severely), while the commander was killed.

Unteroffizier (NCO) Klaus Hubbuch was present at the charge, a charge that may remind one of a modern day successful Pickett's Charge. Present with the *2nd* battalion of the *8th Panzer* regiment, Hubbuch recalls the radio message at the start of the day stating, "The enemy must be decisively beaten today." The company commander was killed just as they breached the South African screen, and the second in command died when his tank was repeatedly hit. Hubbuch goes on to say,

> After a brief fire combat the breakthrough into the enemy laager succeeded. The enemy supply columns, many enemy tanks, and many of ours were burning. Prisoners started coming and soon there were a thousand and many were South African Black and Indian.... The booty of 2-pounders *en portee*, artillery, AT weapons

and machine guns is very high. The approaching night had compelled us to attack without good preparation, and our losses of tanks and tank crews were very high.

But the 5th South African's brigade position had been broken into and the unit would be virtually annihilated. Various small units, collections of men and vehicles, and even individuals would escape and reappear over the following days in the rear, but it had been a costly victory for both sides. The South Africans had lost 3,394 casualties, about three-fourths as prisoners, including the brigade commander. The German force kept pushing on and linked up by the evening with the Axis forces in the escarpment above Sidi Rezegh. German losses were heavy for that day. The *DAK* had lost 72 tanks of the 162 it started the day with, as well as many troops, especially officers at the company and battalion level.

The immediate threat to Tobruk had been stopped, but the New Zealanders were now approaching along the escarpment, and Rommel was about to make a misstep.

The Dash to the Wire and Relief of Tobruk

The reckless manner in which he personally conducted [the Dash] largely contributed to its failure and led almost directly to the defeat of his army.

—General Michael Carver

The Axis had stopped the main Allied thrust. The 7th Armored division, which numbered now only a few dozen tanks, with the intact 1st South African brigade limped off to the south to refit. Now Rommel was thinking of some dramatic move to bring about the defeat of the Commonwealth and how he could help his beleaguered frontier garrisons. This would result in his "Dash for the Wire" which was nothing more than moving the *DAK*, but now with the *Ariete* under his command, to the frontier. The command change had taken place on the evening of 23 November as ordered by Mussolini, who shifted the *Ariete*, *Trieste*, and *RECAM* to Rommel's command.

The Dash would have several purposes. Not only would it

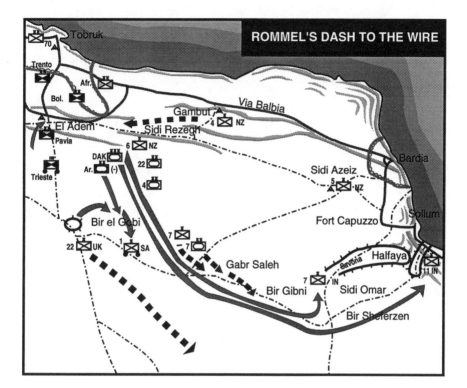

relieve the garrisons along the frontier, but he hoped to find a cache of Commonwealth supplies to replace his own and cut off those of the Commonwealth, and, finally, to break the spirit of the Commonwealth's command. Rommel came close to this achievement which would have brought about an outright Axis victory, but due to luck, the depleted strength of the Axis, and Auchinleck's indomitable spirit, victory was not to be his.

General Cruewell desired to consolidate the victory of *Totensonntag* by remaining in the area of Sidi Rezegh. He wanted "to see the operation tidily rounded off, with the elimination of the broken fragments of XXX Corps and the salvage of the booty." Instead, he would be hustled along with Chief of Staff General Gause in the Dash, and good communications between the various Axis units would remain elusive throughout the Dash.

The *Trieste* was ordered up to the perimeter to stop the Tobruk garrison's breakout and assist the *Afrika* division, while the *3rd Recce* battalion stayed to try to break through along the coast road to Bardia, in the face of the New Zealand division! This part of the German plan was doomed, as the *3rd Recce* was far too weak. *Panzergruppe* headquarters would remain at El Adem, while Rommel would thrust east with the three Axis armored divisions. The *RECAM* would deploy between Bir El Gobi and north to the escarpment. Rommel thought he could crush the remains of XXX Corps in his way and encircle XIII Corps and return in 24 to 36 hours, a very unrealistic estimate. The Allied XXX Corps forces retreating to the south would be missed by this blow. For the first time ULTRA would affect the war at an operational level. ULTRA intercepted Rommel signaling to Europe that they would shortly be operating on the "Sollum front" or frontier. While quickly relayed to Auchinleck, there was not a great deal that could be done to counter this, but at least the Commonwealth was benefitting from this new source.

The Allied command was triggered into a change of commanders at this time as well. On the morning of the 24th Cunningham had come forward to be close to the battle and underwent some rather trying personal times on the heels of the terrible losses of the 23rd. He was going to meet with General "Strafer" Gott and General Norrie; upon his arrival, the three went into a conclave. Rommel, starting his Dash, crashed into nearby British forces, mainly support and headquarters of various units, while one column was approaching the gathering of these generals! The New Zealander Brigadier George Clifton, Chief Engineer of XXX Corps related,

> At that moment all three Generals appeared and mine said, "Get General Cunningham off in his Blenheim (plane) at once!" No time to worry about springs, I drove my precious Ford utility full speed for the landing ground in a run more crazy than any gazelle hunt. Almost unopposed, driving everything ahead like sheep, about twenty German tanks rolled eastwards, completely disintegrating our rear organization and in the course of doing so, having the fun of their lives! We dodged through the thickening mob of runaways, which hurtled across our course, urged on by occasional shell bursts or bouncing tracer. Very fortunally I

knew that particular desert area almost bush by bush because between speed, dust and crossing vehicles, navigation was impossible. More by good luck than judgement, we hurtled down the strip, where the Blenheim was revved up, raring to go. The Army Commander and his staff officer climbed aboard and off she bumped, clearing a crossing three tonner (truck) by inches! That was General Cunningham's last impression of the forward situation. Small wonder he believed withdrawal into Egypt was inevitable.

The upshot of this was General Auchinleck arrived at the front to consult with Cunningham, and though Cunningham recommended withdrawal, several junior officers expressed the desire to continue the fight. Auchinleck agreed to continue the fight, in part knowing through ULTRA of Rommel's supply difficulties, and on his flight back from the front decided that General Cunningham needed to be relieved. But who with? Locked in the middle of a battle, Auchinleck felt that he could not field promote one of the two corps commanders, so, instead, he brought in the "by nature cheerful" Major General Neil Ritchie, the Deputy Chief of Staff, considerably junior to some of the officers at the front, but a tough man who had Auchinleck's ear and would continue the offensive against the Axis. It would later unfold that Ritchie was not always as in touch with the frontline as he should be and that he was too optimistic about circumstances. Ritchie would remain in command until after Gazala.

Ironically the *15th Panzer*, which was in the middle of the Axis Dash to the Wire, had captured Commonwealth plans showing their air landing areas and forward supply depots. But this information was not communicated to Rommel and he would just miss the key forward landing field crowded with over 100 RAF fighters, as well as the supply depots he so desired. As the Axis Dash rolled forward, the 4th Indian went into a defensive stance in and next to the Axis frontier fortifications from where it could not be effectively dislodged.

The Axis forces were able to link up with the garrison in Bardia and some of the outlying fortifications, but were unable to effectively hurt the Commonwealth. The only real result was that many of the various rear area Commonwealth forces were forced to flee to the east, recalled later as the "Matruh Stakes."

As Alan Moorehead, a correspondent of the day would write when he was brought forward to witness the "victory" of the 8th Army, "... we ran. It was the contagion of bewilderment and fear and ignorance. Rumour spread at every halt, no man had orders. Everyone had some theory and no one any plan beyond the frantic desire to reach his unit." But the real fighting strength of the Commonwealth was not hurt. In turn the Axis tank force suffered from wear and tear, as well as expenditure of fuel and supplies. Meanwhile the advance to linkup with the Tobruk garrison at El Duda continued, and XXX Corps continued to recover strength.

The New Zealand advance continued along the escarpment, at two-brigade strength, and had some surprising successes, in part due to the excellent character of these troops. Not only did these troops, ably led, fight their way through to Tobruk, but the division also had the superb 28th battalion of Maori troops—the original native population of former headhunters who throughout the war would have an aura about them of being elite troops. (To cite one example, on 26 November the much depleted *21st Panzer* launched two attacks in the afternoon against the 23rd and 28th New Zealand Infantry battalions which were in position in some captured frontier fortification near Bardia. One of the two landed squarely on the 28th in the gathering gloom of dusk. When von Ravenstein finally withdrew with 76 dead, 6 prisoners, and abandoned equipment on the field, including several vehicles, his *Panzer* had inflicted but eight casualties on the 28th!)

The first linkup with Tobruk was made by these New Zealanders. The final breakthrough by them was a night attack, one of the few forms of warfare the Germans were not adept at in World War II. Yet it was after a particular fierce action on the night of 27 November, that "From the plumed hats of those lying dead they were identified as *Bersaglieri*, and closer examination showed them to be of the *9th* Regiment (*Trieste*). Many of those who went through this night and saw these dead foes in the morning had occasion to sharply revise their opinion of Italians as fighting men." The New Zealand history goes on to say,

Bersaglieri *stretcher bearers in action* (Ufficio Storico).

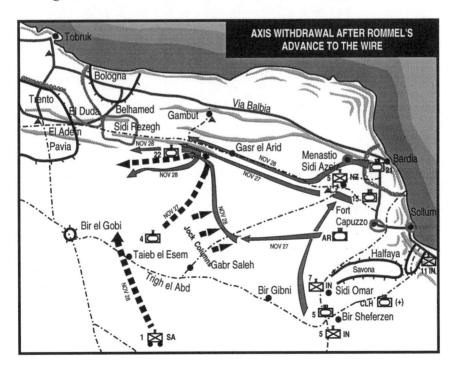

The *Bersaglieri* regiment fought with much greater determination than is usually found among Italian troops and the numbers of their dead and the position in which they lay showed that they had kept their guns in action to the last. Indeed it was reported from several of our men that the first to break under our onslaught were the German troops and that the *Bersaglieri* had been the last to yield.

The Second Battle of Sidi Rezegh

After 4 weeks of uninterrupted and costly fighting, the fighting power of the troops—despite superb individual achievements—is showing signs of flagging.
—Rommel to *OKW*

The linkup had been made. This, combined with the poor results of the Dash and the gathering of the elements of XXX Corps threatening Bir El Gobi, finally forced the three Axis armored divisions to return to Tobruk, a move that Rommel did not necessarily want, but he could not control his forces operating independently as they were. First the *DAK* replenished at Bardia. The *DAK* then advanced from Bardia along the Trigh Capuzzo, which was a road to the south of the escarpments. The *15th Panzer* in this process, on 28 November, overran the 5th New Zealand brigade headquarters and much of its strength. What AT guns the 5th had were poorly arranged, and once the *Panzers* kicked in one side of the laager, they captured 696 officers and men and inflicted 93 casualties. The prisoners ended up in Bardia, which would fall a few weeks later; but before the fall of Bardia, Italian submarines took out all the officers and some of the men to prison camps in Italy.

The *Ariete* swung from much deeper in the desert and then north, linking up with the two *Panzer* divisions at the end of the day in the rear of the rest of the 2nd New Zealand Infantry division. As she started off she was bombarded by artillery. This has been recorded as being accidental fire from the *Savona* division, but most likely was from a Commonwealth formation. The *Ariete* suffered some pinprick attacks from jock columns, composed of numerous but ineffective armored cars and the depleted 7th Support Group. The 4th Armored, now reinforced by reserve tanks and stragglers to 77 Stuarts, and the 22nd Armored brigade of 42 to 50 cruisers (the 7th Armored brigade had been withdrawn to the railhead to rebuild) deployed to stop the *DAK* from moving along the escarpment. The action was pretty much of a standoff throughout the afternoon, with almost equal losses, when the British brigades withdrew to go into laager for the night, instead of remaining on the field of battle. This was a pleasant surprise for the Germans and allowed them to effectively destroy the damaged British tanks remaining on the field of battle as well as recover some of their own damaged ones. This withdrawal was standard British practice at this point of the war, and fully supported by General Gott at the time, but was a poor tactic.

This withdrawal opened up an avenue for the *DAK* to attack the New Zealanders in the corridor into Tobruk on 29 November, with the *Ariete* covering the rear. The 4th and 22nd Armored brigades made some ineffective attacks on 28 November, but the positions abandoned the previous evening were now bristling with AT guns and German tanks, and even the 22nd's attack against the *Ariete* was ineffective as the *Ariete* arrived to complete the concentration of Axis armor for the forthcoming attack on the New Zealanders.

General Freyberg's two New Zealand brigades, along with the garrison of Tobruk, were busily cleaning up pockets of resistance in the corridor they had created. This went on for much of 28 November, and resulted in the capture of 637 men of the German *155th* regiment of the *21st Panzer*. They were now drawing on Tobruk for supply, which had become critical for the New Zealanders due to their constant fighting, and were cut off from the rest of the Allied army on the outside as the *DAK* tightened the ring around the corridor of the breakout.

The outspoken South African brigadier, D.H. Pienaar, commander of the 1st South African brigade, was slowly advancing toward Tobruk from the south, but refused to move quickly to the escarpment unless supported by what remained of the British 7th Armored division. This resulted in their hanging back from the ensuing action on 28 November, and finally on the 30th moving in between Tobruk and Bardia near the escarpment.

For the New Zealanders 29 November was a day of excitement which opened with Major General von Ravenstein, while advancing to reconnoiter, being captured by a New Zealand patrol. The *Ariete* approached a local highpoint which had exchanged hands several times, Point 175, and in the gathering gloom, mistaken identity on the part of the New Zealanders (due in part to the *Ariete* having substantial amounts of captured Commonwealth equipment), allowed the *Ariete*, virtually in a coup, to capture the position from the 21st New Zealand battalion. The *Ariete* inflicted heavy losses, captured 200 men, as well as liberating about 200 prisoners of the *21st Panzer*. It then proceeded to hold off an attack by the weak British 4th and 22nd Armored brigades which never closed to decisive ranges.

These events forced the New Zealanders to retreat from Tobruk (a few joined the garrison at Tobruk) along the Trigh Capuzzo ridge, which over the next few days was successful. The 70th Infantry took up defensive positions, which included the much fought over El Duda. It appeared that the Axis had succeeded in stopping the Commonwealth from breaking through, but the Axis losses had been too high and Auchinleck and Ritchie would not admit defeat. The Commonwealth could introduce fresh troops and equipment, while the Axis could not. Herein would lie the margin of victory for the Allies.

Ritchie decided to bring the 4th Indian division, which had seen some action in assaulting the frontier fortifications, forward to take El Adem. He relieved the 4th Indian with the 2nd South African Infantry division which would proceed with the reduction of the forts on the Sollum front. In the way was Bir El Gobi defended by the *RECAM*. General Gambara, seeing a need to protect the Axis desert flank, had deployed the *RECAM* there. The first battalion of the *Giovani Fascisti* or *GGFF*, deployed at Point 174 along with two *Milmart* 102mm guns, an L tank company, a machine gun platoon, a platoon of 47mm AT guns, and a battery of 20mm AA guns (1000 men) and some minor elements of the *8th Bersaglieri* (1000 men). At Point 182 the second battalion of the *Giovani Fascisti* (660 men) was deployed.

One of the best defensive stands by the Italians took place, once again, here at Bir El Gobi. On 4 December the advancing British army corps detailed the 11th Indian brigade with the 31st Royal Artillery regiment and several Valentine tanks, to clear the

Giovani Fascisti *position at Bir el Gobi in December 1941*(Ufficio Storico).

position so the corps could continue the advance and supply lines to the west of Tobruk could be protected. The Indian brigade brilliantly moved through the night to take up a position to the rear of the Italian position, and attacked at dawn from the west. Both Italian positions were attacked after a short artillery bombardment, each by a battalion supported by a total of 16 Valentine tanks, which made no headway.

The 4th Armored brigade, meanwhile, found the mobile part of the *RECAM* which consisted of five armored cars, four M tanks, and one L tank supported by nine 65mm artillery pieces. The 4th easily won this action, climaxed when a squadron of the 1st King's Dragoon Guards burst into the field depot of the *RECAM*, putting to the torch the *RECAM*'s supplies.

A second reinforced attack against Bir El Gobi went in the next morning at dawn with a surprise attack. Some progress was made, when at noon, yet another reinforced attack commenced. The Official History of the 4th Indian states,

At 1245 hours the artillery laid a smoke screen on the southern approaches to El Gobi; behind it two companies of 1/6 Rajputana Rifles moved to the attack. Four "I" tanks accompanied the assault, but owing to wireless failures fought independently and were not on call by the infantry. After initial progress the Rajputana Rifles were held up. A company of Camerons joined the fray on the left flank. At 1430 hours Lieut.-Colonel Butler (Rajputana Rifles) reported that he had reached the outskirts of a comprehensive defence position organized in depth. His tanks and carriers (Bren) had penetrated the outpost line but were unable to deal with the enemy in their deep and narrow slit trenches. A number of tanks had been knocked out by Molotov cocktails. A similar report came from the Camerons, who added that enemy machine-gun squads had occupied one of the disabled "I" tanks and were enfilading them. At 1600 hours the Rajputana Rifles commander again reported the situation as stalemate....A few minutes later Lieut.-Colonel Butler was killed by a mortar....

In the afternoon the *DAK* arrived and by 1800 had forced the Indians to retreat and had linked up with the Italian defenders. The Indians continued to withdraw and had suffered 25 officers and 450 men as casualties.

Also on 4 December, the Germans launched an attack on El Duda which was repulsed. With this repulse and Rommel's concerns of being outflanked if Bir El Gobi fell, a decision was made to abandon the eastern face of the Tobruk siege line and concentrate all mobile forces to the south. The German story of "Where is Gambara?" arose from this situation. The *Ariete* and *Trieste* was ordered to join the *DAK*. Gambara's command received orders late, the *Ariete* (what was left of it) was harried by jock columns and air attacks (both Allied and Axis) and the *Trieste* was slow in assembling. In addition they had to cover about twice the distance the *DAK* had to, to arrive at the rendezvous point, and like all of the Axis army at this time, they lacked fuel and ammunition. Montanari, the official Italian historian, goes on to say that the divisional commanders of the *Ariete* and *Trieste* "lacked energetic initiative. This coupled with the poor status of communications and problems in the Italian command structure led to the slow arrival and execution of orders." He goes on to quote two messages from Gambara to the divisional commanders. One was, "The commanders are responsible for units not arriving on time to the places they are

Rommel at an Italian command post observing the front; bare-headed officer in the background may be General Gambara (Klaus Hubbuch).

ordered to, or if they go beyond those places" and "I will dismiss any commander who will not stay in communication with headquarters." Unusual orders from one's commander...

By the evening of 5 December Generals Rommel and Bastico knew that no sizeable reinforcements would be arriving before the end of December. One more attempt by the *DAK* combined with Gambara's command (which failed to arrive), to break the XXX Corps attempt to push through near Bir El Gobi on 6 December, failed and General Neumann-Silkow was mortally wounded.

These events caused Rommel to decide to withdraw on

Gazala. Some work had been done in June to prepare a defensive position there, and now it was reoccupied, with the Italian infantry on the north, the Italian mobile forces in the center, and *DAK* to the south, echeloned back to protect the open flank. Over the next few days, the Axis successfully withdrew, partly by fooling the British Corps commanders that they were going to attack, instead of withdrawing.

By 10 December the eight month siege of Tobruk was completely over. Allied forces were moving forward and preparing for their next attack. The Axis Gazala line was the next position the Allies faced.

Some Axis command changes occurred now. Gambara handed over his command to the commander of the *Trieste*, General Alessandro Piazzoni, and became Bastico's full time Chief of Staff. General Max Suemmerman of the *Afrika* division was killed in an RAF attack, meaning all three German divisional commanders had died or been captured in the battle. Bastico also assigned some minor units to Rommel's command. With the Commonwealth attacks of December on the Gazala line, different opinions sprung up in the Axis camp as to whether they should hold or fall back on a better position. Rommel and Navarini both advocated falling back, while Generals Gambara and Gause thought they should stand. In this Bastico tried to be the man of decision and assert his leadership. The decision was made to withdraw.

The Commonwealth mounted an attack on 15-16 December, in part due to ULTRA indicating a retreat by the Axis, using the 4th Indian, the 7th Armored division, the Polish brigade, the 5th New Zealand brigade and some miscellaneous units against the Axis line. The 7th was to raid in the Axis rear (with the 4th Armored brigade arriving in the rear of the *Ariete* and the *Trieste*) while the 4th Indian's 5th and 7th brigades attempted to press through between the *Ariete* and the *Trieste*. So as the Italian infantry was preparing to retreat (Rommel had ordered this for 17 December), the 5th Indian brigade attacked. The Buffs, a British battalion assigned to the Indian brigade, achieved some early successes, but the 4th Armored never arrived due to refuelling and terrain delays, and the *Ariete* counterattacked with about 30 M13's along with 23 tanks of the *15th Panzer* (the

21st Panzer had 19 tanks left). The *8th* and *9th Bersaglieri* were present in the frontline and stopped every infantry attack the 5th launched. Total losses for the 5th were "one thousand men, . . . forty guns, many trucks, and various pieces of equipment." A weak attack by the 7th Indian brigade was also checked that afternoon.

To the north the Poles and the 5th New Zealand had more success against the Italian infantry and created a hole of about four kilometers and captured several hundred prisoners. The *Trento* division filled the hole. This led to some stiff fighting on the 16th between the Allies and the *7th Bersaglieri*. Rommel formed a mobile *Kampfgruppe* of a battalion of *Bersaglieri* and four 88mm guns, and this helped to cover the Axis retreat on 17 December.

The retreat was a success. The main route was through the Jebel Akhbar Mountains. Commonwealth forces did advance across the desert, but not fast enough to "bag" any substantial forces. By 23 December 1941 the Axis were back at Benghazi (preparing to give up that port) and echeloned along the Via Balbia with the Gulf of Sirte to their immediate rear. The RAF tried to harass the Axis retreat as best it could, but winter weather and the rapid fall back made the Air Force less effective than it would have liked. During the retreat, the Axis army called upon an unusual unit to make a rearguard stand near the Lamluda fork in the Jebel Akhbar Mountains. This was a battalion of Italian *Carabinieri* paratroops which had been present in the rear since July. The *Carabinieri* are unique to Italy but are somewhat like a national police force with additional duties. They are considered the senior service and had secured the distinction of being the "1st" battalion of paratroops, though actually two small battalions had been originally formed in Libya under Marshal Balbo in 1938 and had fought well during the retreat to Beda Fomm. The *Carabinieri* paratroops fought from 18 to 20 December, facing some South African armored cars, part of the Central India Horse and two battalions of the 4th Indian division, and "held back the 3/1 Punjabis throughout December 20th, but at dusk a bayonet charge overran the last stubborn defenders." The *Carabinieri* lost 35 dead and 251 missing (mostly captured in the withdrawal).

Indian Prisoners (Ufficio Storico).

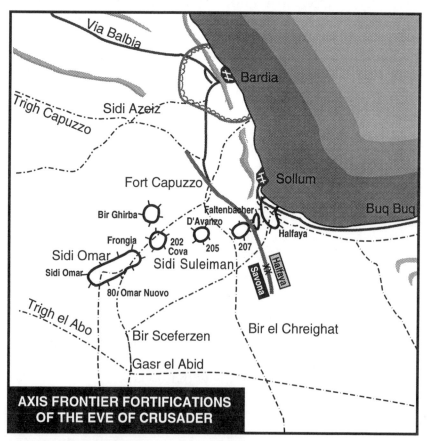

AXIS FRONTIER FORTIFICATIONS
OF THE EVE OF CRUSADER

Some light needs to be cast on the Indian troops. Indian brigades and divisions traditionally had one-third of the units as British, and all artillery are British, though by now some artillery in the war was Indian led and manned. The 4th Indian was particularly noted for its mountain capability and enjoyed duty in the Jebel Akhbar. Of the approximately 200 Indian races, about ten were considered the "fighting races." The Gurkha and Sikh are best known, but the other Indian "martial races" were the Jat, Pathan, Dogra, Islamic Punjabi, Rajput, Mahratta, Madrassi, and Bengali.

Operation Crusader was over, but before the Allies (now truly the Allies with the entry of the United States of America into the war) could continue the advance on Tripoli, Rommel and the Axis military succeeded in reversing the Axis fortunes. Losses on each side had been heavy. Including the Axis fortifications, which surrendered around the New Year, losses were approximately: 1,320 Italians dead, 3,100 wounded, and 13,000 missing, plus about 8,000 (a total of 13,800 Axis troops surrendered in the frontier fortifications) that were lost when the frontier fortifications surrendered. The Germans had just over 1,000 killed and over 3,500 wounded, and 10,100 missing. Commonwealth losses were 2,900 killed, 7,300 wounded, and 7,500 missing or prisoners.

The Sollum Front

The Axis had strengthened their position along the Wire and at Sollum/Halfaya Pass so that the forces stationed there could hold back any Commonwealth attack during Rommel's planned assault on Tobruk, scheduled for 20 November 1941. Operation Crusader started first and fierce fighting would erupt around these fortified positions. Initially there was a combination of outflanking moves by the New Zealanders, bombardments from the sea, and assaults by elements of the 4th Indian reinforced with the 44th Royal Tank Regiment against the extreme end of the line at Sidi Omar and Frongia.

Assaults, while partially successful in areas, were also quite costly, especially in tank losses due to the presence of the German 88's and Italian 105/28 guns. Later the New Zealanders would push on around to cut off Bardia and relieve Tobruk. The 4th Indian, with the 5th brigade of New Zealanders would contain this sector into early December when it was relieved by the newly brought forward and partly trained three brigades of the 2nd South African infantry division. While some Axis supplies were brought in by barge and submarine, and there were discussions of taking the troops out by Italian naval ships, the beleaguered garrisons were doomed. Rommel, who deeply wanted to relieve these frontier forts, could not.

Between 31 December and 17 January in a series of actions the frontier garrisons were reduced and the Axis troops were either killed or captured. Major General Arthur Schmitt, commander of the north end of the line, and the first German general to surrender his command in the war, and 13,800 Axis troops were marched off into the prisoner cages from this action alone. Of General Fedele de Giorgis, commander of the *Savona* and of the south end of the line, Rommel said, "Superb leadership was shown by the Italian General de Giorgis, who commanded this German-Italian force in its two months' struggle."

The Axis fielded at the start of the battle:

In Bardia under Colonel Carlo Pierucci:

2 battalions of the *Savona* and one of the *Bologna*

4th armored car *Genova* squadron

28th GAF (*Guardia all Frontiera*)

282 and *342* battalions of *GAF*

2 *Regia Marina* coast defense batteries (probably 4.7" guns)

2 understrength battalions of Germans, the *3rd/255th* and *3rd/347th*.

Artillery present belonged to the *2nd celere* and the *12th* artillery regiment of the *Savona*. It numbered twenty-six 75-77mm guns, two 120mm, and twenty-two 47mm AT guns, as well as about 55 under repair guns, mostly old 65/17mm guns.

At Halfaya under Major Bach:

1st battalion of the *104th* motorized from *21st Panzer*

10th Oasis company

3rd/2nd celere artillery made up of a battalion of 105/28, one battery of old French 155mm guns, three 88mm AT and three 75/46 Italian guns

At Faltenbacher:

An Italian company reinforced with three 88's and three 75/46mm guns

In the *Savona* sector was General de Giorgis who had the *CLV machine gun* battalion, one *Arditi* company, a company of L tanks, with three *Oasis* companies, in addition to the rest of his *Savona* division. They were distributed as below:

At Cirener:

1st/15 battalion of the *Savona*
2nd battalion of the *2nd celere* artillery; *2nd Oasis*

At d'Avanzo:

A reinforced *11th* company.

At Cova:

The regimental command for the *15th*
The *3rd/15* minus the *11th* company
13th Oasis company
One battery of 65/17 guns

At Frongia or New (Nuovo) Sidi Omar:

3rd/16th battalion
One company of engineers
2nd/12th artillery (two batteries of 75/27mm guns)
One battery of 65mm guns
One battery of 88mm guns
One company of laborers

At Sidi Omar:

16th regimental command
1st/16th battalion
3rd/12th artillery (two batteries of 75/27mm guns)
Two batteries of 105/28mm guns
One battery of 65mm
One battery of 88mm gun
12th Oasis company
One company of laborers

At Bir Ghirba:

The divisional command
One company of *Arditi*
One company of L tanks (15)
One engineer company
One section of 100/17mm guns
Two turrets from Matilda tanks mounted with 2-pounders

Friendly Fire and Atrocities

Many have said the North African campaign was a "clean" war, and it was certainly cleaner than the struggle fought in the Soviet Union and China. But there were cases of wartime atrocities as well as incidents of friendly fire. The acts of friendly fire will first be addressed.

Marshal Italo Balbo was the most prominent loss to friendly fire. As a hero to Italy and for much of the world before the war, he was considered a possible successor to Mus-

solini. The youthful Balbo had been an early supporter of Fascism and led several record setting mass airplane flights across the Atlantic, including one to Chicago in 1933 for the World's Fair (a street is still named for Balbo in commemoration of his visit). For several years he was head of the *Regia Aeronautica*. He was also anti-German, sentiment which made him unpopular in Rome. In April of 1939 while Air Marshal Hermann Goering was visiting him in Tripoli, Balbo had a state dinner and pointedly invited several local Jewish leaders to the dinner.

He might have made a difference in the upcoming fighting, as he was an inspirational and aggressive leader, and long an advocate of invading Egypt. Instead, he would die tragically, shot down by his own AA guns over Tobruk on 28 June 1940, just a week after personally leading the capture from the air of a British armored car that had crossed into Libya. Balbo attempted to fly into Tobruk in a trimotor SM79 he piloted on the heels of a British air raid and he failed to give the proper signal to his AA crews for a complete circle at 300 meters altitude. Additionally, his batteries were under both naval and air force command—and the naval batteries never heard that a visit from Balbo was imminent.

Later charges were made that Mussolini was behind a conspiracy to get rid of a rival. There had been rumors about Balbo possibly leading a *putsch* against Mussolini, and before Italy's entry he had maintained good relations with the French and the British in Africa at the start of the war. Simply put, Balbo was not popular at Mussolini's court. Count Ciano and others had from 1938 been involved in the "Balbo Operation," according to General Viviani in his *Servizi Segreti Italiani 1815-1985* (Italian Secret Service), and included several members of the Italian secret services. Interestingly enough, after Balbo's death the inquiry was run by General Pitassi Mannella, whose immediate superior was General Mario Berti, a Ciano man...still, most likely Balbo

was shot down by his own guns due to faulty communication.

Mistaken identification sometimes occurs, as when an RAF Beaufighter flying to Malta from Gibraltar sighted what appeared to be a SM79 on 3 February 1942. Attacking the plane was Squadron Leader Peter Ruston who shot up what was actually an SM81 transport, forcing it down and killing several civilians, including children. The civilians on the Tripoli to Sicily flight vainly held up children in the windows, but Ruston did not realize his error at the time.

A most unusual instance occurred on 29 April 1942 while a civilian Italian Cant Z506 floatplane was on a flight from Tripoli to Sicily. It flew near a small Axis convoy being protected by a Me-110 piloted by *Unteroffizier* Georg Schleich. Schleich attacked the transport plane, shooting it down and killing two aboard. He apparently realized his mistake, overflew the crash site and dropped his dinghy to the survivors. Tragically he then crashed his own plane with his co-pilot into the ocean, both dying instantly.

Another tragic air incident took place on 9 December 1941, when an Italian pilot apparently went crazy, shooting down two Ju-52's attempting to land at Tmimi. A German pilot, *Unteroffizier* Schultz, took a Me-109 up to shoot the Italian down. Later that month Schultz was shot down, but unhurt, by an Italian fighter....

On the ground, troops found themselves under fire of their own guns, resulting in casualties. The *Ariete* complained several times of being attacked by German Stukas. During Operation Crusader, the

New Zealanders were bombed by the RAF, losing dozens of dead and wounded. Often the errant air attacks took place against poorly marked vehicles or if enemy positions were incorrectly given. This is something that armies want to keep from happening, and certainly they downplay it as it is terrible on the troops' morale, but it can never be completely avoided.

Atrocities too occurred, and the concept of chivalry in North Africa is a bit tarnished. One of the most celebrated events, which is still hidden in the murky past, is the looting of the Derna-Benghazi bulge in the winter of 1940-41. There is no question that during the Allied advance and subsequent retreat there were numerous atrocities. These incidents include the murder of Italian women in Benghazi (the murder scene being photographed by Germans during the advance), photographs of a looted ossuary (reputedly by New Zealand troops), and general reports of destruction, rape, and some reports of murder. Advancing German and Italian troops charged the Australian troops with many of these incidents. Some of the looting charges were supported by the British High Command. Currently the official Australian position is that the atrocities which reportedly occurred may have been caused by the New Zealand troops. However it is speculated that some Australian troops might have done some looting, but only after both Derna and Benghazi had been looted by retreating Italian troops and Arabs. The Australian government apparently does not have a position on the documented case of the murder of civilians in Benghazi by unknown assailants in 1940 and 1941. However, it is known that the local Arab population raped, pillaged, and killed the local Italian civilians throughout the war. The extent of atrocities committed by Allied and specifically Australian troops in this period of the war is still shrouded in the fog of history.

The Italians have put forth a general claim that ANZAC (Australian and New Zealand Army Corps) troops in general often killed surrendering or wounded Axis troops. Sergio Tamiozzo who served with the *9th Bersaglieri* told of a night attack on one of the "R" strongpoints at Tobruk on 30 April 1941, and that during the Australian counterattack he witnessed scenes of atrocities. During the night breakout of Minqar Qaim, at the time of Mersa Matruh, the frenzied New Zealand troops bayoneted wounded and surrendering Germans when they burst into their laager.

When Major Wilhelm Bach, the former pastor, surrendered his command on 17 January 1942 at Halfaya Pass after the Commonwealth victory during Operation Crusader, they surrendered to the South Africans who had them under siege. During the surrender ceremony with many Germans upright and without arms, several were killed and wounded. This was due, not to the South Africans, but to a small contingent of bitter Free French troops.

Sergeant Luigi Castaman of the *Ariete* and tank commander at El Alamein said that during the assault on Tobruk in 1942, when his tank took some prisoners, probably South African, he abandoned the line to escort the prisoners to the rear. An Italian colonel gave him orders to kill the prisoners instead, orders which he refused to carry out.

British agents attempted to rouse the Arabs of Libya and Egypt against the Axis, especially the Italians, in September of 1942. This brought about activities in the Axis rear that led Rommel to note in his diary,

> There is nothing so unpleasant as partisan warfare. It is perhaps very important not to make reprisals on the hostages at the first outbreak of partisan warfare, for these only create feelings of revenge and serve to strengthen the *franctireurs*. It is better to allow an incident to go unavenged than to hit back at the innocent. It only agitates the whole neighborhood, and hostages easily become martyrs.

There was a general attempt to follow the "rules of war" in Africa. Proper policing is required in areas with a civilian population and this policing must be an immediate requirement when occupation begins to avoid incidents. It was the positive attitude displayed by most of the war leaders in this theater and for the most part practiced by all nationalities in Africa, which added a level of dignity to the otherwise dirty business called war.

CHAPTER IV

The Stand at Mersa El Brega and Advance to the Gazala Line

After we have been driving in scorching heat from four in the morning until dusk, ever onward, getting reports from generals and battery and company commanders, he calls a 'halt for forty winks' in the middle of the desert. And there we sleep, the general and his officers and NCO's and enlisted men, side by side as comfortably as we can in our various vehicles. At the first flush of dawn the column starts moving again.
    —Major Carl Cranz on traveling with Rommel in the January offensive

Had not the enemy judged the situation very shrewdly in the middle of January, and after some hesitation taken the right action, the British bluff—for that is what it was—might have succeeded. As it happened, the British High Command took a chance which did not come off.
    —British Official History

The Axis were to go from a position of just holding on to the same line held in February of 1941 to one where they would once again threaten Tobruk directly and Malta indirectly in a rapid winter campaign. Much of Allied and to an extent Axis strategy was built around the control of the Libyan bulge because it allowed greater Allied air cooperation with the beleaguered island fortress of Malta from airfields in and around Benghazi. From there they would go on in to the high summer to deliver a blow which would almost carry Axis fortunes to the Nile. This effort would be led by Rommel, but without the support of Italian arms, the Axis successes of 1942 would not have been achievable. Rommel needed the defensive force of the Italian infantry to protect his base and he would need their motorized and armored forces for victory.

The Axis had received enough reinforcements, especially German tanks, at Benghazi just before it fell in December to launch a spoiling attack against the Commonwealth at Agedabia. The 22nd Armored brigade suffered heavily from this. ULTRA was aware of the increase of Axis tank strength, but 8th Army Headquarters did not appreciate this information and based all their calculations on Axis tank strength as having not received any reinforcements. After the battle of 26-27 December 1941 in which the 22nd lost 37 tanks, Ritchie felt that the 7th Armored division needed to reorganize and the newly arrived 1st Armored was to take over its duties in the Agedabia area. The Axis retired to Mersa El Brega.

While at Mersa El Brega, Rommel ordered an Italian unit to manufacture some dummy 88's to keep the few real ones left (about a dozen) from being air attacked by the RAF. The Italians did such a good job that when Rommel stopped by a few days later, he started to berate the Italian commander for having real 88's out in the open subject to air attack—it was amazing what the creative troops had done with some telephone poles!

A new arrival at the *Ariete* division during the month of January 1942 raised much interest and became quite popular. It was the first two battalions of Semoventi, 75mm 18 caliber howitzers mounted on tank chassises. The 16 Semoventi, along with eight command tank versions, were assigned to the *Ariete* division. It was intended for self-propelled use, and even with its poor armor protection and its slowness, it was quite popular because its gun was capable of piercing 50mm of armor at 1,000 yards. A later report noted that it could not be fired with the door shut, the shells sometimes became stuck in the chamber after firing (the crew needed a pole to fish them out from the

75/18 semovente in right foreground (Ufficio Storico).

muzzle end!), and that the gun could not be fired by the gun layer—he had to order the gun to be fired.

So why now did the Axis receive vital reinforcements?

The Central Mediterranean was now controlled by the Axis, primarily due to the transfer of the *2nd Luftflotte* from the Russian front for employment in the Mediterranean. ULTRA's performance was very effective in the last months of 1941, and the Italian and German High Commands had formed a work group to deal with sea transport plans. It was recognized that the success of Operation Crusader launched by the Commonwealth was largely due to the timely support of the large Commonwealth air and naval offensive against the supply lines of the Axis in Africa. After a series of meetings between Cavallero, Rommel, and officers of the German and Italian navies, it was decided to hold a daily meeting devoted to supply and transport across the Mediterranean. This is interesting in light of the knowledge that no agreements of any kind were concluded between the two Axis powers to define a common direction of the war. The daily meeting, held at *Comando Supremo*, was really a voluntary act of cooperation between officers of good will who tried to send the supplies necessary to Rommel's army to sustain the struggle in the desert. Although

Dismounting Italian **Bersaglieri** *motorcycle troops* (Ufficio Storico).

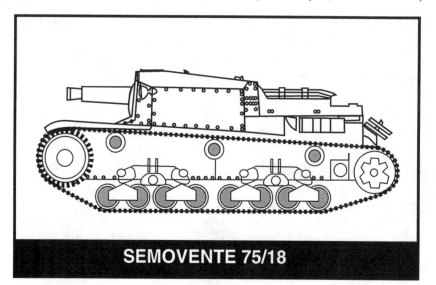

SEMOVENTE 75/18

Breda 51 90mm AT/AA gun (courtesy Lucio Ceva & Andrea Curami).

Cavallero, as Chief of Staff, was often not present, the meetings were held on his behalf to enforce the importance of establishing and maintaining this procedure.

These measures, part of which would result in the Italian "battleship convoys" to Africa using portions of the main Italian fleet to protect troops and supplies to Africa, allowed the arrival of not only the Semoventi, but 51 Pz III's and Pz IV's and 16 armored cars which were disembarked with enough supplies to allow Rommel to launch some local and effective counterattacks. While many troops arrived by air, additional tanks, trucks, and ammunition would arrive throughout January and later that winter and spring via these battleship convoys, to rebuild the Axis strength in Africa. To do this Rommel regrouped his motorized units behind the screen of the Italian infantry of the *XXI Corps,* now made up of the *Pavia, Trento,* and *Sabratha* divisions. The *Sabratha* had its normal two infantry regiments but also had attached a battalion of the *San Marco* marines (it arrived in November) and the *Raggruppamento Giovani Fascisti.* A new *X Corps* was formed under General Benvenuto Gioda with the *Bologna* and *Brescia* infantry divisions.

The motorized portion of the Axis army consisted of the *DAK*, and the *Corpo d'Armata di Manovra*, now called *XX Motorized Corps*. The *Afrika* division was in reserve and renamed the *90th Leicht* (Light). The *90th* consisted of the *155th* and *361st* infantry regiments, a battalion of newly arrived German paratroops under Major Burkhardt, and a mixed battalion of artillery and AT/AA guns. The German forces now became *Panzerarmee Afrika* on 22 January.

The Italian army was reorganizing, bringing the firepower of Italian units up, while reducing manpower. This was the AS42 model, or *Africa Settentrionale* 42 (North Africa) TO&E. By mid-January the *Ariete* had the *132nd* tank regiment of two battalions, of three companies each. The *8th Bersaglieri* regiment had two battalions, each of two rifle companies and one 81mm mortar company. The *132nd* regiment of artillery had four battalions, two with 75/27mm guns and two of the new Semoventi. The reduction of the *8th* was due to dispersing the third heavy weapons battalion among the other units. This new style *Bersaglieri* company had one rifle platoon, one machine gun platoon, one 20mm AA/AT platoon, and one 47mm AT platoon. It had been planned to build the armored division up to 9,000 men with an armored car battalion, a Semoventi battalion, a full strength tank regiment (three battalions), the *Bersaglieri* regiment with two battalions and an AT battalion, and the artillery getting a 90/53mm AA/AT battalion and a 105/28mm howitzer, but this goal was never obtained.

The new AS42 model for the Infantry divisions was a 7,000 man unit of two regiments each with two battalions and a mortar company (employing the effective 81mm mortar). Each battalion would have four companies. The artillery regiment would have two battalions of 75/27 field guns, two battalions of 100/17 howitzers, and one battalion of 88/55 (German) or 90/53 (Italian) AT/AA guns. Additionally, supply and other services were reduced to keep the supply burden down. It was planned for the *Trieste* to have two regiments of two battalions each; a tank battalion; an armored car battalion, and with the artillery regiment would give a strength of 6,700 men. This new organization was never fully realized, i.e., there were not enough 88 or

Italian 105/28 gun (Ufficio Storico).

90mm AT guns, and captured British vehicles were used in lieu of the armored cars.

The counterattack launched by Rommel was viewed as a necessity to prevent a renewed Commonwealth attack. Such an Allied attack could be successful against the widely scattered thin line of strongholds held by the Italian infantry which had suffered serious losses.

Rommel suspected that his Italian allies were unable to keep his new offensive secret, so the officers in the know were very limited. This was really the effect of ULTRA—ironically, after 1941 ULTRA could not read the highgrade Italian army cipher, while the *Luftwaffe*'s was particularly easy to read. General Bastico, *OKW*, and *Comando Supremo* were not informed of his planned attack. General Kesselring was only informed of the offensive on the eve of its launch. General Gambara was informed since he supplied trucks and fuel to the Germans. It was probably because of this fact and other actions in support of Rommel, without Cavallero's knowledge and against his wishes, that Gambara was fired on the spot shortly after the offensive unfolded. At the time of Gambara's departure it was stated that he had fallen out of favor with Cavallero for his "insubordinate behavior" and that an embezzlement scandal existed among his subordinates. It is interesting to note this evolution of Gambara's support of Rommel, as well as his not following the chain of command, as leading to his fall. While he may have said in an Italian mess, as has been reported, that he wanted to "Live long enough to lead an Italian army against Germany," by the spring of 1942 General Gambara supported General Rommel in many areas, had good contact with him, and approved of his methods of warfare.

The counterattack began on 21 January 1942, 0830, with the *DAK* fielding nine Pz IV's, 66 Pz III's, and 22 Pz II's. The British commanders, Auchinleck and Ritchie, were in Palestine studying the new offensive against Tripoli, code named Acrobat. The 7th Indian brigade was stationed near Benghazi. The few Commonwealth units in place formed the support group of the 1st Armored division and two battalions of the 200th Guards brigade (formerly the 22nd Guards), which were totally surprised by the attempt to encircle them with the *DAK*, German *90th Leicht* division, the *Marcks Group* (made up of about half of the *90th*), *Ariete*, and *Trieste*. The Axis realized by the 24th that they had not bagged the enemy due to their rapid retreat. In the following days units of the 1st Armored division were routed by the *DAK*. The rough and tumble Axis advance continued until the seizure of Benghazi on 29 January.

While the 7th Indian brigade was able to retreat in a mad dash across the desert without many losses, the inexperienced 2nd Armored brigade suffered badly. An overconfident Auchinleck and Ritchie had seemed too sure of the inability of Rommel's forces to mount an attack. Churchill signaled, "I am much disturbed by the report from the 8th Army, which speaks of evacuation of Benghazi and Derna. I certainly have never been led to suppose that such a situation could arise."

With the conquest of Benghazi, Rommel saw the possibility of the pursuit toward the east, and was covered by Hitler's instructions and by Goering's activity in Rome. Cavallero maintained the opinion that the logistical situation did not allow the seizing of Tobruk. Many writers have described Cavallero's flight to Libya at this time as an attempt to stop Rommel's advance, which is not perfectly accurate.

When Cavallero arrived at 1245 on 22 January to settle the difficult relations between the Axis commands in Africa, he knew little of the operations then in progress. He was accompanied by Enno von Rintelen, German military attache, and Kesselring. First he saw Bastico, who was against the continuation of the attack beyond the capability of his supply, since he feared that the "thrust" could be transformed into a "race forward." Cavallero met with Rommel and Kesselring on 23 January, and the results are reported very differently in both sides' minutes. Cavallero asked Rommel to hold the front at Mersa El Brega and to hit the enemy with limited offensive operations thrusts. By 27 January the advance was approved by Cavallero and the *Duce*, which was essentially approving what Rommel had already accomplished.

The Axis advance eastward arrived at Derna, which was occupied on 3 February. At the same time General Ritchie established a line of defense from Ain El Gazala advancing XXX Corps from the Egyptian border to cover Tobruk. Ritchie also began to lay down mines from the coast to the deep desert, which was also ordered by Rommel on 5 February. The Commonwealth used many mines from Tobruk's defenses, and upwards of a million mines were laid by both sides that winter and spring. Among other improvements to the Allied position was the extension of the railhead from Egypt to Belhamed, near Tobruk.

The reconquest of Cyrenaica was complete with a brilliant maneuver and with heavy Commonwealth losses. It was in this period that Rommel began to receive the famous "Fellers" or "Gute Quelle" (Good Source) intercepts which helped him in the counterstroke, as Hans-Otto Behrendt, former G2 officer in the *Panzerarmee* later wrote. Now the question was, who had the strength to move first?

Tanker Luigi Castaman posing with Fiat-Revelli Model 1935 8mm machine gun (Luigi Castaman).

The Build-up to Gazala

North Africa may well have been the theater in which the war was waged in its most modern guise. . . It was only in the desert that the principles of armored warfare as they were taught in theory before the war could be fully applied and thoroughly developed. It was only in the desert that real tank battles were fought by large-scale formations.

—Rommel

Both sides built up their forces in the following months for a momentous battle in the desert. The Commonwealth wanted to launch an attack by June to relieve the pressure on Malta by extending the range of the RAF. The Axis wanted to deliver a one-two punch by taking Tobruk and following that up with the seizure of Malta in a combined air-sea assault.

From 1 February 1942 to 1 June 1942 the numbers of the Axis tanks grew from 227 (185 Italian, 42 German) to 548 (276, 272). By comparison, the 8th Army had 770 tanks on 1 May. In early

March there were 128,000 Italian soldiers of every kind in Africa, of which 39,000 were in the seven divisions at the front with Rommel, who also had 25,000 men in his three German divisions. Both sides had better lines of supply, with the Axis using Benghazi, and the Commonwealth using Tobruk. However, the Axis were able to bring to Africa in the month of April some 150,389 tons of supplies and equipment of the 151,578 tons shipped, against 47,588 tons arriving in March. May was also a good month: 86,439 tons arrived of the 93,188 tons shipped. The combined Axis effort at sea and in the air had helped to bring about this improvement.

On 17 March Rommel flew to Hitler's HQ to support his view of the importance of a decisive blow in North Africa. Hitler wanted to engage as many Allied troops as possible in the Mediterranean theater, while he won or lost his decisive war in Russia. On those immense plains the past winter losses were so severe that Hitler could not send more troops to Rommel. In Hitler's view, Africa was only a secondary front to be held to help the weak Italian ally. Also the *Kriegsmarine* (German navy) had proposals, based on the evaluation of the Mediterranean as a suitable theater for decisive action, for seizing the British positions of Suez and Basra. Hitler discounted this proposal made by Admiral Raeder. Interestingly enough, the appreciation of this situation by the *Kriegsmarine* was different from that made at the start of the war. According to the research of Dr. Gerhard Schreiber of the German Federal Military Historical Office, there was a specific interest by the *Kriegsmarine* in obtaining the control of ports in the Mediterranean and influencing the command and use of the Italian navy.

In February 1942 the Egyptian government was forced to change parliamentary leaders by the British. There is no question that the war put great sums of money into the Egyptian economy, but many Egyptians felt that they were but slaves to the colonial masters. In this change, the British forced a new government into power which was headed by Nahas Pasha. To future leaders like Gamal Abdel Nasser and Anwar Sadat, this was an afront, but they could do little about it.

It is in this strategic context that the new Axis offensive was planned. At the end of April Mussolini and Hitler met at

Klessheim, a castle near Salzburg, where an agreement was made for the schedule of the operations. The "Big Plan" was: first Rommel's army had to attack and defeat the Commonwealth forces deployed at Gazala while the *Regia Aeronautica* and the *Luftwaffe* launched a massive air offense against Malta. Then before the continuation of the desert operation, Operation *Herkules/C3* (the invasion of Malta) would be accomplished, and then the thrust against Suez—the so called Operation *Aida*— would be launched with the support of all available aircraft. This air force availability was the fundamental problem. But Hitler had already decided to consider the Malta operation only an exercise study when he met his Italian allies on 29/30 April. Hitler was afraid to carry out the operation as he doubted the Italians would give proper support, primarily naval, to German paratroops once committed to the attack.

On the other side the strategic situation was influenced by events in the Pacific theater, where the necessity of stopping the Japanese tide drained resources both in the Middle East and Western Desert. Nevertheless, the Prime Minister bombarded his commander on the scene, General Auchinleck, with exhortations to take the initiative, personally take command of the 8th Army, to attack Rommel, etc. The friction between Auchinleck and Churchill at this time was one of the factors which led in August to the removal of the former. For Auchinleck, it was not the time to attack, since his major problem was the number of tanks available for action. It was felt that a ratio of 3:2 was needed to contest the German *panzers* (and 1:1 to contest the Italian tanks). However the Middle East did receive reinforcements, including the new American built Grant tank.

The Grant tank was a welcome addition to the Allied forces "for it provided the means of killing German tanks and anti-tank gun crews at ranges hitherto undreamed of. And this could be done from behind the heavy armor of a reasonably fast and very reliable tank." This was not a surprise to the Axis, because its presence was known and in the order of operation issued by Rommel, the tank was commented on, but somewhat discounted because its 75mm gun was hull mounted in a sponson. It was short of spare parts, and had ammunition ineffective beyond 700 yards. Called the "Pilot" by the Axis, the M3 tank

American-supplied Grant tank, backbone of the 8th Army by the time of El Alamein.

had some disadvantages, primarily the slow handling of the main armament. Yet the Grant's additional 37mm gun was the same as the Stuart's and gave it some extra punch, and its armor protection was thick and well designed. For the battle of Gazala, it would lack its best armor piercing shot, and would still give a good account of itself. The first of the new Crusader Mark II tanks were also beginning to arrive, still unreliable, but with thicker armor. Auchinleck feared that an operation launched too early could fail like Brevity and Battleaxe the previous year. Thus he agreed with General Ritchie, the commander of the 8th Army, that no major offensive operations could be launched before June. Buckshot was the nickname of the offensive operation, but as it become clear that Rommel was about to attack, Ritchie prepared for the defensive.

His plan was to hold the front with the two forward divisions of Gott's XIII Corps (1st South African and 50th Infantry) covered by minefields in a series of defensive boxes. The Free

Destroyed British Crusader tanks, probably after Gazala (Luigi Castaman).

French brigade was at Bir Hacheim. Norrie's XXX Corps with the 1st and 7th Armored divisions had to react to Rommel's maneuver and were in reserve behind the lines. Other troops were at Tobruk (2nd South African) and east of Tobruk (5th Indian).

Norrie had:

167 Grants
149 Stuarts
<u>257</u> Crusaders
573

The armored brigades of the 1st and 7th Armored divisions had the tank types divided into squadrons, thus for instance the 10th Hussars of the 2nd Armored brigade would have one squadron of Grants and two of Crusaders. The 1st and 32nd Army Tank brigades had 110 Matilda and 167 Valentine tanks. These two brigades were parcelled out in driblets to various commands. Finally, Ritchie had received 112 of the new 6-pounder AT gun which had slightly better penetration than the German 50mm AT gun, though it would not have capped ammunition for this battle. They were distributed to the motorized infantry and AT batteries of the Armored divisions, but little training was given with them.

The deployment of the 8th Army forces was often criticized. Ritchie was considered not only incompetent in view of his reactions during the battle, but for failing to execute the deployment changes urged by Auchinleck, who recommended concentrating the armor. It should be noted that Ritchie was probably not dismissed after the January defeat as he had strictly followed Auchinleck's instructions.

Auchinleck also instituted more use of the brigade groups in answer to the German *Kampfgruppe* or battle group, which ultimately were unsuccessful due to lack of training, especially in coordination between the various arms. He was also instrumental in reorganizing the British Armored divisions so that they had a larger infantry element and less tanks, much like the German *Panzer*. The new division had a brigade group made up of three armored regiments, a motorized infantry battalion, along with a combined field artillery and AT regiment. A second brigade group had three motor battalions and a similar amount of artillery and AT guns.

The ULTRA assessment of the situation gave General Ritchie a fairly good picture of Rommel's attack intentions. The date of the enemy offensive was reported likely before the end of the month, but the direction of the main Axis thrust was thought to be on the center, while a maneuver around Bir Hacheim would be a diversionary attack. In the second week of May Rommel moved the motorized part of the *90th* next to the *XX Motorized Corps*. The *XX* switched with the *X* so as to have the *XX* in the next most southerly position, next to the *90th Light*. ULTRA also revealed the amount of supply available to the Axis, hence, an idea of how many days they could fight.

The Italian *XXI Corps* was left to the north with the non-motorized part of the *90th*. An attack in the north along the Via Balbia was always considered a possible Axis avenue of assault, but one not used in the course of the war. ULTRA revealed that the *Ariete* and *Trieste* were taking up the positions of the *X Corps*, but the move of the *90th* was not suspected. By 11 May, plane sightings indicated that at least the *21st* or the *15th* had moved south, which was part of the deception plan developed by the

Axis. The Commonwealth knew the Germans could make either a frontal or a southern flank attack, but assumed a frontal attack because the other *Panzer* division was probably to the north. Plus there were numerous ULTRA revelations about a seaborne (*Hecker* brigade group) or a paratroop attack (Rommel did have a battalion of paratroops available), or both. With the assumption that the *90th* was still up north with one *Panzer* and a seaborne flanking capability, we can understand why Ritchie suspected the attack would come in the middle.

"Venezia"

Despite warnings from Italian Military Intelligence (SIM) that British armour was positioned behind the Ain El Gazala line to intervene quickly, and despite Bastico's misgivings, Rommel estimated that he would need only two days to wipe out the RAF, three to eliminate British armour, and five to capture Tobruk.

—Dr. James J. Sadkovich

...the Afrika Korps was a tightly woven fighting force, whose commanders had a common tactical doctrine and a high sense of discipline. In contrast it is no secret that personal relations between some of the British commanders—particularly in the armored divisions—could not have been worse, and there was a general tendency to regard orders as a basis of discussion.

—South African Official History

Rommel's plan for the attack on the Gazala Commonwealth position was based on evaluations of the enemy which were somewhat different from reality. Axis intelligence units had failed to identify certain Allied units and positions on the eve of battle. The 22nd and 32nd Armored brigades were thought to be far from the Gazala line. The 3rd Indian Motorized brigade south of Bir Hacheim and the 29th at Bir el Gobi were also surprises, as well as the 201st brigade at the Knightsbridge strongpoint. The 150th brigade box at Gor el-Ualeb would be a great surprise and block Axis supply and communication for part of the battle before finally being cleared.

But, taking into account the available information, Rommel's

Rommel receiving Colonial Order of Silver, also called Italy's Silver Star, from the hand of General Ettore Bastico on 27 April 1942. This was an Italian award given for military action in the colonies. Special thanks to Marcello Ravaloli for identifying the medal (Klaus Hubbuch).

plan was good. This was a classic envelopment maneuver with all the motorized and armored divisions driving south of the enemy front and then encircling it, striking north to the sea. The lengthy preparatory movement should be made with two points of regrouping, A and B, the latter being the attack position in the southern part of the front line. To deceive the Commonwealth, Rommel held the armored and motorized divisions behind the center of the front and planned a diversionary attack in the north with Italian infantry and some tank units which should later join his units to the south. It was planned to destroy the superior Royal Air Force by the second day of the attack by the Axis air forces. Finally, the *Hecker* brigade group was to make an amphibious landing in the rear between Tobruk and the Gazala line and set up a roadblock one day after the start of the battle. This force was to issue from the small port at Derna outside of

Tobruk. To support the *Hecker* brigade group and attack Allied ships entering the port were several Axis submarines.

The *Panzerarmee* should, in Rommel's order of operation, "destroy the operating British army deployed in the area Bir Hacheim-El Adem-Acroma-Ain el Gazala, and finally will seize the Tobruk fortress." The destruction of the 8th Army was supposed to be complete in three days, while on the fourth day the Axis forces were to be poised before Tobruk. This schedule would prove to be rather optimistic.

The *Panzerarmee* had the following tanks available:

    53 Pz II
    242 Pz III
    _38_ Pz IV
    333 German tanks
    228 Italian M13 & M14
    561 ready for action

It is interesting to note that the ratio of tanks between 8th Army and *Panzerarmee* was just what was desired by Auchinleck: 3 to 2. The best tanks on the German side were 19 Pz III Ausf.J, or Special, with long barreled 50mm gun (it used the German AT gun) and four Pz IV's with the long 75mm L43. The Germans began the battle with a total of forty-eight 88mm guns, and a very small number of captured Soviet built 76.2mm AT guns. The Italian M14 was primarily with the *Littorio* armored division.

Tactical hints were issued by Bastico at *Comando Superiore Africa Settentrionale* to the units dependent on the employment of artillery. Italian doctrine had called for the mass employment of artillery, but with the German arrival in Africa, the Italians had learned to have pieces detached to every strongpoint, especially in an AT role. Now with an increased number of Italian AT guns in North Africa, Bastico urged the employment of the field artillery as a concentrated mass to blast the enemy's position. The employment of massed Italian batteries would compensate, in part, for the inferior precision and range of Italian artillery. The majority of Italian artillery in North Africa at this point in the war was built under French and German license granted *before* World War I, or was, like the 100/17

One of the few Italian modern artillery pieces in action, the 149/40 produced by Ansaldo (Ufficio Storico).

howitzer, built by Austria-Hungary and was booty from World War I.

The key to victory in the approaching battle would be the destruction of the Commonwealth armor. Part of it would be destroyed in the initial fighting, in which the Axis armor was hurt as well, especially in fighting the effective Grant tank. Then it would be a combination of the armor losses in the Commonwealth attacks on the Cauldron, in which the *Ariete* would play a decisive role, and the battles of June 11-13 in which the counterattacking *DAK* effectively destroyed the 2nd and 22nd Armored brigades. The Italian *XX Motorized Corps* would ably support the *DAK* in this later endeavor.

On the night of 26 and 27 May the enormous wave of armored

Typical hodge podge of Italian and captured material in 1942; in background are two Italian '41 armored cars, a British Humber and a Bren Carrier.

fighting vehicles roared from behind the Axis front toward the south and arrived near Bir Hacheim, the well built Free French strongpoint.

There was a stop for refuelling the vehicles. Bir Hacheim is mentioned in Army Order n.50/42 of 20 May 1942, issued by Rommel, with the words: "Enemy who would be in the Bir Hacheim area should be attacked and defeated." Intelligence information spoke of the 1st French Brigade at a strength of 5,000/6,000 men, depending on support from the 7th Armored division. In the area were supposed to be "some small mine-fields," but not a fully fortified box. Thus for the *Ariete* there was only a possible enemy to watch and perhaps to attack. Going forward about 7 kilometers south of Bir Hacheim, along the same line of the *21st Panzer* division, which was rolling south of the *Ariete*, the two advanced tank battalions of the *Ariete* saw at 0600 "a big enemy stronghold" two miles away. This stronghold began to lay down an artillery barrage. While the 88- and 90mm

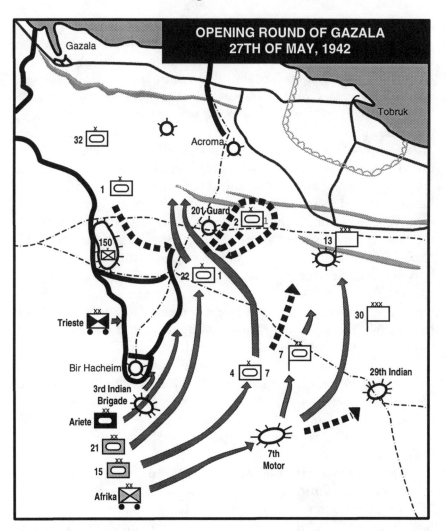

guns fired against the stronghold, the tanks went forward at 0620.

In accord with the *Nizza* recce unit report, the stronghold was a little hill occupied by Indian troops entrenched with artillery and AT guns (though the brigade had only 30 of the authorized 64 2-pounders). The commander of the 3rd Indian Motor brigade, Brigadier Filose, reported he was "facing a whole bloody German armored division," which shortly after would become "the *Ariete* division, with a few German tanks." From the interview and war diaries explored by Francesco Viglione in his essay devoted to that morning, the *21st Panzer Division* was advancing south of the position and there is no mention in the war diary of the *21st Panzer* encounter with the Indian brigade. According to written orders, the commander of the *Ariete* ordered the attack on the enemy. The *Ariete* war diary says that "At 0710, overcame with a rush the very strong enemy reaction, the *Ariete* tanks penetrating deeply into the enemy position. The garrison, composed of colored and Congolese troops, surrendered for the most part, [including] about one thousand men and one general [this was Admiral Sir Walter Cowan, an elderly hero of World War I] and three colonels." According to Commonwealth histories there were two assaults, the second one referred to two hundred tanks. The *Ariete*'s attacking tanks, in reality, numbered 110-115. They were also supported by two battalions of *Semoventi*. The major actor in the Indian defense was the 2nd Field Artillery regiment. The *Ariete* losses were 23 tanks and a total of 30 dead, 5 or 6 missing, 40 wounded. After the charge, the M13s continued to advance, and since the third battalion with the *Bersaglieri* arrived late, the Indian brigade commander, Filose, was able to escape with some troops. The Indian losses were 200 dead and 1,000 prisoners. Note that in Michael Carver's book, *Tobruk*, he states that the admiral was captured by a German tank, while in the Viglione study, the 72-year-old admiral surrendered to Major Pinna, commander of the *X* tank battalion.

After the fight with the 3rd Indian Motor brigade, the *Ariete* tank battalions continued their movement as ordered toward the "C" area, which was northeast of Bir Hacheim. One of the battalions, the *IX* of Colonel Prestisimone, changed direction approaching the stronghold of Bir Hacheim. The reason is still unknown; since there was not any order to do so, there could be many reasons: the battalion commander had lost his tank, the only one with a reliable compass; or the desire to silence the guns to the left that fired some shells against the tanks; or the fact that a good trail from the desert oasis of Giarabub to Bir Hacheim passed the unit's front, and it could be blocked by this change of direction. In any case, the tanks arrived at 0815 before the Bir Hacheim minefield, where there was barbed wire. The tanks charged the barbed wire and tried to pass the minefields, but 31 tanks and one Semovente were lost in the process. Of these, 10 tanks overcame the minefield and were stopped by the AT fire. There were 124 casualties among the Italian tank crews from this attack. Ironically, one of the wounded tank men recounted, as he was captured by three Free French Foreign Legionnaires, that they were Italians from Venice!

Concluding the description of this later attack, Viglione wrote that:

> Prestisimone, following his sanguine and impulsive nature, reverted 25 years back to his young Lieutenancy and the bayonet charges of World War I. He sought to show proof of his courage from those times in this attack. He forgot that he now had the responsibility of 60 tanks....

Viglione spoke in favor of Prestismone's bravery, but this attack was primarily a failure in the face of the unsuspected minefield.

In the meantime the offensive was continued with the German *Panzer* divisions going north. The self confidence of the *Panzer* units was shaken when the Pz III met the Grants. The *15th Panzer* received a sharp welcome by Grants of the 4th Armored brigade, while the *21st* repulsed the 22nd Armored brigade after two hours of hard fighting. The Grant tank had revealed itself as a bitter surprise to the Germans and it was only the 88mm AT guns which saved the tanks of the *15th Panzer* from greater losses. Both British formations suffered severely from the German tanks and AT guns, while one-third of the German tanks were lost on the first day and the *Ariete* suffered heavily. Communications at the end of the fighting between units of the *DAK* and the *XX Motorized Corps* were difficult because the units were scattered.

The *Ariete* resumed the movement at about 1200 hours, while the *Trieste*, which was much disorganized, was greatly delayed and dispersed. At evening the mass of the *Trieste* was still behind and was suffering from an acute case of command breakdown. Communication during movements was terribly difficult for the Italian motorized units. Eventually the *Trieste* got things sorted out and cut its way across the minefields, *north* of Bir Hacheim.

Although Ritchie and Norrie did not employ their tank units in a concentrated mass, the situation of the Axis armored and

Italian manned 88 (Ufficio Storico).

motorized units was not too good. The enemy was much stronger than foreseen. The long supply lines around the untouched Bir Hacheim fortress were exposed to British attacks, which were conducted by small jock columns and elements of South African and British armored cars.

The second day was spent trying to find a way to the sea, but without any success. Kesselring ordered the *Hecker* brigade group to proceed, but Rommel regained contact that afternoon and the plan for the landing of the *Hecker* brigade group was cancelled.

In the following days the *DAK*, *90th Light* and the *XX Motorized* formed a front toward the north and east against the uncoordinated Commonwealth tank attacks, without being able to break the resistance of the "boxes" left in the rear along the

Gazala line. The perimeter was called the "Cauldron" by the Commonwealth.

The east front held by the *Ariete* was heavily attacked on 29/30 May, but the 88- and 90mm AT guns (and even some old 76mm Skoda guns from World War I) were able to form an anti-tank screen to protect the *Ariete* and the *DAK*'s rear and their lines of communication. On the afternoon of 29 May heavy tank attacks were made on the screen. At 7:30 a.m. 30 May, without any artillery preparation, enemy "tanks came suddenly attacking out of the cover of the Trigh's downward steps, firing with all guns" as later wrote the commander of the *14th* battery, Lieutenant Calabresi. The two gallant British tank attacks were conducted by the 2nd and 22nd Armored brigades, both of which suffered heavy losses. In the case of the 2nd, it was left with only 30 tanks, mostly Grants. The Italian manned 88mm and the 90mm guns proved very effective, although suffering high losses. One Italian battalion lost 49 men and five 88mm guns, having fired some 1,748 rounds. A charging Crusader tank at one point closed to 200 yards of a 88mm gun that was running out of ammunition, before being stopped. It was at this point that Lieutenant Calabresi was wounded in the leg and was shortly thereafter awarded the Iron Cross 1st Class by Rommel himself at the hospital. Michael Carver would later write that this failed Commonwealth attack here and elsewhere around the Cauldron was "the turning point of the battle."

One British staff officer later wrote that this typified the bad tank tactics then in vogue with the British army. He said,

It was not so much recklessness that was needed as a properly coordinated attack using all the fire-power available in a properly thought-out tactical plan designed to destroy the enemy's anti-tank guns....If, instead of a series of uncoordinated advances at the enemy on a wide front, which came to a halt when the leading tanks were knocked out by guns which had not been located or neutralized, a concentrated attack on a limited front, supported by the concentrated artillery available to an Armoured Division, had been delivered, after a systematic attempt to locate and destroy by (High Explosive) fire all the anti-tank guns within range, better results would have been obtained. There was no depth and weight in our attacks and nothing to follow them up.

What was needed was a tactical plan....What was needed was a deliberate attack, not just one more "charge."

This was followed up on 4/5 June with yet another attack with both armor and infantry against the Italian line in "Operation Aberdeen." The concept was that the infantry was to make a breech and allow the armored to punch through and exploit into the rear of the Axis position. The plan was poorly coordinated and the infantry only made a partial lodgment. Part of the problem was that the Allied artillery was targeted on an already abandoned Italian position, as the *Ariete* had fallen back. The *15th Panzer* did support the *Ariete*'s left in this action and helped defeat with losses the 2nd Highland Light Infantry, after the 156 tanks of the 22nd Armored brigade were thrown back by the anti-tank line. The 2nd Armored brigade received several orders, and counterorders, and so effectively did nothing. By the end of this action, combined with the severe losses of the 32nd Army Tank brigade in its attack to the west against the *DAK*, Rommel had once again gained the initiative.

This battle shows that attacking prepared Axis positions supported by powerful anti-tank guns was simply not good tactics. The British clearly paid for it with heavy losses. Interestingly enough, both the British Official History and Michael Carver simply refer to the Italian defense as an attempt "to pierce the screen which lay west of them, thought to be Rommel's rearguard." The fact that it was essentially an Italian defense is not noted.

The British tank strength was broken in the Cauldron and with this defeat the Commonwealth superiority held at the start of the battle had vanished. Combined with the Italian linkup through the minefields and the re-establishment of a secure supply line, the Allied effort was waning quickly and victory was with the Axis. It can be argued that it was the Italian contribution at the Cauldron along with the linking up and resupplying of the *DAK* which gave the Axis victory at Gazala.

Rommel's tactics were, at this time, to resist the Commonwealth armored attacks while attacking the unsuspected and dangerous boxes. In this way the 150th brigade stronghold, at Sidi Muftah, was seized on 1 June after two days of attacks by

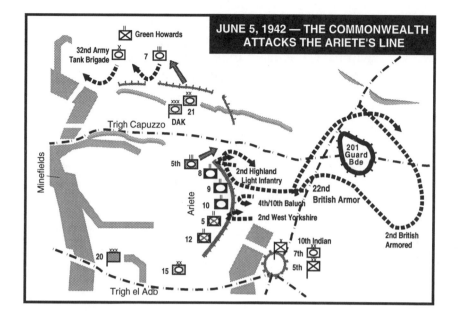

JUNE 5, 1942 — THE COMMONWEALTH
ATTACKS THE ARIETE'S LINE

Green Howards

32nd Army
Tank Brigade

7

21

Trigh Capuzzo DAK

Minefields

5th

8

2nd Highland
Light Infantry

9

22nd

10

4th/10th Baluch British Armor

Ariete

5

2nd West Yorkshire

12

10th Indian

20

7th

15

5th

201
Guard
Bde

2nd British
Armored

Trigh el Adb

Rommel standing in his staff car; note the assortment of vehicles in midground (Klaus Hubbuch).

15th Panzer, 90th Light and *Trieste.* Colonel Westphal and General Gause of the General Staff were wounded, and the commander of the *66th* regiment of the *Trieste* was killed in the action. This box was very dangerous because it harassed and menaced the only passage the Italian *X Corps* had opened in the minefields for the movement of supply. Without those supply columns to the *Panzer* and motorized divisions the Axis motorized units would have been crushed. In the attacks on the British boxes an important part was also played by the *Luftwaffe*, especially by the Stukas.

Bir Hacheim was garrisoned by the Free French and consisted of upwards of 1,200 pillboxes, anti-tank and field artillery, as well as anti-aircraft positions manned by 3,826 men. *Fliegerfuehrer Afrika* attacks against Bir Hacheim were frustrating as Rommel would not adequately reinforce the ground forces to take the Free French fort, and Stuka losses mounted to 14 that week. Kesselring went out to Rommel's HQ to protest this situation. In the next wave of attacks against Bir Hacheim on 10 June 1942, Kesselring had 124 Ju-87s followed by 76 Ju-88s attack Bir Hacheim. Immediately after this air assault the Italo-German attack followed up and this combined pressure forced Free French General Koenig to order a breakout that night of his command to Allied lines. Between 2 and 5 June Bir Hacheim had been invested by *90th Light* and *Trieste*, before it was taken on 10/11 June after many attacks, with heavy air support. In the dark of the night on the 11th some 2,700 French (including 200 wounded) were able to escape from the area. Over 1200 air attacks were made on this fort before its final capture.

It was now Rommel's turn to unleash the *DAK*, with their rear now secured, against the Commonwealth before Tobruk. He had received some armored reinforcements (he now had 27 Pz III Specials, as well as six of the Pz IV Specials). The general counterstroke ordered by Rommel on the afternoon of 11 June was deadly: while *21st* and *Ariete* attacked from the Cauldron toward the east, the *15th Panzer* surprised the Commonwealth units from the south overrunning signal and command posts and equipment, disrupting the headquarters of the 10th Indian brigade, 7th Armored division and 5th Indian division. A series of battles were fought in which the Commonwealth decisively lost the initiative and was forced to abandon the fortified front at Gazala so it would not be cut off and captured. 12 June was the worst day for the British armored forces: the concentric attacks of the 15th and 21st Panzer, the last supported by the Ariete's artillery, destroyed the bulk of the British tank brigades with a pincer maneuver. The way was now open to the sea and to Tobruk. The tank battles of 11-13 June critically reduced Commonwealth tank strength.

Ritchie had until this point displayed a rather optimistic attitude. While earlier Rommel had contemplated a possible retreat in defeat, the situation had reversed itself, especially after the surrender of the 150th brigade. On 13 June the remainder of British armor concentrated around the Knightsbridge box of the 201st Guards. But the soft pressing of the tired 21st Panzer on Rigel Ridge became harder in the afternoon and when the tanks moved to help the Scots Guards at Rigel Ridge the 15th Panzer also attacked. The end of the day saw about 70 tanks left to Ritchie, and of these some 20 were the slower infantry tanks. At this point the order to retreat was unavoidable. The Axis reported that evening they had captured 3,100 prisoners, 115 tanks destroyed or captured (by 13 June the actual loss in the last three days of battle had been 138 tanks), 96 artillery pieces and 37 AT guns destroyed or captured. On the 14th the supplies at Belhamed, including over a million gallons of fuel, were destroyed on Ritchie's orders. ULTRA at this time indicated that the Axis would not press on against Tobruk, but this was due to messages involving Bastico, Kesselring, Hitler, and Cavallero, but not Rommel.

On 16 June Auchinleck granted permission to leave Tobruk garrisoned and in the enemy rear. This was a change from the winter of 1941/42, as Auchinleck had decided not to leave Tobruk isolated in the enemy rear. This was to enable the Allies to fall back further into Egypt if the need arose and because of the unfavorable situation in the central Mediterranean for the Commonwealth. Supplying Tobruk would be even more difficult in 1942 than in 1941. By falling back into Egypt, it would be easier to make a defense closer to the Allied supply base and increase the distance of the Axis supply lines. But Ritchie decided an attempt was to be made to hold the Tobruk-El Adem area as a new deployment of the 8th Army, taking into account the fact that the enemy was supposed to be logistically near the end of its tether and that attrition had to have been great after so many battles. Moreover the 8th Army could count on a continuous flow of tanks, repaired and new, from the Nile Delta.

The two advanced divisions of XIII Corps managed to slip through the enemy units to retreat toward Egypt to form a new Army reserve. The 1st South African moved along the coast with protection of the 1st Armored division, thanks to the fact that the *DAK* was too tired to push to the coast. The 50th headed toward the south through two corridors open in the stretched line of the *Brescia*. In the fight with the 50th, the *Brescia* lost 28 dead, 26 wounded and 57 missing, capturing 27 armored vehicles, 300 trucks and 200 prisoners. The bulk of the 50th saved itself in this way, while the 9th Durham Light Infantry battalion (151st brigade) was compelled to retreat and join the South Africans. Some minor rearguard units were taken prisoner. Knightsbridge was abandoned by the 201st Guards as well. But the stand at Tobruk-El Adem-Belhamaed using Tobruk as a fixed position was not to be. The tank formations to the south were too weak and the South Africans and the 50th were in retreat. Churchill also intervened to urge the Tobruk defense, and Auchinleck thus agreed not to abandon the fortress. A strategic British calculation was that no major penetration in Egypt could be made with Tobruk in British hands. Moreover the resources committed by Hitler in the Mediterranean did not allow an Axis stand in Egypt in face of the superior Commonwealth forces, which could be so readily rebuilt.

During the discussions between Ritchie and Auchinleck, and while the interventions of Churchill were taking place, Rommel pushed decisively against the fortress after the important air facilities at Gambut were secured. Gambut, the large British airbase, had to fall and the border be approached before Rommel could turn on Tobruk. With Gambut's fall, Allied airpower was far enough back that the final assault on Tobruk could follow. With the area surrounding Tobruk cleared, it was now Tobruk's turn.

On the 20th the southeast perimeter was attacked after a

terrifying Stuka attack and an artillery bombardment. The Tobruk sector targeted for the Axis attack was pounded by both Ju-87's and CR-42's. A former translator for Rommel, NCO Spitaler, remembered during the fall of Tobruk that the Indian soldiers he saw were "shocked" by the air attacks. "One must see the Stuka attacks of that day to understand the fall of Tobruk," he said. Rommel also used the Stukas in a new role by having them drop their bombs on the minefields, each bomb detonating mines and clearing a path for his advancing troops. As Heinz Schmidt wrote of the assault,

> Our combat engineers jumped up and advanced. They carried explosives with which to destroy further wire entanglements. Then hell was let loose.
>
> Heavy fire from the defending 11th Indian brigade met us. From the flank one machine-gun steadily raking us with long bursts, but the combat engineers pressed on relentlessly. They sent up Very lights as signals to the artillery. The barrage crept farther. Then they lit their smoke candles.
>
> This was our signal. Under cover of the smoke screen we swept forward. A few men fell. But rapid strides soon took us to the first trench. It was empty. We had cover now, and a good field of fire. Through the shell-fire from Tobruk, which was now falling behind us, our motorized infantry with anti-tank guns and *Panzer* support was rolling on toward the gap.

The *21st Panzer* division and the *15th* brigade opened the passages in the minefields in shorter time than the other units: the *15th Panzer* asked as a "loan" for some 88mm pieces from the *Ariete* and they helped open a passage. The *Ariete* took longer in opening two passages. The *8th Bersaglieri* regiment slipped across near midday, attacking the 2nd Cameron Highlanders' position. The *Trieste* engineer units arrived too late in the morning and in the daylight fell under Commonwealth artillery fire and the passages were not cleared. Tanks of the *Ariete* were then ordered to exploit the passage of the *21st Panzer* and the *Trieste* was ordered to follow. In the afternoon the resistance of the defending troops began losing strength.

The Axis were through and into the fortress. It was this quick move forward and the inability to quickly respond to the Axis threat which spelled the doom of the garrison. The Germans were particularly quick in moving forward and deploying as

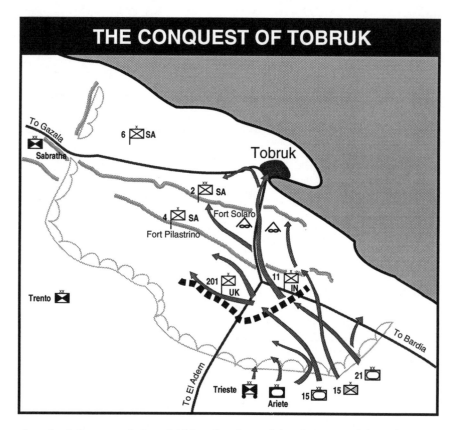

THE CONQUEST OF TOBRUK

they led the attack in, shifting back and forth to quickly advance forward the line. The goal was to split Tobruk in half, and this was being achieved. No South African infantry had been fought yet, and now the Axis were in the rear, and not to their front.

By the 21st the defense of Tobruk had collapsed and almost the entire garrison was captured. Approximately 33,000 prisoners, 2,000 vehicles, and 5,000 tons of food had fallen into Axis hands. Only 2,000 tons of fuel were captured. This is important because Rommel would use the argument of the captured supplies to support his view of the exploitation of this incredible success.

War is not so chivalric an affair: about the captured booty from Tobruk, Ciano noted in his famous diary on 6 July: "...there is violent indignation against the Germans because of their behavior in Libya. They have grabbed all the booty....The only one who succeeded in getting plenty for himself, naturally, is

Cavallero and he has sent the good things to Italy by plane....Cavallero may not be a great strategist, but when it is a question of grabbing, he can cheat even the Germans." It is interesting to note that when Rommel was informed about South African General Klopper's intention to surrender, he ordered the bulk of *Trieste* to move to Sidi Rezegh; and after the fall of Tobruk, at 0945, "All the units must round up and prepare for further advance."

Axis plans about Malta needed to be decided now that Tobruk was secured. Kesselring first arrived in Africa to speak with Rommel on the question of the air units now to be delivered to the Malta operation. "The British are on the run, we should give them no chance to regroup. A later attack on the Nile Delta will need stronger forces and mean higher casualties." Kesselring argued against this, he felt that the air forces needed to rest and Malta needed to fall so that supply lines could be made more secure. But Rommel refused on the ground that the enemy was in complete crisis. He was informed by the "Gute Quelle" intelligence that the situation of the Middle East Common-wealth forces was so bad that an immediate exploitation of the success would allow the Axis, as Rommel signaled Rintelen, to "destroy the enemy and thus open the way to the hearth of Egypt."

The same day Tobruk was assaulted, Mussolini wrote a letter to Hitler asking for fuel for the Malta operation. Cavallero and the navy also supported the need for the Malta operation. In mid-June Malta had received some supplies from a convoy which was almost destroyed, but these few supplies had been enough to cause further troubles to the Axis convoys. Thus Rommel's proposed advance into Egypt was opposed as too dangerous in view of the activity of the Malta forces. This view was also held because the air units were concentrated in the Gazala and Tobruk battles and would now be needed in Egypt. There was simply not enough air strength to deal with Egypt and Malta.

Rommel asked the *Fuehrer* directly for permission to continue the offensive and Hitler agreed against the view of Raeder and Kesselring. The *Kriegsmarine* staff of Raeder argued in favor of the seizure of the Suez area, combined with the employment of

Commonwealth prisoners (Ufficio Storico).

surface ships against the Murmansk convoys and the submarine war in the Atlantic, before America's growing strength turned the tide. Hitler then wrote the famous letter to Mussolini who was enthusiastic over Rommel's victory and ignored Cavallero's advice. Cavallero was sensitive to the political need not to disagree with Mussolini, and came around. The result was that Rommel was allowed to continue the pursuit of the 8th Army, which was retreating in confusion into Egypt. At the end of the meeting with Bastico and Barbasetti on the afternoon of the 22nd near Bardia, Rommel showed his intentions by ending the lively meeting with the words: "I now invite you for lunch at Cairo."

Rommel won the argument, partly due to Hitler and Mussolini's support, as well as to the mirage of the defeat of the Commonwealth. It was thought by Hitler and Rommel that there was little to stop them from rolling into the Delta and crossing the Nile.

Rommel receiving Colonial Order of Silver, also called Italy's Silver Star, from the hand of General Ettore Bastico on 27 April 1942. (Klaus Hubbuch).

So as the Axis pushed toward Egypt, *Luftwaffe* losses quickly mounted due to well supplied RAF attacks from fully developed and secure Egyptian bases. The threat of the invasion of Malta was ended forever. Accurate losses are difficult to obtain for Gazala, though it is clear that the 33,000 prisoners taken at Tobruk and the breaking of Commonwealth armored strength at Gazala were certainly reason enough to promote Rommel to field marshal. Italy, in turn, promoted Bastico and Cavallero to field marshal.

Gazala is a classic example of an Axis victory. The Commonwealth did not lose this battle by their inept tactics and leadership alone, though these certainly contributed to their defeat. Nor did the Germans win the battle by themselves. They needed not only the secure rear base protected by the Italian *XXI* and *X Corps*, but they also needed the victories supplied by the *Ariete*

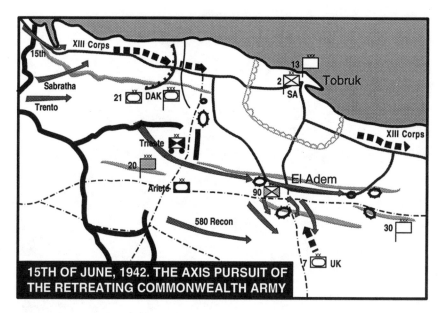

15TH OF JUNE, 1942. THE AXIS PURSUIT OF THE RETREATING COMMONWEALTH ARMY

and *Trieste* divisions, especially at the Cauldron. It was the destruction of the motorized and armored portions of the Commonwealth army which allowed for the advance of the Axis and the taking of Tobruk. The Italian contribution to this victory, so often overlooked in the histories of the War in North Africa, was vital for the victory of the Axis in the summer of '42.

Rommel's Goals

In the high summer of '42 Rommel was moving on the Nile Delta. What to do when it fell? Rommel envisioned three strike columns and two phases to capture Egypt. He issued orders before the battle of Alam Halfa for three columns to strike into Egypt. The *Bismarck* group made up of the *21st Panzer* and *164th Infantry* would head for Alexandria. Its value as a naval base would be over, even if it did not fall immediately.

The *DAK* made up of the German *15th Panzer* and *90th Light* would head for Cairo. The key was to occupy bridges across the Nile, but the seizure of the city would have been a tremendous psychological blow in itself. The *XX Corps* made up of the *Trieste, Ariete*, and *Littorio* had to eliminate the British defenses on either flank of the *DAK* thrust, and then seize bridges, capture the key airfield of El Fayum, and the Delta region between Cairo and the coast.

The second phase would see the slower Italian units advancing and having the *XXI Corps* of the *Trento* and *Bologna* relieving the *Bismarck* group at Alexandria, while the *X Corps* of the *Folgore* parachute and the *Pavia* and *Brescia* infantry divisions moved forward to Cairo, releasing the *DAK* to push for the

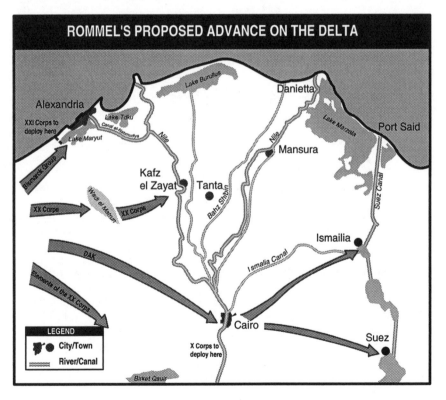

ROMMEL'S PROPOSED ADVANCE ON THE DELTA

cities of Suez and Ismailia on the Suez Canal.

The fall of Alexandria and Cairo also might have triggered an Egyptian army uprising against British control. Egyptian officers had approached the Axis on this point. This occurrence would certainly have hurt the ability of the Commonwealth to hold on.

On 10 August 1942, Rommel had a meeting with Barbasetti di Prun, a special envoy from *Comando Supremo* who discussed what was to be done. They discussed special means by which German paratroops were to seize bridges on the Nile, for which command of the air would be required—and disputed. Major Sillavengo and his elite combat engi-

neers of the *31st Guastatori* battalion had been ordered by Rommel on another occasion to prepare to bridge the Nile if need be. So these were some of the elements that the Axis considered for their seizure of Egypt.

After the fall of Egypt, Rommel foresaw three strategic columns. One would advance up the Nile, eventually retaking the *A.O.I..* One column would push into Arabia to seize Aden and control the Red Sea. Finally, the main thrust would be into the Middle East with an eventual linkup to the Germans in Russia and a move onto India. Facing the Axis would be up to 700,000 Allied troops, but many were rear area troops and military units that were not of frontline quality.

The Good Source

The history surrounding the Colonel Fellers messages that were intercepted and decoded by *SIM (Servizio Informazioni Militari,* the Italian Secret Service) has been clouded in controversy. Some sources state that the American diplomatic "Black" code was compromised in September 1941. It has also been written that the Germans were the ones who broke the code in the autumn of 1941.

In our research we have concluded that the following is the history of the Fellers intercepts. In the first part of December of 1941, before the outbreak of war between Italy and the United States, the Penetration Section (P) of *SIM,* headed by Captain Manfredi Talamo, secretly entered (read bur-

glary!) the U.S. Embassy in Rome and photographed the secret code used by the American military attache, one Colonel Fiske. The same code was being used by Colonel Bonner Fellers, the military attache in Cairo, to communicate with Washington every day. Colonel Fellers had been in the Middle East for some months and at the time of Operation Crusader had been with the Stuart tank equipped 4th Armored brigade, where he evaluated and reported on the performance of the Stuart, first used in combat there. His short messages discussed what had transpired each day and often listed Commonwealth units, especially armor, and their losses.

Fellers' transmissions were intercepted and decoded by *SIM* who passed them on to *Comando Supremo*, which made inadequate use of this information. *SIM* also passed the information on to the German headquarters in Rome which forwarded the information on to the German command in North Africa, where Rommel made excellent use of the information gleaned, referring to it as his "Good Source." *SIM* did not send the code to *Abwehr*, the German Secret Service, in Berlin, which most likely points out a typical "turf" battle between the Axis partners.

On 10 July, with the destruction of Captain Seeholm's *621st Radio Intercept Company*, the Allies discovered in the captured paperwork information which led back to Colonel Fellers. The "Good Source" had dried up.

However, there is some question as to why a German tactical intelligence group would have strategic information with them furnished by their ally—there is no logical reason

for this. Professor Lucio Ceva's recent research has uncovered that the "Good Source" apparently dried up on 25 June, and not on 10 July with the destruction of the *621st Radio Intercept Company*. Churchill had been informed on 10 June 1942 by British intelligence about Fellers. This was due to ULTRA intercepts of messages between Kesselring and Rommel's command. Even at this point of the war ULTRA could not read high level Italian radio traffic, but they could read the German traffic.

Between the dates of 10 June and 25 June 1942 British intelligence sent only "developed" messages through Fellers to mislead Axis intelligence, and also not to give away the fact that British intelligence had been reading Axis radio traffic. That mission was accomplished. So on the eve of the decisive battles for the Egyptian delta, Axis intelligence was crippled, while Allied intelligence continued to develop and grow.

Folgore Parachute Division

Although Italy parachuted supplies and officers just after the 1917 battle of Caporetto to reach isolated units, send messages, or establish an intelligence service behind enemy lines, the birth of the Italian paratroops was not a simple affair. The parachute was seen primarily as a means to escape from an airplane on its way down, but was used in minor ways during military operations in the 1920s and in sporting events.

The Soviet maneuvers of the thirties which featured largescale em-

ployment of paratroops created interest in Italy; supplies were successfully dropped in the Ethiopian campaign. This caused the Army General Staff to authorize the first paratroop battalion in June of 1936 (though its actual forming was delayed), while the next month saw the *Regia Aeronautica* founding the first paratroop school.

The tactical employment envisioned for them was minor sabotage, since the difficult Italian terrain had the Army thinking it could not employ large units. The paratroops were viewed as an irregular weapon which would be connected with the Italian spy network working behind the enemy lines as part of the "Fifth Column." Mussolini saw the paratroops as a unique propaganda weapon that would show off the *elan* of the Fascist regime.

The armed forces and the fascist militia contested each other over the years between the wars for the right to form these particular units, and delayed their inauguration until Marshal Italo Balbo, Governor of Libya, formed the first paratroops unit from volunteers of the Libyan soldiers called "Ascaris." This happened in 1938 and during that year a mass air drop was successfully accomplished. Two battalions were formed along with the parachute school at Castel Benito outside of Tripoli. Their official title was "Infantrymen of the Air" and they were all volunteers. The main problem was the parachute itself, which resulted in many deaths during the training and thus a demand for better equipment. After this early Salvador model there came the D.39 and D.40, the latter being able to restart the training and the formation of other units. The two Libyan battalions had a total strength of about 300 men, with some 50 of them being Italian. In 1940 the Libya paratroop battalions became part of the national scheme for paratroop training and in the homeland the Royal Parachute Schools of Tarquinia and Viterbo began to work under control of the *Regia Aeronautica* according to a Royal Law Decree of 1937, which delegated to the air force the duty to organize the parachute schools. Ad-

ditionally, a third battalion of Italian paratroopers was organized in 1940 in Libya. This was in fact a true case of cooperation between air force and army, because the army general staff was responsible for the tactical employment of the paratroops.

The first paratrooper units under this new scheme were formed on July 1940, three battalions at the start, one of which was made up of *Carabinieri* (Italian National Police). Both the officers, and unusually for the Italian army, the NCO'S, were carefully selected from many volunteers and were well chosen. This was usually one of the weak links in the Italian army, but not in these units. Additionally, the Italians were caught up in the propaganda and early wartime successes of the German paratroops and wanted to aspire to their success, as well as remembering their own *Arditi* from World War I, who were Italian assault troops used late in the war to help break the Austrian front.

In the autumn of 1940 the training went slowly because of the high loss rate due to the poor quality of the parachute. Only with the introduction of the new type in March 1941, the IF.41/SP, modeled on the successful German one, did the development of paratroops in Italy begin to forge ahead.

Considering this state of affairs, no actions were taken with the paratroops, though *Comando Supremo* considered several projects, including a descent on the Corinth Canal, several islands in Greece, or even an attack in the *A.O.I (Africa Orientale Impero*, the Italian East African Empire). This latter idea was given serious thought, but the Italians did not have enough SM82's (their standard three engine air transport) to move substantial numbers and thus they would be dependent on German help for air drops into Ethiopia.

As to action, the Libyan paratroops, along with the Italian paratroop battalion formed in Libya, merged into the *Tonini Mobile Group* (named after Lt. Colonel of the Engineers Goffredo Tonini, their commander) and fought in front of Derna in January, delaying the Australian advance. It was destroyed in the defeat at Beda Fomm. It should be noted that Graziani never considered employing these troops, though a lack of air transports would have colored any proposed scheme. Marshal Balbo, before his death in the first month of the war, wanted to raise two divisions of paratroops and to employ them in an attack against Egypt!

In July 1941 the *Carabinieri* paratroop battalion was sent to Africa and participated in Operation Crusader. It covered the flank of the exhausted *Ariete* armored division at the end of that operation, and was destroyed in the Jebel Akhbar Mountains in the retreat. The *Carabinieri* paratroops fought from 18 to 20 December, facing some South African armored cars, part of the Central India Horse and two battalions of the 4th Indian division, and "held back the 3/1 Punjabis throughout December 20th, but at dusk a bayonet charge overran the last stubborn defenders." The *Carabinieri* lost 35 dead and 251 missing (mostly captured in the retreat). Many of these troops, along from Tonini's group, did survive and would add their experiences to the pool of knowledge that was developing at Italy's parachute school.

Only one minor airdrop operation occurred at this point in the war. This took place at Celafonia and Zante in Greece. It was executed by the *2nd paratroop battalion* at the end of April 1941. It was largely a propaganda gesture because the Germans were occupying all of Greece and this was an opportunity to seize some islands. It was personally urged by Mussolini, and though with only three planes available, there was no resistance, and it was successful. It did give some lessons to the Italians on the use of paratroops which would be helpful later in their training.

The first large paratroops unit of the Italian Army was formed on 1 September 1941, as the *1st paratroop division* under command of General Enrico Frattini. It was composed of two infantry and one artillery regiment, plus the *8th Engineer battalion*. The artillery regiment was equipped with the light transportable 47/32 AT gun.

From June 1942 the division was called *Folgore* (Lightning) from the nickname of the *1st regiment*. The planned invasion of Malta (operation *C3* or *Herkules*, as the Germans called it) was the main duty of the new division which was trained at Tarquinia and Apulia for that operation. When the operation was cancelled, it was the opinion of General Student, the German leader of the Crete airborne invasion, that the division was ready for employment against Malta and that the only weaknesses were in the armament and equipment, but Student thought it was possible to remedy this with the German units that had to operate with the *Folgore*. During this period of training there was one

175

German paratroop battalion stationed at Tarquinia and General Bernhard Ramcke spent a great deal of time working with the Italians in an unusual act of cooperation between the normally uncooperative Axis partners.

The division, renamed *185th* and *Africa Hunters* for deception reasons, began to arrive in North Africa from mid-July 1942 on, when two things were clear: the Malta operation was cancelled and there was an urgent need of fresh troops on the Alamein front, where the fatigued Italian infantry battalions were attacked almost every day by units of General Auchinleck's 8th Army. It is no exaggeration to say that the paratroop division lived for the invasion of Malta, and the decision to send it on 14 July to Africa deeply disgusted the thoroughly trained men.

At the time of the arrival in Africa the division had the following organization:

1st Paratroop division (from 27th July 1942 known as the 185th)

186th paratroop regiment (5th, 6th, 7th battalions)

187th paratroop regiment (2nd, 4th, 9th, 10th battalions)

185th paratroop artillery regiment

8th pioneer engineer battalion (functioned like a demolition or assault engineer unit, or *guastatori* of the Italian army)

Each regiment was to have three battalions and one 47/32 anti-tank company, with the artillery battalions also equipped with the 47/132 guns.

The *3rd* and *11th battalions* remained in Italy along with the headquarters of the *185th Infantry*

regiments. From these units was eventually formed the *Nembo* division. Some sources said the unit originally had 3,800 men, and that to Africa were sent 2,676 men (this is probably in July, but at El Alamein the division would have 3,000 men).

At the beginning the division was employed among other units from Deir el Munassib and Qaret el Himeimat and took part in some fighting, but displayed particularly strong activity in no man's land by night. The division was then regrouped and reorganized in three ad hoc battle groups called *"raggruppamenti"* for the Alam Halfa battle, also called the "six days race":

> *Ruspoli* in the north with the *5th* and *7th* battalions, plus the *2nd* artillery battalion
>
> *Comosso* with *9th, 10th*, and *3rd* artillery battalion
>
> *2nd* battalion, reduced, with some minor units

During the battle the division had to cover the left flank of the main thrust, in cooperation with the *90th Light* division, the *Ramcke Fallschirmjaeger* brigade, along with some *Brescia* infantry units. The *Comossa* battalions were thus hit by the Commonwealth attack called Operation Beresford in the night between 3-4 September 1942. In 20 hours of fighting the paratroops had some 200 dead and wounded but bloodily repelled the attack of the New Zealanders. On this occasion Brigadier G. H. Clifton was captured along with many vehicles and weapons. The capture of Brigadier Clifton was simple enough; his driver drove his jeep at Clifton's direction up to some khaki clad troops, who turned out to be *Folgore*. Along with Clifton was captured "a number of documents and marked maps."

After the battle, the *Folgore* was assigned its own divisional sector which was hit by the British attack launched on 30 September by the newly arrived 131st British Infantry brigade supported by tanks of the Royal Scots Greys and heavy artillery fire. The green infantry was repulsed with heavy losses, also thanks to a new tactical procedure put in action by the *9th battalion* commander during the 3-4 September fighting: he let the enemy advance *into* the defensive position and then counterattacked by surprise from several directions. The *X Army Corps* HQ was opposed to such a tactical procedure, but allowed this. The result was that the *9th battalion* lost 45 men against estimated enemy losses of nearly 400.

The idea proved sound, after three weeks, when the newly reorganized 8th British Army launched the main offensive to put Rommel and the Axis army out of Africa. On 23 October 1942, in the southern sector, the *Folgore* was attacked by 44th Infantry and 7th Armored (Desert Rats) which also used Scorpion tanks for the minefield (specially equipped tanks with flails for making crossings through minefields), but casualties were high for little in the way of gains, because of artillery and molotov cocktails. The molotov was employed due largely to the ineffectiveness of the 47/32 anti-tank gun which for one kill against a British tank needed 20 hits! Two Free French battalions were repulsed by the *5th Folgore battalion* in the fighting at Naqb Rala on 24 October and later pursued by armored cars of the *33rd German Recce* unit which unfor-

tunately killed enemies and allies alike. On the following day the 4th Armored brigade and 69th Infantry brigade attacked the *Folgore* at the Deir Munassib position but lost 22 tanks gaining only the forward positions. Further attacks launched by 50th Infantry and 7th Armored against the *Folgore* failed again with considerable losses. The *Folgore* officers claimed the destruction of 110 tanks, while others were towed out of the battlefield because the Italian engineer commander did not follow the order to destroy the immobilized British tanks. The situation had in the meanwhile compelled Montgomery to change his plans, for which the southern attacks, which lasted three days, were suspended. The new plan would be *Supercharge* and was launched in the north toward the coast. In the south the battlefields remained quiet until the retreat order of 2 November given to the *Folgore* and *Bologna* divisions of the *X Army Corps*, which condemned the units to a hopeless retreat in the desert. Only some minor motorized units reached the coast.

The Commonwealth forces of 1st Armored division closed the pocket around Fuka on the 5th. The final organized resistance by the *Folgore* was put up by the remnants of the division thanks to the fact that they had hand towed several 47/32 guns.

Only a few hundred survived to join a newly rebuilt *285th Folgore* battalion under Captain Lombardini which participated in further fighting with the *Trieste* division in Tunisia. Again it was employed as an infantry unit, though with more independence than an organic battalion of the *Trieste*. After the Mareth battle the battalion was some 200 men strong and fought the last time at the Takrouna stronghold where it was utterly destroyed.

Many of the survivors of the North African battles returned to Italy where they joined the *185th Folgore* regiment, which was part of a new paratroop division This division was called *Nembo* (rain cloud) and was recruited with less exclusivity and not as well trained for the most part. In 1943 the *Nembo* appeared as below:

Nembo (known as the 184th)

183rd paratroop regiment (*10th, 15th, 16th* battalions)

184th artillery regiment (*12th, 23rd, 14th* battalions)

185th paratroop regiment (*3rd, 8th, 11th* battalions)

184th guastatori engineers

Due to lack of planes and secure air space to drop paratroops the Italian army employed this unit strictly as an infantry unit. Part of it was used in suppressing Yugoslav partisan activity in Gorizia. They, like the *Alpini*, or mountain troops, were quite effective at this type of warfare, employing pack mules, and being comfortable in the mountains and other difficult terrain. After the

fall of Tunis, the *183rd* regiment and *184th* artillery regiment of the *Nembo* was transferred to Sardinia due to fear of an Allied invasion. Parts of the *Nembo* would go on to fight in Sardinia, covering the retreat there, as well as in Calabria, fighting the British 8th Army.

Italy also proposed building a third division, the *Ciclone* or Cyclone, seeing four battalions organizing in August of 1943. Both the Italian Navy and the Air Force organized some minor units, mostly for the planned invasion of Malta, and there was one ineffective drop in North Africa for sabotage purposes by some of these units. All it achieved was the destruction of some Allied planes near Benghazi. Many of the men were quickly captured in this attempt and it may have been revealed to the Allies through the ULTRA intercepts.

While not fully utilized in the war, the Italian paratroop units, and especially the *Folgore* division, personified the best in the Fascist Italian military effort in World War II. It also pointed out the weaknesses of that effort as well, coming too late and too little, and not employed in the fashion they were designed for.

The Logistical Nightmare, Axis Reinforcements, and ULTRA

Reading the *Rommel Papers* gives a good view of the logistical problems faced by the Axis. Not only do the *Rommel Papers* discuss the lack of sufficient supplies to the German

and Italian troops in Africa, but there are many archival papers which give testimony to the continuous demands for more fuel and ammunition, and the need to bring

TYPICAL ITALIAN TRUCK

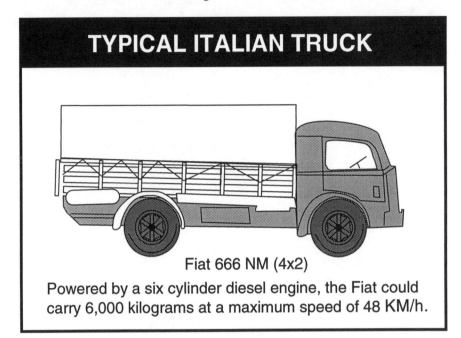

Fiat 666 NM (4x2)
Powered by a six cylinder diesel engine, the Fiat could carry 6,000 kilograms at a maximum speed of 48 KM/h.

them first to Africa and then to the front line. Interestingly enough, the convoys to North Africa was one of the few areas of co-operation between the two Axis partners. In the winter of 1941 a high level commission was established dealing with "traffic with Africa," and met almost every day. Participants often included German Field Marshal Kesselring and Admiral Arturo Riccardi of the *Regia Marina* (Royal Italian Navy).

Among Rommel's remarks there are also claims against the High Commands in Rome and Berlin, and open charges of treason against the Italian Navy officers who "sabotaged whatever they could." Such charges have often been accepted without any reconsideration by historians and are repeated in many historical works appearing on the campaign. The bitter accusation by Rommel against the "treasonable"

officers of the *Regia Marina* has been discovered only in later years as a cover operation mounted by the British in order to keep secret the role of ULTRA. But how valid is this acceptance? Did not Rommel also wish to protect his reputation, or did he fail to see another dimension to the overall situation facing Axis forces in North Africa?

To these claims General Enno von Rintelin, at the time the liaison envoy of the German High Command to Rome, answered in a postwar article that "supply should serve the operations, but also the operations had to take the logistical situation into account." Von Rintelin felt that the general situation did not allow the sustained effort Rommel wanted without a radical change in the overall situation, such as the seizure of Malta. The *Regia Marina* produced detailed figures to demonstrate that the majority of

THE DOVUNQUE FAMILY

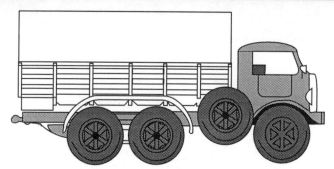

Troop Carrying version of the Breda Dovunque 41.

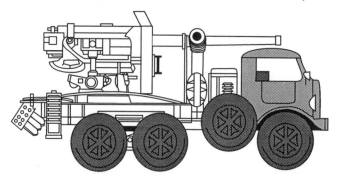

Italian 90mm Anti-Tank Gun Mounted on a Breda Dovunque. The Breda Dovunque could carry 7,500 kilograms with its six cylinder diesel engine at a maximum speed of 53.5 KM/h.

Earlier model of the Breda Dovunque, the "35". This shows how the four wheel drive vehicle could go over large obstructions. One of the more successful Italian truck designs of the war, but too few were available.

supplies sent arrived on the African shore. Among these figures are the following: 896 convoys sent to Libya, with the transport of 206,402 men, of which 189,162 arrived safely; and 2,245,381 tons of various materials, 1,929,055 of which arrived on the Libyan shore. Tunisia received 72,269 men while 5,468 were lost during transit; of the 433,601 tons of material arriving, 127,000 additional tons were lost.

According to these figures, the *Regia Marina* claimed that it made a maximum effort to transport the reinforcements to Africa and that it was successful in this job. Another example of this is during two of the hottest months, both literally and figuratively, July and August of 1942. In those two months the Navy disembarked some 140,000 tons of supplies in the various ports of Libya and Egypt, as follows: Tripoli received 35,669 tons, Benghazi 60,500, Tobruk 47,071, and Mersa Matruh 1,927 tons of supplies. In July 274,337 tons were shipped of which 11,661 tons were lost; while in August 253,005 were shipped and 45,668 lost. In September losses were 15,127 tons out of 197,201, and in October 32,572 tons were lost out of 205,599 tons of shipping employed. The problem was that it was mostly tankers that were lost, largely due to ULTRA. But there is no denying that Italy successfully shipped a great deal of men and supplies to Africa.

The *Regia Marina* claims of having done its duty need to be weighed against Rommel's remarks and possibly the failure to move the landed supplies to the distant El Alamein front. This may have been a bigger problem than either Malta's

Strike Forces or the disputed command of the Central Mediterranean. In the latter case, it must be recalled that at the time of El Alamein many of the Commonwealth shipping attacks originated from Egypt, and not Malta. In the ultimate analysis the main reasons for the supply failure to sustain a major campaign in this theater of war were naval warfare in the Mediterranean and the difficulties of land communication in North Africa.

How exactly did ULTRA affect the shipping of Axis supply and reinforcements?

An important role in the Allied actions against the Axis supply route to Africa was played by the ULTRA intercepts and decoding service which enabled the British to read the messages sent through the Enigma code machine widely used by the Germans, but also by the *Regia Marina*. This important intelligence operation whose existence was revealed only in the 1970s was based at Bletchley Park near London and was greatly helped by the rudimentary computer which sped the decrypting analysis required to read key signals.

The direct effect of ULTRA, which has also been called "the true traitor," with reference both to Rommel's accusation and to post war controversies in Italy, was a long list of sinkings of merchant ships in the Mediterranean. Some 37,800 intercepted messages of the *Regia Marina* show that the intelligence service had an important role both in the Mediterranean war and in the supply situation of the troops in Africa.

The breaking of the German *Luftwaffe* code ("red" code) enabled the British to acquire useful information, although this information was often a small puzzle piece set in one large unknown picture, or the information was partly discounted by local commanders in view of the little importance generally ascribed at that time to such military activity.

It should be noted that while the Luftwaffe's "light blue" code used in the Mediterranean had already been broken at the time of the Afrika Korps disembarking in Tripoli in 1941, ULTRA was also able to read the secret code of the Regia Marina, which was employing, among other means, the C38m code machine produced by the Swedish company Hagelin from the time of the Spanish Civil War. Another unlucky means of transmission used by the Regia Marina was the Enigma D type German code machine, which was partly responsible for the Cape Matapan naval defeat, which could be read by the British as early as the autumn of 1940. Messages concerning the African convoys were sent with the Hagelin machine whose code was broken in June 1941.

The increasing effectiveness of Bletchley Park in this decoding activity led to some important successes against the Axis supply route for Africa in the autumn and winter of 1941. An example of the ULTRA effect is the damage done the Giulia convoys, only half of which reached Tripoli on 11 October 1941, on the eve of Operation Crusader when the Axis desperately needed supplies. But at that time, several problems affected the Bletchley Park activity in the intercepting, decoding and sending of summaries to local commands. These, in turn, did not always pay full attention that the source deserved. As a result, it seems that the famous Duisburg convoy was sunk without or

with very little help from ULTRA on the night of 8-9 November 1941. On the other hand the Maritza and Procida tankers were both sunk on ULTRA indications. Of course it was not only the increased effectiveness of the ULTRA service that caused many ship losses to the Axis. The general situation in the Mediterranean periodically changed as the shifting of the Luftwaffe units to and from the Russian front weakened or strengthened Axis control of the central Mediterranean.

In July 1942, at the peak of Rommel's drive on the Nile, ULTRA became very effective, having broken an army supply key, as well as improving on the breaking of the Scorpion key for liaison between the German Army and the Luftwaffe.

The Alam Halfa battle was an ULTRA success not only because Rommel's plan was well known in advance, but also because all the important tankers sent to Africa were accurately followed by intercepts and for the most part sunk, as was the Giorgio, Picci Fassio, Sanandrea and Abruzzi, ships whose names are closely connected with the second attempt by the Axis to force the El Alamein position.

On 17 October ULTRA intercepted the Axis tanker schedule which enabled them to pay great attention to these ships during the third battle for El Alamein. Thus 12 ships were sunk during the month of October, two of which were tankers (plus the Panuco burned but not sunk); and another 11 were lost during November 1942.

A total of 86 ships and nine naval craft were sunk thanks to the intervention of ULTRA. Of course, some of these would have been sunk in any event, but the general effect of ULTRA, which was involved in 40% of all the merchant ship losses, was vital.

Some Prisoners and Their Fate

Prisoners of war (POWs) are a natural fact of war, and World War II in North Africa produced many. It was customary to move them out of the theater as quickly and conveniently as possible, so risk of their being liberated would be minimal. In the case of Axis prisoners, many ended up in North America, even performing some labor operations while there. The Allies would place agents among the top officers in hopes of obtaining valuable information.

The Axis shipped their prisoners back to Italy, Germany, and occupied Europe, which was relatively easy as the supply ships arriving in Africa could carry back little other than the wounded or prisoners. This led to some unusual and still not completely resolved incidents involving prisoner laden ships.

The British did attack merchant ships transporting Commonwealth POWs from Africa to Europe. In light of information supplied by ULTRA London may have known that a ship contained prisoners, as well as their nationality, but getting "the word" to a particular stalking ship, plane, or especially submarine, was not easy.

Dr. Alberto Santoni in *Il Vero Traditore (The Real Traitor*, a study of ULTRA and the war in the Mediterranean) was first to discuss this issue; it has also been mentioned in appendices of the official *British Intelligence in World War Two*.

Four ships were involved. The *Bosforo* sailed from Tripoli on 6 February 1942 with 250 British POWs as reported on the 7 and 8 of February by ULTRA; destroyers based on Malta had tried but failed to locate the *Bosforo*.

On 14 February a message was sent from London stating that the ships *Ariosto* and *Atlas*, with 294 and 150 POWs respectively, had sailed on the 13th from Tripoli and were due to arrive on the 16th at Palermo. There were attacks against the convoy, and the *Ariosto* was sunk by the submarine P38 at 2200 on the 14th with 135 POWs dying.

The third case was after London signalled on 9 October 1942:

> *Loreto* will sail from Tripoli at 9.00 a.m. of the 9th, speed 7 knots, and should arrive to Naples at 07.30 a.m. of the 13th. It will transport 350 POWs.

The *Loreto* was sunk by the submarine *Unruffled* (P46) along with a hundred Indian POWs at 1732 on 13 October, four days after the word went out from London.

The last case involves the *Scillin* which was sunk by the submarine *Sahib* (P212). The *Scillin* sailed on 13 November 1942 without escort and when lost, 830 British POWs went down with her.

A warning about the prisoners on the *Scillin* does not appear in the London OIC (Operational Intelli-

MOST SECRET.

FOR THE PERSONAL USE OF THE ADDRESSEE ONLY

OPERATIONAL INTELLIGENCE CENTRE SPECIAL INTELLIGENCE SUMMARY

ITALIAN CONVOY SITUATION   O.I.C/M.C.38
7th February 1942.

DTPT

INS   MK

Part I AT SEA

Southbound

5679   BOLSETA (2400) from Tunis. Due Tripoli 0800/ today. Note:— Was   2316
sighted by aircraft in position 45 miles S.E. of Kerkennah at 2300B/6,

Northbound

5695   MONVISO (8600) from Tripoli. Due Palermo 0745 today.   2330
5718   Note:— Was sighted by A/C at 1000B/6. 35 miles East of Kerkannah,
at 1640B/6 when 12 miles south of Pantellaria and again at 2240B/6
when 50 miles 060° from Cape Bon.

5730   BOSFORO (3648) escorted by T.B. CALLIOPE sailed from   2352
5733   Tripoli at 1800/6. Speed 10.5 knots. Due PALERMO 0915/8. She is   2361
5755   carrying 250 British prisoners.

Coastal

5745   ACHAIA (1800) sailed from Tripoli 1500/6 for RAS EL ALI   2359
where she is due 0900/8.

5722   EMILIO due BUERAT 0800 today from Tripoli.

PART II LATE REPORTS

Nil

PART III FUTURE MOVEMENTS.

Southbound

5540   TRAPANI (1800) escorted by a T.B. was ordered on 31/1 to sail   2247
5545   from Trapani for Tripoli as soon as ready. Tanker ARONDIDE (6000) 2265
5543   escorted by destroyer PREMUDA was to follow one day later. No   2264
confirmation of these sailings has been received.

Northbound

5733   The following Steamships are ready to sail for TRIPOLI for Italy but 2355
are held up for lack of escorts:— PISANI. BENGASI. ATLAS. BEPPE.
ARIOSTO. DELIA AND ANNA MARIA.

PART IV FRENCH TRAFFIC.

5757   A French convoy of 5 merchant vessels escorted by a T.B. and   2366
a minesweeper will pass C. Bon at 0800/7 proceeding to Sfax from
Bizerta. A minesweeper leaves SFAX for KERKEHAH at 0700/7.

Distribution.

1st Lord	A.C.N.S. (F)	D. of P.	N.I.D. 8.E.I
1st Sea Lord	D.O.D.(F)	D.M.I	N.I.D.3.
V.C.N.S	D.D.I.C	A.C.A.S.I.	

This is a reproduction based on the original document.

gence Centre-Admiralty) dispatches. But this case and the previous *Loreto* one does have a witness in the naval intelligence papers of the Public Records Office. It is the long report of the Admiralty dated 20 Nov. 1942, without protocol number and unsigned, titled *Italian Ships Transporting POWs*, which says:

> The Mediterranean authorities are always informed of the ships transporting POWs. Two of these ships were sunk while returning to Italy: *Loreto* sailed from Tripoli on 9th October 1942 and was sunk by submarine P.46 on 13th October and the information that the ship had POWs on board was signalled to Mediterranean authorities on the 8th. *Scillin* was sunk by P.212 on 14th November 1942 and the message was transmitted to Mediterranean authorities on 13th November, specifying that the ship was transporting POWs.

To avoid such tragedies in the future, the same 20 November 1942 report supplied the names of 29 Italian ships used for transporting POWs between 9 June and 1 August 1942 and between 21 August and 20 November 1942, with the ports, dates of sailing and arrival, and number of POWs on board. This would serve to identify the ships equipped for the transport of POWs, and avoid their sinking. In conclusion, it can be affirmed that it is difficult to abort war missions in progress, especially those of submarines.

CHAPTER V

The El Alamein Battles

Well, Briel, you will advance with your men to Alexandria and
stop when you come to the suburbs. The Tommies have gone.
When I arrive tomorrow we'll drive into Cairo together for coffee.
—Rommel to the commander of the 606th Flak Battalion

The battle plan was typical of Rommel: hasty, reckless, unrealistic
and based on poor information. But he counted as always on the
moral factor to make nonsense of rational calculation.
—Correlli Barnett

The British pride themselves on being good losers. I'm a damn bad
loser. I'm going to win.
—Auchinleck

On 23 June 1942 Rommel's spearhead entered Egypt, driving on the El Alamein chokepoint with the intention of pushing on to the Nile. The reasons why Rommel made this decision (which was later to be much criticized) was the supposedly depleted, confused, and low morale condition of the battered 8th Army. The perception of the weak state of the 8th Army was endorsed by one of the famous intercepted "Gute Quelle" signals sent from Cairo by the local American military attaché, Colonel Fellers, to Washington. Moreover, Rommel had ample supplies captured at Tobruk (though little of it was fuel).

But the decision implied the cancellation of the projected invasion of Malta, because Axis air power was insufficient to handle both operations at the same time. Although opposed by

Kesselring, Cavallero, and von Rintelen, among others, Rommel firmly held his opinion, asking only for the *Fuehrer's* decision. Hitler probably never actually planned to order *Herkules* or the *C3* operation against Malta. Records from the *Fuehrer* headquarters and the meeting with Mussolini on the schedule for the Malta invasion at Klessheim support this conclusion. Rommel got the answer he wanted. Hitler persuaded Mussolini on the point by telegraphing to *Il Duce* that "it is only once in a lifetime that the Goddess of Victory smiles," and Mussolini replied the following day to Hitler "...that the historic moment has now come to conquer Egypt."

The decision to advance or not is debatable with the information at hand. Rommel was enthralled by the dream seemingly at hand, and he was sure he would capture Alexandria by 30 June, although the state of depletion of the advancing Axis forces was great. Moreover the speed of the advance diminished through attrition of the vehicles and weapons of the Axis army. Facing the Axis was an Allied army which was feeding in reinforcements from throughout the Middle East. We often think of an empty desert leading to the Nile Delta, but it should be remembered that Churchill complained to General Alan Brooke (later Field Marshal Viscount Alanbrooke), Chief of the Imperial General Staff, that in the Middle East there were 750,000 men, asking "where are they, what were they doing, why were they not fighting...?" Of course, many were rear area personnel, but as Churchill wrote to Auchinleck, "...there is no reason why units defending the Mersa Matruh position should not be reinforced by several thousands of officers and administrative personnel..."

A big change was Auchinleck taking personal command of the 8th Army, sacking Ritchie on 25 June, at the urging of Churchill and many others. Auchinleck would now lead from the front. He acted virtually as a "Corps, Division, Brigade and even Battalion Commander," and this control helped to stop the Axis. He also viewed the 8th Army not as an army that would make a last stand, but as an army that would continue to fight, throughout the Middle East if need be. From now on it would be a fluid defense. All medium and heavy artillery was also placed under

Italian truck mounted 20mm AA gun; sometimes used in an AT role (courtesy Lucio Ceva & Andrea Curami).

Auchinleck's direct orders, thus giving the headquarters a real punch.

The negative aspect of this decision to view the defense as fluid was that some in the army were looking over their shoulder, wondering where they would retreat to next. This attitude would not change until later when Montgomery took command. Auchinleck also continued forming mixed brigade sized fighting units, a tactic adopted before Gazala, and this was resisted by the Commonwealth army, as it forced them to operate in a way they were neither trained nor designed for. Additionally, there continued to be friction between the various services: ANZAC troops had rivalries with the Pommies (British), just as the infantry in general felt poorly supported by the Armored units. The Commonwealth army could not fight together as a team.

One must realize that when the *DAK* (the *15th* and *21st Panzer* divisions) crossed the Egyptian border it had only 44 serviceable tanks. Rommel considered that there were but two Commonwealth divisions facing the Axis. In reality, after the retreat on the Mersa Matruh position the 8th Army had the 50th division and the 10th Indian, the 20th Indian brigade of the 5th Indian division and the 2nd New Zealand division. The 1st and 7th Armored divisions, although depleted, were defending the long open southern flank, but were held back in part due to incomplete British intelligence on Axis tank strength. One Allied estimate was that the Axis had 339 tanks (220 being German) compared to the 155 with the 8th Army on 26 June. In reality, the Axis had built up a total of 104 tanks (44 Italian) by the end of June.

After 24 June the RAF began dogging the advancing Axis columns. Not only was the available strength concentrated in the support role for the retreating Commonwealth forces, but the enemy was constantly bombarded by the RAF, bombing it even by night with the help of the Albacore, a naval torpedo bomber, launching flares. As the Axis advanced they approached the RAF bases while the *Regia Aeronautica* and *Luftwaffe* were busy moving forward.

Meanwhile on the Alamein line XXX Corps (Norrie) organized the resistance with the South Africans, preparing for the probable enemy blow, while the 9th Australian division was arriving from Syria.

On the afternoon of 26 June the *DAK* advanced into the center of the British deployment, while the *XXI* and *X Corps* advanced north near the Matruh perimeter and the *XX Motorized* hit the south. The *21st Panzer* division was stopped by the 29th Indian brigade and minefields after having routed "Gleecol," one of Auchinleck's jock columns. This was, along with "Leathercol," one of the tactical brigade strength mixed forces groups. Leathercol was slammed by the *90th Light* division which took 400 prisoners and continued ahead until midnight. Fighting on the 27th and 28th, the *DAK* was able to reach the Fuka area, cutting the retreat route of the British divisions. Axis forces tried on the 28th to open the defensive perimeter of Mersa Matruh but without success. The *Trento*, with the *7th Bersaglieri* regiment, had to attack from the Charing Cross trail to Matruh, and the *90th Light* attacked from the east. Lieutenant General W.G. Holmes, commanding the Allied position, attempted to free his two divisions by breaking out eastward which was partially

British prisoners being taken to the rear under Italian guard (Ufficio Storico).

successful. The capture of Mersa Matruh by the *90th Light* and *7th Bersaglieri* regiment followed, and some 2,000 more Commonwealth prisoners were taken.

General Freyberg, commanding the 2nd New Zealand division, decided fighting from Mersa Matruh would invite disaster and so had positioned his men to the south in the open lands. Early in the morning they became involved in an exchange of fire with the *21st Panzer* in which an artillery shell landed among the divisional staff. One of those wounded was General Freyberg, who was hit in the neck. This was about his thirtieth wound from two wars (Freyberg once said that being wounded twice was easy, the bullet had to enter and had to exit - hence two wounds!). The *21st Panzer* moved away and past the New Zealand position, and in the process scattered much of the 2nd

Mussolini in Africa after the victory at Gazala, waiting to enter Cairo, a fate he was not to enjoy; Colonel Pedini, left, looking at Mussolini, and Colonel Scalabrino in the car standing (Luigi Castaman).

New Zealand's tail, or truck support. The New Zealanders were cut off by the Axis advance and realized that to avoid disaster they would have to move off that night.

During the retreat from Mersa Matruh the New Zealanders engaged in one of their most dramatic actions of the war. Moving in the night to escape the Axis forces, part of the division, motorized by dint of stuffing troops into whatever vehicles they had, stumbled into the laager of the *21st Panzer Division*. During the ensuing action, the night lit up with flares, gunfire of all sorts, and as trucks careened through the encampment, General Freyberg, swathed in bandages around his head, looked out on the bedlam and shouted that this was "By God! another Balaclava." But unlike the Light Brigade that was destroyed at Balaclava, the 2nd New Zealand division would live to fight another day.

Il Duce, caught up in the successful Axis advance, and sensing that the fall of Egypt was imminent, personally piloted his plane to North Africa. Arriving at Derna, he had a transport bring his white charger to the front to ride into Cairo!

Rommel's incredible success at Tobruk, and then at Mersa Matruh, resulted in the opening of a crisis in the 8th Army.

Rommel's rapid advance also hindered the planned halt at Fuka that Auchinleck desired. This halt was impossible because Auchinleck was determined to save the units of the disorganized 8th Army and he realized that he could not reorganize under pressure at Fuka. The confused retreat of the 8th Army to El Alamein following the fall of Mersa Matruh was recognized by Rommel, who urged his troops forward in the race against time, before those British retreating columns had the chance to reinforce the defense of the Alamein line. In Egypt, with the fall of Mersa Matruh and the Axis advance to El Alamein, the "Flap" now came into full swing.

The Flap was the slang term for the panic that now gripped much of Egypt. The Royal Navy was hurriedly evacuating Alexandria as a naval base and demolition units were stationed at key installations, and in the process failing to properly notify the army of this evacuation. In Cairo, the requests for passports out of the country shot up, and the British embassy was so busily burning vital documents that a plume of smoke could be seen rising above its offices. Many tail elements of the Allied armies were evacuating to Palestine and elsewhere. Exhausted stragglers and units sent to fortify the Delta region came from the front, creating the impression of a massive retreat by the 8th Army. Where would it end and what would it lead too? Would the Mediterranean and Malta fall together and would Turkey be outflanked? Would the valuable oil fields of the Middle East fall to the Axis advance?

Rommel was confident, in view of the retreating 8th Army, but one key goal had not been achieved. The capture of Mersa Matruh had not brought about the destruction of the 8th Army. The pickings were actually quite slim. Nor was he warned by any intelligence that the 1st South African division was in position and ready at El Alamein. In contrast, the Axis divisions were further depleted and were only shadow spearheads due to fighting and losses from May until July. Tanks and trucks suffered breakdowns, thus delaying the rebuilding of units with men, guns, fuel, ammunition and food. Each step east toward the Delta was one step further away from supplies arriving from Europe. The total strength available to the *Panzerarmee* at the end of June was reduced to 55 medium German and 70 Italian

Rommel conferring with a German and Italian officer (Klaus Hubbuch).

tanks, 330 German artillery pieces and 200 Italian, 15 armored cars, 2,000 German infantry and 8,000 Italians. This was simply not enough to overrun the strong Allied position, now partly defended by fresh troops. Moreover, most of the Italian infantry was still marching on foot in the desert to reach the front.

On 1 July Rommel was still confident of taking the new line of El Alamein before the British had the chance to strengthen it. The forces facing the *Panzerarmee Afrika* were the 1st South African of General Pienaar, deployed on the north, the 6th New Zealand brigade at Bab el Qattara, and the battered 4th and 5th New Zealand brigades reorganized behind it. The 1st Armored division (consisting of the 7th Motorized brigade, the 22nd and 4th Armored brigades—the 7th Armored had transferred its strength to it) of General Lumsden faced Rommel with some 150 tanks. Auchinleck was aware from intelligence sources that an enemy attack was planned against the center of his line in the afternoon.

The attack plan was similar to that used at Mersa Matruh, but it became a head-on assault. The *90th Light* division would attack on the center along with the *DAK*, break through and then envelop the enemy position, the *DAK* turning it from the south. The south flank would be covered by the Italian *XX Motorized Corps* and by the *Littorio* armored division. The latter was depleted and had suffered many losses due to air attacks, and while attacking a British tank and artillery group, proved again the M13 no longer a fit tank for fighting in 1942. At the same time, two battalions of the *Trento* division and the 7th *Bersaglieri* regiment had to attack the El Alamein position from the west to engage and hold down the defense.

The *21st Panzer* found in her advance an important strong-point in the center of the British line, and attacked it, losing an entire day and 18 tanks, but capturing 2,000 prisoners and 30 guns of the 18th Indian brigade. At the same time the *90th Light* was blocked by the strong artillery fire from the boxes of the 1st South African division, which also panicked the men in the *90th Light* and brought artillery losses. The artillery barrage also hit the *7th Bersaglieri* which was unable to gain terrain against the west side of the perimeter. The day had certainly not achieved the results hoped for by Rommel.

That night the impression that Rommel gave to the Italian liaison officer to *Panzerarmee*, General Mancinelli, was positive, since he reported that enemy "forces deployed south of the [18th Indian brigade] will retreat during the night in the southeast-east direction...." In Rommel's mind, the battle was still in process, but 2 July was not any better.

The *DAK* was heavily bombed and the *Trieste* lost some 60 trucks from RAF air attacks. Its mobile strength was reduced to one reinforced company for each regiment. The *90th Light* division experienced the same artillery barrage of the previous day, which compelled Rommel to try a new move along the Ruweisat ridge with the *DAK*. This encountered a Common-wealth countermove and engaged the 1st Armored division and the 7th Motorized brigade which led to a halt in the evening. The *DAK* now had but 20 tanks in the *21st Panzer* division and six left in the *15th Panzer*.

On 3 July, Auchinleck maintained the defensive posture which foresaw the firm defense of XXX Corps, while XIII Armored Corps would hit the south flank, enveloping the advancing enemy. Rommel asked the *Comando Superiore Africa Settentrionale* to send the infantry battalions of the non-motorized Italian divisions to the front as quickly as possible. He asked for Stuka support, which was ordered, but the *Luftwaffe* and *Regia Aeronautica* airplanes were still in the rear because of the lack of motor transport for support services. The *Ariete*, which had six or eight tanks and 1,000 men, advanced south during the night while the *Trieste* was ordered to cover her flank, but, instead, remained in the same place due to the disorganization caused by the enemy air attacks. At dawn the *Ariete* saw that their position was in a large depression and that it was partly surrounded by enemy forces. The division remained under British fire that morning for hours and when one of the two advancing New Zealand columns overran a *Bersaglieri* battalion of the *Ariete*, the remnants of the *Ariete* then broke and escaped toward the northwest, leaving a great deal of war booty on the field, including some valuable 88mm and 90mm AT guns. It would have been better to try to retreat in some way before this, since the losses were high. This was a sign of the strain which affected this good unit, and the fault remained on the shoulders of her commander, General Francesco Arena, who pushed too far ahead without proper reconnaissance and support. The remnants of the *Ariete* fell back behind the two battalions of the *Pavia* and *Brescia* deployed on El Mreir, which formed at that moment the "*Brescia* position" (also deployed on the ridge were two battalions of the *9th Bersaglieri*). The *Brescia* repelled a New Zealand attack thanks to the intense fire they developed.

Rommel would later bitterly criticize the *Ariete's* stand here, but it appears the main problem was that the *Ariete* was too weak, and the initial attack was poorly supported and launched into a bad piece of terrain. Of the 531 losses of the division, about 350 men were prisoners, while the rest were dead and wounded.

Rommel then launched an attack on the British center with the *21st* and *15th Panzer* divisions, which was checked by the 1st and 2nd South African brigades, and by the 22nd (with 56 tanks) and 4th Armored brigades. The 4th's war diary reported that "fighting was very heavy and continued to be so until last light." It was becoming clear that the drive on the Delta had come to a standstill and that the conquest of the Nile was to remain a dream. That day the RAF flew some 400 missions against the Axis at El Alamein.

Auchinleck's intelligence services continued to collect a good deal of information about his opponent's intention, learning among other things that on 4 July Rommel would not attack.

The weakened 1st Armored division, mechanically unsound and with some poor radio equipment, now counterattacked the depleted *15th Panzer* division, while it was covering the retreat of the *21st*, causing a somewhat confused retreat of the *115th* regiment. Another attack was also launched at night against a battalion of the *Brescia*, which lost some positions but repelled the attack. The 4th Armored brigade was so weakened from these actions that it was ordered withdrawn to the rear on 10 July to be reorganized as the "4th Light Armored Brigade Group."

In the following days Rommel regained his optimism and began to plan a new attack on the south end of the British line, but his intentions were clear to Auchinleck because of the effective use of ULTRA. Auchinleck, forewarned, concentrated on an attack against the weak Italian *XXI Infantry Corps* deployed before the El Alamein defensive perimeter. The attacks were launched by the 26th Australian brigade of the 9th division and by the 2nd South African brigade, reinforced by 32 Valentine and 6 Matilda tanks. While this latter attack failed, losing seven tanks out of eight available, the Australian attack hit two battalions of the newly arriving and poor (it was a hodge podge of rear area troops and not a tight integrated unit) *Sabratha* division, which was deploying to relieve the *7th Bersaglieri* regiment. One battalion of the *Sabratha* was overrun, while a battalion of the *Sabratha* and the *Bersaglieri* were isolated. The Aussie attack succeeded in capturing two battalions of the *3rd Celere* artillery regiment and the headquarters and commander of the *7th Bersaglieri*. The remaining part of the *Celere* was also isolated. Navarini, commander of *XXI Corps*, immediately sent a battalion of the *7th Bersaglieri* and a battalion of the *46th Artillery* to block the road, while Rommel sent an ersatz battalion of the *90th Light* and part of the *382nd* regiment of the newly renumbered and just-flown-in *164th* German infantry division to the action. The *164th* was just arriving from Crete, without its vehicles. The *164th* had most recently been on garrison duty, but it had been specially redesigned for service in North Africa. Like the *90th Light*, it had been heavily reinforced with AT guns, primarily of the Russian 76.2 type.

The *99th Heavy Artillery* battery, equipped with long range 149/40 guns, ended up firing point blank against the attacking Australians. Rommel had not only lost the initiative, but also the precious *621st Radio Intercept Company*, whose value was high for tactical intelligence, which was overrun, and its Captain Seeholm killed. Attempts by Axis troops to regain the lost terrain failed and the renewed Australian attack launched at night against a completely surprised battalion of the *Trieste* captured 250 men. Also the isolated Italian battalions were for the most part overrun by the Australians while the new South African attack in the afternoon against the combat engineers of the *32nd Guastatori* battalion and another battalion of the *Trento* was checked by confusion and the fire of the *Trento's 46th Artillery* regiment. The total losses of Italian units in those two days were 700 men of *Sabratha*, 550 artillerymen, 250 of *Trieste*, headquarters personnel and two *Bersaglieri* companies of the *7th* regiment (350 men), plus the *3rd* battalion of the *24th Artillery*, with 20 men and a total of 30 artillery pieces. Also the attacks launched by *21st Panzer*, the German *382nd* regiment and a battalion of the *Sabratha* did not make progress, in spite of the mass employment of *Panzerarmee* artillery and air support.

The *Sabratha* was originally formed in Libya from collected personnel of various duties intended for garrison work. Moreover her officers had not prepared or trained the battalions. A better solution was not to employ this unit until properly broken in but pressure on local commanders to send men to the front was high. Rommel's need for a unit as poor as the *Sabratha* convinced Mussolini to send the *Folgore* paratroop division to the desert. This move made Operation *Herkules/C3*, the invasion of Malta, an impossibility.

On the afternoon of 13 and 14 July attacks were launched again against the Tel el Eisa (which is Arabic for "hill of Jesus") bulge but with very few results. At the same time tactical groups of the *Ariete, Littorio, 90 Light, 164th Infantry* division and *3rd*

Recce pushed the front about 10 miles eastward without substantial opposition.

Rommel had planned another attack against the 9th Australian division but Auchinleck, who knew where the *DAK* divisions were, launched an attack against Ruweisat Ridge on the night of the 15th using the 4th and 5th brigades of the 2nd New Zealand division and the 5th Indian brigade, while the 2nd and 22nd Armored brigades of the 1st Armored division had to protect the operation and stay poised to exploit any success. The attack fell on the eight battalions of the *X Corps, Pavia* and *Brescia* divisions, an estimated 4,000 men. The night attack overran a battalion of the *Brescia* and slipped partly through strongpoints which had holes of a mile between them, actually reaching the divisional artillery and the *Brescia*'s headquarters. The commander, General Lombardi, was captured with his staff, but succeeded in freeing himself only to be severely wounded shortly thereafter by an air attack. The attackers then began to clear the strongpoints, attacking them from various directions, but many of these strongpoints resisted, hindering the advance of vehicles and equipment. The scattered Kiwi infantry were then attacked by armored groups of the *15th Panzer* and later in the day by other arriving German units which collected a total of 1,600 prisoners. Later this action evolved into a further successful German counterattack which regained the positions seized by the Commonwealth and an additional 1000 Allied prisoners. The Allied armored finally did intervene but too late to affect the outcome. Thus a deeper bitter feeling spread further among Commonwealth troops about the untimely British tank support. The sector remained quiet while Auchinleck launched another attack with the excellent 24th brigade of the 9th Australian division against Tel el Makh Khad on the Miteiriya Ridge.

This attack launched by two infantry battalions and by the 44th Royal Tank Regiment pierced the line between the *Trieste* and *Trento* divisions, destroyed one *Bersaglieri* company and the few remnants (about 100 men) of the *32nd Guastatori* battalion, and encircled another battalion of the *Trieste* division. The *32nd Guastatori* had been a companion battalion with the *31st Guastatori*, arriving in time to take part in the attack in June against Tobruk. During this Australian attack it fought until the end. A battalion of the *Trento* was sent to plug the hole but a battalion of the *46th Artillery* was destroyed and another was forced to fire at point blank range to save itself. With the counterattack of the German recce units the front was stabilized; the Australians had collected 700 prisoners and suffered about 300 casualties. This Allied strategy of hitting the Italians, and staying away from the Axis armor, was hurting the Axis. Rommel wrote that day, "the enemy is using his superiority, especially in infantry, to destroy the Italian formations one by one, and the German formations are much too weak to stand alone. It's enough to make one weep."

That evening Rommel had a meeting with Bastico and Cavallero and said to them that he was probably not in a situation to continue to hold the line, and a retreat would probably be in order, unless of course reinforcements and supplies arrived quickly. Rommel was rather depressed and afterwards explained to Generals Navarini and Nehring that the Deir el Shein strongpoint should be held, but much of the Ruweisat Ridge should be abandoned. German and Italian units should be alternated to mitigate the weakness of the latter, a process called "corseting." After the Germans and the Austro-Hungarian Empire established a joint command in World War I, a similiar procedure had been adopted.

Relations between the two Axis partners is a subject that has not been fully analyzed. Italian General Roncaglia remarked later that relations were correct, but it was difficult for Germans to take orders from Italian territorial headquarters. Relations between the troops, he says, were "never cordial, because an irritating sense of superiority of the Germans, who saw, and this was true, our shortcomings in many fields." After El Alamein, another Italian general wrote that between commands, relations were correct, tactical collaboration willing and fruitful, but there was no comradeship between soldiers. This may be due to the defeat at El Alamein and the disasters in Russia, as many reports show relations between the two Axis partners as being quite good in the summer of '42, as they enjoyed together the high tide of success.

The report Rommel sent and the words he pronounced face to face to Cavallero were highly pessimistic. ULTRA intercepts

Italian and German officers observing an artillery bombardment in the distance (Klaus Hubbuch).

gave Auchinleck the impression that the enemy was ready to collapse, having lost most of the German and Italian artillery, and having only 42 tanks in the *DAK* and 50 Italian tanks. But Rommel also reported the loss of four Italian divisions which was an exaggeration and this gave a further false impression of near collapse that ULTRA reported. In reality, the position was improving daily with the laying of mines and barbed wire, and general digging in. It was not uncommon for 1,000 mines to be laid in a night, and it was done by all nationalities. There were Italian, German, French, and even captured Egyptian mines up and down the Axis position, designed for different tasks from killing a man to blowing up only from the weight of a tank—but all deadly.

So Auchinleck, believing the Axis forces were actually as weak as they appeared to be in ULTRA intercepts, launched the next well prepared attack on Deir el Abyad-El Mreir to destroy the bulk of the Axis forces and especially the *DAK*. He was pressed by Churchill, whose political situation needed a victory as his party had been crushed in an election in late June in a seat thought to be safe. In a vote of confidence on 1 July the opposition hit him with the telling line, "The Prime Minister wins debate after debate, and loses battle after battle." The attack, under control of XIII Corps, would be made again by the 2nd New Zealand and the 5th Indian divisions supported by 2nd, 22nd and 23rd Armored brigades.

The attack was executed on the night of 22 July and went badly, becoming confused when it ran into unknown Axis strongpoints. The 6th New Zealand suffered from the fire of two German battalions in strongpoints and was counterattacked and overrun the following morning by the *8th Panzer* regiment, losing 500 prisoners. New Zealand Brigadier Kippenberger had predicted before the battle that such losses might occur referring to the lack of armored support for his infantry. The 161st Indian brigade had to occupy Deir el Shein defended by the two battalions of the *Brescia* and a battalion of the German *104th* regiment. The attack was repulsed but gained some ground thanks to the intervention of the 23rd Armored brigade. It was for this action with the 23rd Armored that Gunther Halm received the Knight's Cross, the second youngest German ever to receive it, from Rommel's hand. He earned it by being the gunlayer on an anti-tank battery (Russian 76.2mm AT gun) that, after suffering under a fierce preliminary artillery barrage, sprang to life and knocked out nine advancing British tanks, including the commander's tank, while under heavy fire and with the battery suffering casualties. The British were forced to retreat.

The following counterattack by the *5th Panzer* regiment destroyed 40 tanks and damaged 47. The other British armored brigades had many problems in passing the unknown Axis minefields so the 2nd eventually lost 20 tanks and was blocked by the *15th Panzer*, while the 22nd made but a probe against the *Ariete*, as the general attack petered out.

The Australians also attacked that day with the 26th and 24th brigades with help from the 50th Royal Tank Regiment. The 26th attacked initially without tank support and gained little ground, then later renewed the attack with tanks. After the capture of about 60 men of a battalion of the *155th*, the other Axis units (*61st* regiment of the *Trento* and German *200th Regiment*) checked the attack, which also ran out of steam. A battalion of the *Trento* had saved one flank from penetration, and was so cited in the *Panzerarmee* daily summary. Also new attacks launched by the Australians later made limited gains and took 100 prisoners, overrunning a unit of the German *361st* regiment while the *Trento* gave stiff resistance. Another night attack launched in confusion by a battalion of the 14th Punjabis toward Point 63 of Ruweisat resulted at dawn in the loss of the battalion and company commanders due to the spirited leadership of the *19th* regiment of the *Brescia*. Rommel, who was thinking of retreating during the day, was satisfied in the evening of 17 July with the heavy enemy losses, especially in tanks (146), and was more optimistic. In any case he ordered General De Stefanis of *XX Motorized Corps* to study a possible retreat west in case of a British breakthrough. On the Allied side, bitter feelings were fanned yet again against the armored formations because of their ill-coordinated support.

Nevertheless, another attack was tried again on the night of 27 July by the 24th Australian brigade and by the British 69th brigade supported by 2nd Armored brigade. Only limited ground was gained by the Australians who overran a battalion of the *164th Infantry*, while the 69th destroyed a company of the German *200th Regiment* and one battalion of the *Trento*, but suffered 600 casualties in accomplishing this. The 24th lost 400 men here. Intervention of the German *33rd Recce* caused the loss of 22 tanks by the 50th Royal Tank Regiment and the attack was called off. It should be noted that the Axis minefields had been substantially strengthened by this time.

Auchinleck and the Commonwealth army had stopped the Axis advance, largely by depleting the Axis infantry in the middle of July. He had then tried to destroy the *Panzerarmee*, but failed in that endeavor. The end result was a standoff. A month of fighting had stopped the Axis drive on the Nile, but Rommel was clever enough to avoid the possible destruction of his army. A general comparison of the losses of two sides gives an advantage to Rommel: against 7,000 Axis prisoners, of which some 2,000 were Germans, the Commonwealth forces had lost 13,000 men.

According to Rommel's data, from 26th May to 30th July 1942, he took 60,000 British prisoners and destroyed 2,000 tanks, while sustaining the following losses:

Losses:	Deaths	Wounded	Prisoners
German	2,300	7,500	2,700
Italian	1,000	10,000	5,000

The state of the Italian infantry at this time is revealing. Apart from the low level of training of the infantry units, who in many cases were rushed to the front without the necessary weapons training, there was the poor rotation of men who had been in Africa for up to three years. "Rest and Relaxation" (R&R) to the quiet rear, in order "to remove from the mind of the survivors the conviction that for them now the only possible outcome will be death, a deforming wound, or capture by the enemy," was simply impossible at a reasonable rate. Not only was R&R impossible, but the same men had to walk some thousand miles in the desert in the hottest of summer temperatures. There was little time or opportunity for swimming in the Mediterranean. Advances and retreats were made on foot in these temperatures. Many refitted battalions were sent to the line during the night of their arrival and collapsed immediately. Rommel was criticized for employing the *Sabratha* in this fashion (in both cases, each battalion destroyed was at the wrong place at the wrong time).

On the other hand, cases of surrender were less publicized in other units. This applied to both German soldiers who were also near exhaustion in July, especially toward the end of the battle, and new Commonwealth units which were also easily captured.

Alam Halfa

If Auchinleck had not been the man he was—and by that I mean the best Allied General in North Africa during the war—Rommel would have finished Eighth Army off.

—General Fritz Bayerlein

Given our full knowledge of the gamble, the attack ought never to have begun.

—Marshal Kesselring

August was a bad month for Axis fortunes. In the Soviet

Union the failure of the summer offensive began to be apparent, as the encirclements formed by the *Panzer* divisions in the Ukraine came up empty of Russian troops and the oil fields in the Caucasus remained too distant, as the good months of weather were passing and winter (and Stalingrad) were approaching. In Africa, as of 16 September 1942, the newly renamed *Deutsch-Italienisch Panzerarmee* (*Armata Corazzata Italo Tedesco*) was recovering from the difficult battles of July, which had stretched supply lines and left very few chances to reach the Nile.

This German-Italian *Panzer* army also saw a reorganization. Commanded by Marshal Rommel, it served directly under *Comando Supremo* and Marshal Cavallero, while Bastico as head of *Comando Superiore Africa Settentrionale*, was responsible for administrative and logistical duties and for the defense of Libya.

The Allied side was changing too. The balance of forces was shifting with the American decision of "Germany First," which brought the immense resources of the United States to the Mediterranean to fight the Axis. The results would be clear after a couple of months' build-up.

On 3 August Churchill arrived in Cairo where he met with General Smuts of South Africa (who had fought as a Boer against the British and with them against the Germans in World War I), General Wavell, and General Corbett, Auchinleck's Chief of Staff. Then he summoned Auchinleck, and also visited the 8th Army (without telling him), and he made up his mind to relieve him. Auchinleck had never won the victory the PM needed during the terrible month of July. Auchinleck received the news by letter on 8 August. His successor was General Harold Alexander for the Middle East Command and Gott for the 8th Army. Gott was shot down while flying to take command and died from the exploding aircraft while on the ground trying to save other crew members. The second man on the Prime Minister's list, General Bernard Montgomery, was named the new 8th Army commander starting 15 August (Montgomery took command two days early, which created a rift between him and Auchinleck).

Reinforcements continued to flow to the front in an unprece-

Commonwealth determination and American equipment, Montgomery and a Grant tank typify the 8th Army late in the North Africa campaign.

dented manner, thanks in part to President Roosevelt, who had promptly sent 300 Sherman tanks and 100 self-propelled artillery pieces when the news of the fall of Tobruk arrived while meeting with Churchill in Washington. The overall scale of Allied reinforcements is sometimes forgotten. July and August saw 820 artillery pieces, over 7,800 vehicles, and 368 tanks being shipped from the United Kingdom alone, while North America sent 7,989 vehicles in those two months, and this despite the war with Japan. It should also be noted that much of the foodstuffs required for the Commonwealth army were by now coming from India, which was much closer than the United Kingdom. Additionally, it must be noted that the new British 6-pounder AT gun was now widely distributed among various units. This gave the Commonwealth formations a lot of tank stopping power. A large convoy with 100,000 tons of reinforcements and supplies was due to arrive at the end of August at Suez, which was also a reason for Rommel to attack, before it could change the strength ratio even more.

Montgomery quickly went to work. Among the new measures introduced by the commander of the 8th Army was the concept of creating a counterpart to the *DAK*, formed with two armored and one motorized divisions. This *corps de chasse* would be X Corps with the 1st and 8th (or 10th) Armored division and the motorized 2nd New Zealand, and while it differed from the *DAK*, in that the *DAK* had to spearhead any major advance, it did create a force that could exploit success. The jock columns were ended and formations were to fight as coherent units in the future—no longer as *ad hoc* combinations.

Without going into the much discussed quarrel between Montgomery and Auchinleck and their respective abilities, the various changes at top level in the Middle East signalled that the wind had changed. The corps commanders were changed in the so called "Cairo purge," and only Chief of Staff De Guingand and Lumsden (X Corps) remained who were not Monty's new men. Additionally, the fact that neither General Freyberg nor General Morshead were appointed corps commanders upset the Commonwealth nations. This was because the British army did not think a "citizen soldier" should command at the corps level without having made a lifetime commitment to the army, contrary to what was the practice in South Africa, New Zealand, and Australia.

Over the years Montgomery's abilities have been called into question. His ego was overly large, he was too careful, and he was a man of narrow tastes (being totally devoted to the military). However, he had trained and excellently commanded the 3rd Infantry division in the campaign in France in 1940, and this with the pall of defeat and the shambles surrounding the British troops that spring. Unlike previous commanders in the desert, Montgomery was popular with the ANZAC troops, as he had grown up in Tasmania and communicated well with them. He also moved the army headquarters near to the headquarters of the RAF, so that both could better co-ordinate their actions. He also envisioned that a decisive battle had to be fought to establish the Commonwealth ascendency over the Axis, and the El Alamein battles would achieve this. This would not be a mobile battle, but a more static one, which was what Montgomery was better at. While he may have been, as was once quipped, "the greatest World War I General of World War II," his methods of employing overwhelming strength backed with excellent intelligence due to ULTRA did achieve success, and this, after a period of many defeats, was important to the Allied cause. That Monty established an expectation of victory is often overlooked by those who study his later campaigns, and contrasts favorably with his predecessors. He did improve the overall ability of the Commonwealth army. He improved them to an extent that victory would be theirs.

Just one example of his effect is in one of his numerous visits to the frontline troops. On one such visit to the 9th Australian division he noticed some gunners by one of the new 6-pounder AT guns. He asked them what they thought of it and was informed that they had not fired it yet with live ammunition as there was so little available for it! Within two days orders had been issued to fire off half of the available 6-pounder ammunition in practice. Monty's orders stated, "Unless the men are trained to shoot we shall do no good on the day of battle however great the number of rounds we have saved ready for that day." Before Rommel's attack, the Alam Halfa position was reinforced because Montgomery considered it a key position. The newly arrived 44th Infantry division was chosen to defend the Alam Halfa ridge, and the plan also foresaw that Rommel's thrust would not go too far beyond the ridge before turning north to bag the entire 8th Army.

Meanwhile, Rommel did not lose hope in receiving more attention from the OKW, including two more promised Panzer divisions and plenty of supplies. Bastico visited Rommel on 29 July, thinking "(Rommel) was serene and sometimes fantasized about those far objectives of which he had spoken to me with great enthusiasm after the fall of Tobruk. The arrival of reinforcements had changed his (pessimistic) attitude." Rommel again thought that his fantasy could become reality. On the other side the long and dispersed tail of the Axis army brought to the front, along with replacements, two new units: the Italian *Folgore* parachute division and the German *Ramcke* parachute brigade.

The number of Axis tanks continued to increase to 234 German and 281 Italian (234 being medium tanks). The Italian tanks were always the same, more obsolete than ever, because the few improvements of the M14 were not enough to keep up with the rate of evolution in other countries. The Germans could now field 64 *Panzer* III and 27 *Panzer* IV's with long barrel guns. The armored formations were generally brought up to full strength, although the shortage of trucks was a major problem among the Axis units and its logistical organization. The German divisions lacked 1,400 trucks and the Italian motorized units could only motorize services, guns and weapons, as well as one-third of the troops.

The infantry divisions had to rely on their feet and bring their weapons up by hand. According to Rommel's claims, not one German truck arrived in Africa during the El Alamein fighting until early August, although his supply papers said at least 25 arrived in August. Too little, of course, but it points out Rommel's tendency to exaggerate. The strength of a typical Italian division at this time was about 5,000 men (*Trento*; 5,200; *Brescia*; 4,300; *Ariete*; 7,200). At the beginning of August the availability of aircraft of the Italian *5th Squadra Aerea* was 144 fighters (98 ready), 7 bombers (4) and 40 assault (27) for the east sector which was commanded from Fuka. At the end of August there were 298 planes available to *Fliegerfuehrer Afrika* and 460 for the *5th Squadra Aerea*. About one-third were fit for action. The RAF performed 2,500 sorties and the U.S. Air Force about 180 during the coming battle and they outnumbered the Axis air forces.

In the Mediterranean the Axis were losing the war at sea. Operation Pedestal, a convoy battle to resupply Malta, was a costly Allied victory, but Malta had received enough supplies to allow her a respite and to rebound as a thorn in the Axis flank. Axis convoys also had difficulty in disembarking enough sup-

Rommel addressing troops (Klaus Hubbuch).

plies in Tobruk, which could only handle 1,000 tons of supply a day. This was further reduced by heavy bombing by the RAF on 8 August, with a result of a reduction of 20% in Tobruk's capability. Mussolini would say after the battles of August, "In August 1942 the Italo-German offensive at El Alamein failed. Not because the soldiers failed to fight as splendidly as always. But we must remember that in war, victory is won or lost at sea, rather than on land."

Meanwhile, the plan of attack was known on the Allied side, since a detailed account sent by Rommel to Berlin was decrypted on 17 August. It lacked only the date, which was known to be the end of August.

The plan foresaw the attack of the Axis motorized formations against the southern part of the line, and then, as at Gazala and Mersa Matruh, the drive north and the encirclement of the British forces.

Rommel had no other choice than attack because a retreat on Libya with the non-motorized units would have spelled disaster, and in any case Hitler would not allow it. In fact, on 26 July, General Walter Warlimont, deputy chief of staff of *OKW*, arrived

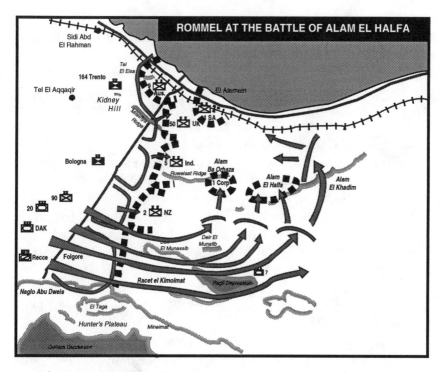

ROMMEL AT THE BATTLE OF ALAM EL HALFA

in Africa to be sure that Rommel would not abandon the El Alamein position.

According to Colonel Mellenthin, who was at the time a staff officer of Rommel's army, "the General Staff of the *Panzerarmee* did not believe that we could break through to the Nile." Such an attitude was coupled with Rommel's intention to resign because of ill health, but also for his mentally depressed state, probably due to the continuous strain he had been under for years. On 21 August he signalled to Berlin this state of affairs, recommending General Guderian for his replacement. Since this was impossible because Guderian was out of favor, settling in on his vast estate given to him by Hitler, Rommel retained the command of the army for the coming offensive, and would leave after it for Germany. It should be noted that one reason the senior German officers were as loyal to Hitler as they were was not just due to their loyalty oaths (similar oaths were given to the Weimar Republic), but that Hitler literally bribed them. As pointed out by Gerhard L. Weinberg, senior generals and field marshals received immense secret nontaxable pay bonuses which, in effect, doubled their army salaries (or more), and the best were given estates. While the senior staff received these rewards, the German army would go on to shoot approximately 25,000 of its own soldiers for breeches of discipline in the course of the war. It was this stick and carrot routine in the German army which would have such a deep effect throughout the war. This method or process contrasted strongly with British, American, and even Italian practices in the same period.

Facing the Axis tanks were 935 tanks of the 8th Army. Of these, 713 were effective and of the following types: 164 Grant, 370 Valentine and Crusader, and 179 Stuart tanks.

The so called Six Days Run, or Battle of Alam Halfa, began on the night of 30 August with *Brescia* trying to secure a fixed flank position in cooperation with the *90th Light* toward Alam Nayil with a mixed group of eight battalions of the *Brescia*, *Folgore* and *Ramcke*, and a battalion of *Bersaglieri*. They were formed in two columns which advanced and secured Deir El Angar and Deir Alinds ridge.

Further south things began to go wrong very soon, since the minefields were revealed to be much deeper than expected and took too much time to be cleared in face of strong opposition by the British 7th "Desert Rats" Armored division. Surprise was clearly lost and moreover the RAF's air attacks night and day were highly effective and many senior officers fell in the first hours. The Rommel plan to advance 50 kilometers east in the moonlit night had failed and Rommel was about to call off the offensive, but insistence by Bayerlein convinced him to continue. The main attack would be launched on the western edge of the Alam Halfa ridge, instead of the eastern one. The divisions had to advance in a disruptive sand storm. The *21st Panzer* attacked first, followed by the *15th*, which was delayed, and was not able to reach the objective of Point 132. Instead it attacked Point 102 and was hurt by the defense of the 22nd Armored brigade which had its Grant tank hulls buried with just the turrets exposed and supported by the 44th division's artillery. Moreover the attack was suspended because, as Rommel reported, "petrol stocks were soon badly depleted." The following day only the *15th Panzer* attacked, because the *21st* had to refuel, but the *15th* was forced by fuel consumption and the Common-

Rommel with a large mapboard on the telephone at the front (Klaus Hubbuch).

wealth's strength to give up the attack. On the following morning Rommel called off the attack and began to retreat, while the 7th Armored division was attacking the right flank (where an anti-tank screen was established), and all were under continuous attack by the RAF.

Montgomery was satisfied with the progress of the battle. Now he would try to cut off the main body of the motorized Axis troops with a dashing attack. About 400 tanks were concentrated in the area between the New Zealanders' positions and the Alam Halfa ridge, in a good position to cut the Axis supply lines. But at Rommel's request, Kesselring had ordered bombing and this hurt the Commonwealth forces. An infantry attack was ordered on the Axis flank in "Operation Beresford." The 132nd Infantry brigade led the attack while the 6th New Zealand brigade had to cover her flank and create diversions, supported by a few Valentine tanks. The attack fell on the positions of the eight mixed battalions of the *Brescia* sector, and suffered many casualties, 697 men for the 132nd brigade and 275 for the 5th New Zealand. One of the *Brescia* battalions suffered heavy casualties from the 5th New Zealand brigade, but not the 500 men, as claimed later by General Kippenberger, while in the sector of the *Folgore* and *Ramcke* battalions things got worse. The 6th New Zealand brigade joined the battle attacking the *Trieste* and *Ramcke*, and falling also on the *90th Light* division, but the attack failed after much turmoil in the area and many casualties were the result. Montgomery understood that a large scale attack was too much a risk with his incompletely retrained army, and against a general of Rommel's caliber. Thus the Alam Halfa battle, or six days run, was over.

Summing up the losses of the operation, they were:

Losses:	Men	Guns	Tanks
Allied	1,750	15	67
Axis	2,855	53	47

The reasons why the Alam Halfa offensive failed were argued by Rommel in his papers. A great emphasis was placed on the fuel problem, but also the solid Commonwealth resistance and the mastery of the air by the RAF. The battle was prejudiced by the lack of surprise, which Rommel would remember later in Germany, quoting the story of his attack plan being handed over to the British by an Italian officer ("superior" officer was later added). Only with the ULTRA revelations is it possible to know how much of the Axis defeat was due to ULTRA. At the time *Comando Supremo* made an inquiry asking for the interrogation minutes to *Deutsch-Italienisch Panzerarmee* headquarters, and the chance to make joint interrogations of British prisoners declaring that it was Italian treason that was the source of information to the Allies. The minutes were to be brought to Rome by Colonel Mellenthin, the German intelligence officer who was leaving the front due to sickness, but he brought only minutes relating the very generic interrogation of one British NCO. Cavallero replied to Rommel and complained also to the OKW, but probably there was now a readiness to believe in treason. The poison of this entire episode is that it had the Germans thinking Italian officers were giving information to the Allies, while Italian officers thought the same of their German counterparts. ULTRA's effects reached much deeper into the Axis camp than the knowledge of the enemy that it gave to the Allies.

The fuel shortage was used by Rommel as a lightning rod for all the supply problems he had. To him, this was why he had problems with the offensive. Rommel's records say that 5,714 tons of fuel were sent to Africa and only 954 arrived in August, for a total of 10,908 tons arriving in July-August. The Italian navy has data relating to the fuel disembarked in Africa in the period July and August 1942 with a total of 44,498 tons of fuel of all kinds arriving. It is difficult to reconcile these figures because the contemporary data does not provide details. According to the Navy's figures, the *Giorgio* tanker reached Tobruk on the 28th with 2,516 tons of aviation fuel and the *Gualdi* with another 1,216 tons on the 30th. The ship *Sportivo* then arrived at Tobruk with 800 tons of fuel. In view of this data, the concern should be: "arrived too late" or "the wrong type of fuel" and "where" and "did it arrive at the front?" As General Warlimont wrote in his memoirs, at Berlin the Allied air superiority was commented on more often than the supply question.

The key points here are the effect of ULTRA which not only supplied vital information to the Allies, but also the dominance in the air of the Allies. This, tied to the superior and growing forces of the Allies, coupled with a growing confidence in their ability to defeat the Axis, spelled doom for the Axis. Lack of Axis supplies are an important factor, but not as vital as where and when they arrived, while the story of Italian traitors revealing war plans on an unprecedented scale is but a myth. (This entire re-examination of the war situation at this time points out the need for a balanced approach to researching the war in the Mediterranean.)

Alamein

Rommel, Rommel, Rommel, what else matters but beating him!
—Churchill

When (Rommel) had twice attacked unsuccessfully before
Montgomery's offensive he should have withdrawn at once to
Mersa Matruh...I told (Hitler) we had lost the initiative from June
1942 onwards, and that a nation which has lost the initiative has
lost the war.
—Mussolini

After the failure to break through at Alam Halfa, Rommel was forced on to the defensive because of the growing preponderance of the 8th Army. Yet the actual perception of the daily growing strength of the British Army facing El Alamein was at the time viewed somewhat optimistically, considering the defeat about to befall the Axis. Although the Axis logistical situation was very difficult, the approaching battle was faced with confidence.

Rommel went on sick leave in Germany and was temporarily replaced by General Stumme, who arrived from the Russian front. ULTRA revealed that Stumme was in command on 8 October, along with some returns on the available Axis tanks and aircraft. Also the supply situation was accurately followed by the 8th Army intelligence officers, who gained a picture of progressive strain following a short good period after the battle at the end of August. Affecting the German-Italian *Panzer* army was not only the fuel shortage, due to increased transport problems and ship sinkings, but also a food shortage, which resulted in illness among the troops. Rommel's intelligence was much worse after July: both his intercept company and the "Good Source" were no longer available, however the rebuilt *621st Intercept Company* was able to produce enough acceptable intelligence to give a good summary of Allied strength and the date of their attack.

One Axis problem in Africa was the long extended front running to Tunisia. For the control of such a large territory, Hitler insisted in April that the inferior *Pistoia* Infantry division be sent to Africa as a defense force against amphibious operations. The increasing possibility of a landing in the rear of the army deployed at El Alamein also worried Rommel. Limited Allied operations in the rear were carried out, among them a complex Long Range Desert Group operation in mid-September, but this was generally unsuccessful, apart from the destruction of about thirty airplanes. An attempted landing at Tobruk failed in the face of coastal artillery fire and the *San Marco* Marine battalion stationed there.

On 30th September the British 136th Infantry brigade launched an attack against the most prominent position of the Axis line on the El Alamein front: the Deir el Munassib position, but the attack failed against a sector held by a *Folgore* battalion with heavy losses.

On the frontline Italians and Germans were laying hundreds of thousands of mines to fortify the front against the approaching Allied attack. The minefield zone was about five to seven kilometers deep, organized in two continuous lines with connections forming boxes. Between the two main armored groups (each made up of a German and an Italian Armored division), deployed north and south, there were also two strips running in an east-west direction to stop the easy encirclement of penetrating armored forces. The line of resistance was then formed with a continuous line of battalion strongpoints. Each battalion would have control over 3,000 meters of front and only in the central sector were there double lines of strongpoints.

According to wartime reports, the Commonwealth artillery increased its effectiveness to a great extent at El Alamein over that of their opponents. The Italian artillery, for instance, was unable to match the Commonwealth because it lacked the range of the Commonwealth guns. Thus the Italian artillery was continually deployed forward to make up for their lack of range.

Stumme had two corps, the XXI and X, deployed on the strongpoints. From north to south the XXI, with the "corseting" *Trento* and *164th* infantry divisions new to the front, and the *Bologna* division were reinforced with two battalions of the *Ramcke*. The X Corps was deployed south of Ruweisat with the *Brescia*, *Folgore* and *Pavia*. Also in the *Brescia* sector were two other battalions of the *Ramcke*. The mobile units were deployed in two main groups: *15th Panzer* with the *Littorio* deployed in the north, and *Ariete* and *21st Panzer* south along with the *Kampfstaffel* group and the *33rd Recce*. The *90th Light* and *Trieste* were deployed along the coast to defend against a possible British landing along the coast.

Speaking of "divisions" is not entirely correct, since the Italian infantry division corresponded to a British brigade and the German divisions were also depleted. The number of German tanks fit for action on 23 October was down to 250. The 289 Italian tanks were always the same and now incapable of matching the Grants and Shermans. It is true that before the battle additional Italian Semoventi arrived (48 total). But, again, it was too little, too late. Italian tanks were distributed as follows:

Ariete	129
Littorio	116
Trieste	34

(figures don't reconcile because they changed daily)

The *Panzerarmee* had 48,854 Germans and 54,000 Italians. Of the Germans, 32,474 men were fighting troops.

On the other side the sheer weight of the American war mobilization began to affect the situation in the Mediterranean. Air superiority was now shifting definitively into Allied hands, U.S. Air Force planes bombed the Axis troops daily, and a lot of American tanks, guns and vehicles, the best available in the desert, flowed to reinforce the 8th Army. U.S. Headquarters Army Air Forces, Middle East was also established.

The German strategic picture showed that in September Generals Halder and List were dismissed by Hitler because of the failure to reach the oil fields in the Caucasus, while General von Paulus was involved in the battle of Stalingrad with its dismal future, and the German High Command was finding itself without any practicable strategy. In the Mediterranean the Axis was chained, locked into waiting for the next enemy move. This initiative was to be utilized as a joint American-British invasion of North Africa. By 25 July the decision for Operation Torch had been made, and plans for the November 1942 invasion with a large scale landing of three separate forces, two American and one mixed American-British on Vichy French North Africa, was moving forward.

The forces available to Montgomery for the defeat of the Axis forces in Africa were three army corps with seven infantry and four armored divisions, with two attached armored brigades. A total of 230,000 men were in the 8th Army, 195,000 of them ready for fighting along with 1,229 tanks available and perhaps another thousand in the rear depots. On 23 October about 1,000 were ready for action. Also the air superiority was gained not only because of the greater strength ratio of the Allies, but also because of the possibility of more sorties for the RAF than for the Axis air forces (about 1,000 against 340). Nearly one thousand guns, mostly 25-pounders, were available to bombard enemy defenses.

The British attack plan, as elaborated by Montgomery, was a slow and methodical crumbling of the Axis field defenses, which would lead to a breakthrough and a final collapse of the enemy. This was a classic concept of a battle of attrition, very different from the others fought in the desert to this point. Because of the unique feature of the El Alamein line, one could anchor one flank on the sea and the other on the impassable Qattara Depression. It was not designed as a brilliant operation, but a sure and sound victory after many years of suffering at Rommel's hand. The choice of the date was conditioned by the timing with Torch, so it was decided to begin the attack thirteen days before the landing, partly to influence French North Africa and Franco's Spain, and partly because of the need for a "British" victory before the American intervention could play a significant role. Moonlight would be essential for the start of the land battle because of the need to pass through the minefields, while a daylight attack was considered impossible for the amount of casualties it would generate.

The Montgomery plan foresaw two pincers, north and south of the line formed by the XIII and XXX corps, while X Armored was to exploit the success. Montgomery would later recall that he changed his mind and the southern attack would be only a secondary attack to avoid the *21st* and *Ariete* and would be shifted north, but at the time he hoped this attack would do the trick. The 8th Army commander explained to his immediate

Royal Artillery in typical desert dress, firing a 5.5 inch gun.

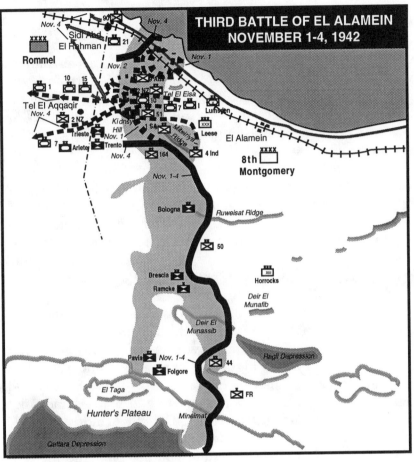

THIRD BATTLE OF EL ALAMEIN
NOVEMBER 1-4, 1942

subordinates his intentions in mid-September. On 6 October he changed his plan because it was too ambitious, and ordered Operation Lightfoot. This plan envisaged the 9th Australian, 2nd New Zealand and the 1st South African divisions opening the way through the minefields and into the Axis defenses to the line called "Oxalic." On the morning of the 24th the tanks of X Corps were to be in position to advance beyond the Oxalic line. Some days before the offensive, the RAF launched a violent air offensive that denied the Axis planes any reconnaissance activity and gained the mastery of the air.

At 2030 on 23 October 1942, the battle of El Alamein began with an artillery bombardment which was like a hurricane hitting the enemy positions. Axis reaction was slow due to lack of ammunition and the destruction of communications. Although the Australian infantry reached part of their objective, the Oxalic line in the rear of the defensive position, overrunning two battalions of the Italian *Trento* and one of the German *164th*, the tanks found greater difficulties than expected in passing the minefields. Metal detectors were used, although much of the work was done the old fashioned way with engineers probing the ground with bayonets.

In the south, the attack of the 44th Infantry and 7th Armored struck the *Folgore* and suffered many casualties for little gain. The 7th Armored used Scorpion tanks (anti-mine tanks armed with flails, or chains, to explode mines) for the minefield in this area, but lost many tanks from artillery fire and even Molotov cocktails, and some hundreds of men. Two Free French battalions were repulsed by another battalion of the *Folgore* and then were hit by the *33rd Recce*'s armored cars.

About this time General Stumme disappeared and was later found dead, probably from a heart attack. Rommel was immediately alerted, while the command was assumed by General von Thoma. On the following night further attacks by the Australian and New Zealand infantry divisions allowed two armored brigades to pass over the former Axis line of resistance, but again with some loss and difficulty. The 4th Armored brigade and the 69th Infantry brigade attacked the *Folgore* at Deir Munassib, but lost 22 tanks while gaining only the forward positions.

In the north the 8th Army gained a positive result when the Axis armor launched some desperate counterattacks, and were repelled by British firepower, but further attempts on the 26th by the British tanks to break out failed due to Axis resistance, while other attacks of the 50th Infantry and 7th Armored divisions in the south against the *Folgore* failed also with considerable losses. The general situation compelled Montgomery to change his plans. The new plan was called "Supercharge" and was launched on the night of 28 October toward the coast, hoping to form a pocket and then drive on Fuka. In the meantime Rommel arrived from Germany and resumed command of his army on the morning of the 26th. The British advance on the coast failed in the face of enemy resistance by a combined German and Italian unit, and became embroiled in the minefields. Rommel's reaction was to move the *90th Light* from the coast to the menaced point. In view of this result Montgomery turned again to the previous attack direction, regrouping his attack forces. This took some time and the British were unable to continue the offensive until 2 November.

Montgomery had foreseen about ten days of fighting for the defeat of the Axis army, but Churchill was becoming disappointed and was pressing Brooke. He sent a message to Alexander not only to give compliments to the 8th Army, but also to press his generals. ULTRA closely followed the situation of the Axis forces and particularly the supply situation. Three tankers were sunk and most of the fuel that arrived landed at Benghazi and had to be transported to the front line hundreds of miles distant. Tanks were consumed quickly: the *Littorio* had 30 tanks left and there were a hundred altogether for the two *Panzer* divisions. The *Ariete* still had a hundred tanks. The infantry had suffered (*Trento* and *164th* especially). At this point the only hope for Rommel was that Montgomery would call off the offensive. He was also thinking of retreating to Fuka but this would mean the loss of the nonmotorized part of the *Panzerarmee*. Therefore, he asked permission from *Comando Supremo* to fall back on Fuka in case of an enemy breakthrough, and requested 1,500 trucks for the transport of the German and Italian nonmotorized infantry. This was refused on the grounds that *Comando Supremo* simply did not have that many trucks available, and since Rommel wanted to retreat from El Alamein, he would do so if he had the trucks. It should be noted that among the Axis high command there was a poor understanding of the actual situation with Cavallero and Kesselring still fairly optimistic. Contributing to this false optimism was the lull after the failed attack of the Australians on the 28th and before the start of Supercharge.

Before the launching of Operation Supercharge, Montgomery had to reconcentrate his units and prepare for the attack, foreseen for the first hours of 2 November. Some 487 medium tanks were collected, many from the rear area repair centers, in the 1st and 8th Armored divisions and the 9th Armored brigade. ULTRA made it clear that Rommel was employing the *21st*

Two resting Germans at the time of El Alamein (Allesandro Massignani).

Panzer in the north to free the *125th* regiment of the *164th* infantry division and the *7th Bersaglieri*, which were still half isolated, deploying the *Trieste* at the point of attack. The Allied attack was preceded by a seven hour attack by the RAF which disrupted communications in the *Panzerarmee* and shocked the defending infantry. Two German and two Italian battalions were wiped out by the 151st and 152nd Infantry brigades (of the 51st Highland division) which reached their objectives. The following attack with 94 tanks of the 9th Armored brigade was somewhat confused and checked by an anti-tank curtain and artillery fire at dawn. The 9th Armored (now directly attached to the 2nd New Zealand for close support) remained with 19 tanks after the loss of 75. But the anti-tank screen was almost destroyed, losing 35 guns, while the wounded *Littorio* tank commander reported that he had lost most of his tanks. The attack was checked and the continuing fight on the following day resulted in the loss for the 8th Army of a total of 200 tanks, but Rommel was at the end of his resources. Moreover the damages to communication were so serious that von Thoma did not know that the menaced sector was that of the *15th Panzer*.

Rommel at the front (Klaus Hubbuch).

Von Thoma launched an armored counterattack with the *21st* and the *15th Panzer* in the area of Tel el Aqqaqir. The remnants of the *Littorio* and the tank battalion of the *Trieste*, a total of about 50 M tanks, were employed alongside the German divisions and were also sacrificed in this attack. Against the prepared position of the 1st Armored division supported by air power, and warned by an ULTRA intercept, the attack failed, leaving the *DAK* with but 35 tanks.

Montgomery now ordered XXX Corps to attack south with the infantry. An attack by 51st Highland and 4th Indian divisions succeeded in destroying a battalion of the *104th* regiment, *21st Panzer*, and part of the *Trieste*.

Von Thoma's evening report was depressing and convinced Rommel to order the retreat on Fuka, while on the same day the corps commanders were instructed that a possible retreat would take place on the 5th. To Hitler it was reported that the *Panzerarmee* was preparing for retreat in case of a breakthrough by enemy formations, which was sure to happen because there was nothing more to oppose them. Only on the morning of the 3rd, due to an error of the officer in charge in the *Fuehrer*

Hauptquartier, the message was shown to an angry Hitler. The reply was received by Rommel in the afternoon, which included the words "victory or death." Meanwhile the infantry divisions were retreating partly on foot, partly on some of the few trucks available (the Italian command had found some 150 and tried to send them to the front). It was impossible to instruct the *X Corps*, which was marching on foot to Fuka, of the new order from Hitler to stand and die, or the *Bologna* division either, while the divisions in the northern sector were still on the line. The *Bologna* received the order to come back to the Alamein line on the evening of the 3rd.

The holes in the front allowed the British armor to penetrate and attack on 4 November the last defensive screen put up by the Axis, and Rommel was forced to order "fight to the last shot." The Axis were aided by the fact that Montgomery had ordered two pursuing corps to advance in the same area, so there was much confusion, as various units became entangled as Allied columns fought to move forward. The *Ariete* was employed with its tanks as a last reserve, but it was impossible for the M tanks to achieve anything other than being targets. In one after-action report, a previous commander of the *Ariete* division reported that his division,

> ...during the day of the 4th November was facing a group of some 200 tanks, most of that type (Sherman and Grant). Against them, which were also reinforced by 25-pounder guns brought forward under the protection of a smoke screen to within about a thousand yards range, the *Ariete* tanks had to receive very hard blows without any chance to inflict any damage to the enemy.

But they fought as Rommel had ordered—to the end.

General Wilhelm Ritter von Thoma was personally involved in the concluding engagement of the *DAK* at El Alamein. A man wounded over 20 times in two wars, he was wearing all his medals and orders on his chest that morning as he prepared to make this final stand. The initial Commonwealth tank assault was stopped, but then the Allied artillery was hauled forward and slowly turned the remaining elements of the *DAK* into wreckage. He fought with his *Kampfstaffel* and by mid-day he could be seen "dressed in a correct field uniform with epaulettes and decorations, standing beside a burning tank, impervious to

Rommel overlooking wide expansive desert with some vehicles in midground (Klaus Hubbuch).

Desert column moving forward with Rommel in staff car at the lead (Klaus Hubbuch).

the heat, the sand, the bullets which still whistled close," and was captured. He could no longer support a government of "unparalleled madness" knowing that this order to stand and die "is the death warrant of the army."

This last resistance, along with a successful defensive stand by the *15th Panzer*, was enough for the retreat of the motorized remnants of the *Panzerarmee*, since the pursuit was not resumed until the next day, and so slowly that only rearguards and out-of-fuel troops were captured. Rommel, in fact, had a meeting with Kesselring, who now recognized the actual situation and proposed to Rommel that he consider the *Fuehrer* order as advice rather than an order, on the grounds that it was impossible for any further resistance. The retreat was ordered at 1530. The *DAK* and then the *XX Corps* with remnants of *Ariete, Littorio* and *Trieste* began to move westward. The *Bologna* was abandoned as was the *7th Bersaglieri* on the coast. The *X Infantry Corps* had not received the 150 trucks requested and was asking for water and help in the desert.

The pocket closed around Fuka on the 5th by the 1st Armored division contained few stragglers but the advance was continued with some difficulty due to rough terrain and general confusion. The next move of the pursuing 1st Armored was slowed again by the fact that it ran out of fuel advancing on Mersa Matruh. On the 6th heavy rain further slowed the pursuit, and the retreat alike.

The victorious 8th Army had suffered in the battle 13,500 casualties: 2,350 dead, 8,500 wounded and 2,260 missing. Some 500 tanks were disabled, but only 150 were totally destroyed; and having control of the battlefield, the Commonwealth was able to recover many tanks. The Axis casualties are difficult to calculate, but should have been 4-5,000 dead, 7-8,000 wounded and 35,000 prisoners, although the latter were often administrative personnel rather than fighting troops.

The battle of El Alamein was one of the preeminent battles of the Second World War. Its significance was more political than military, and it marked, along with the Torch operation, the turn of the tide of the war in the west.

The performance of the *Panzerarmee* was quite good, although a large part of its equipment was now obsolete or inferior to the

British-American equipment. As has been noted, the strange thing was not the fact the 8th Army won, but that they almost lost. Rommel's influence was very important because he enjoyed great popularity among his troops, Italian and German alike, and was given much credit from both *Comando Supremo* and the Italian commanders in Africa. The same was not the case for other officers of his staff. Cooperation between German and Italian units was generally good until battalion level was reached, also thanks to Rommel. It must be remembered that although many tactical procedures were similar, many others were not, and in more general terms there were numerous differences between the two military systems, as many people who served in both armies have observed.

In this context the story popularly spread that the Germans took all the trucks, leaving the Italians in the lurch was largely created by clever British propaganda. Much of the responsibility for the conduct of the retreat was also on the shoulders of *Comando Supremo*. It is true that many German units disengaged without informing the Italian units attached to them, as was the case with the *7th Bersaglieri*, whose survivors and relatives are still speaking about this today. But part of this was due to the word getting out quicker to the Germans than to the Italian units, which was a factor of the efficiency of their respective command structures.

The main goal of the Axis retreat at this point was to move far enough west so that the RAF attacks would cease, as they could operate effectively only so far from their air bases. But the retreat was on, one that would not stop until Tunisia was reached. The high tide for the Axis had passed and defeat and destruction lay ahead.

Tanks

Draw the enemy's tanks into ground of your own choosing and destroy them there.
—Erwin Rommel

The decisive weapon in the desert war was the tank. While the anti-tank gun, especially powerful ones like the 88mm, 90mm, or 17-pounder, would influence the war, as well as planes, supplies, and the men operating them, it was the tank that captured the public's attention, and was the weapon of penetration that could force the surrender and destruction of numerically larger forces. It was German military doctrine, combined with excellent weapons under a brash and insightful tank commander named Erwin Rommel, that would decisively affect the course of the war in the desert.

So what is it like in a tank in the desert?

The fact is that armored warfare makes big demands on the skill of the tank crews in driving, navigation, gunnery, inter-communication, rapid recognition of many types of vehicle, and running repairs.

....we gained experience of the desert, of close leaguering at night, of "brewing up" (tea time) quickly and of spotting vehicles in the mirage which made them look fifty feet high. We got practice in filling up and repairing vehicles in the dark without lights; we sorted out supply problems, and we learned to put up with the glare from the sand and great heat...and to manage on very little water. It was our first experience of thirst and not having

enough water to quench it. During the heat of the day it was trying, but the cool nights eased it, and it was practice for later on when we had even less. It was decided to leave the front (machinegun) gunner out of action and to use his turret for stowing kit, ammunition and supplies (on the Crusader I).

...the (Pz III) tank surges across the battlefield. Its tracks churn up dense and choking plumes of sand. The noise inside is deafening. The 320-horsepower Maybach engine roars and races as the driver shifts up and down through the manual gears. The hot spent-shell cases clatter around the metal deck. The tank stops, the gun barks, and then again continues until the enemy is destroyed or the target is lost. Here in the open the rules are the same for both sides. Every tank commander instinctively dreads the sight of enemy tanks appearing on his flank. He and his opponent both try to come up behind low rises, "hull down," so that they can open fire while exposing nothing of their bulk. Both know the penalty of error—entombment in a blazing tank, with the hatch jammed and flames licking toward the ammunition racks....(when a tank "brews up") Long tongues of flame would curl out of every orifice. The shells and machine gun bullets inside would begin exploding until the whole hull seemed to bulge and convulse. Glistening rivulets of molten aluminum would run from the dead engine like tears, congealing on

ARRANGEMENT OF ARMOR ON THE PZ. III

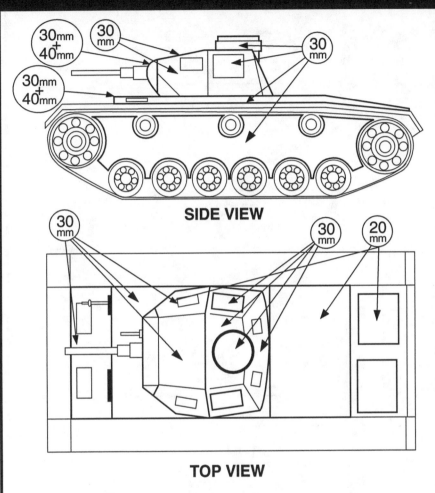

SIDE VIEW

TOP VIEW

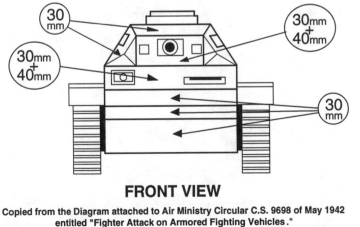

FRONT VIEW

Copied from the Diagram attached to Air Ministry Circular C.S. 9698 of May 1942
entitled "Fighter Attack on Armored Fighting Vehicles."

ARRANGEMENT OF ARMOR ON THE PZ. IV

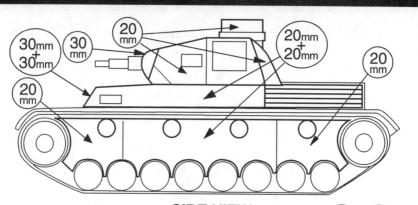

SIDE VIEW

TOP VIEW

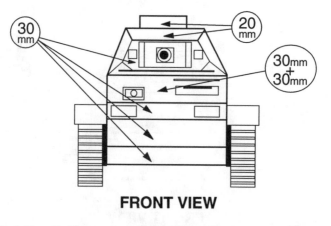

FRONT VIEW

Copied from the Diagram attached to Air Ministry Circular C.S. 9698 of May 1942
"Fighter attack on Armored Fighting Vehicles."

THE ITALIAN M.13/40

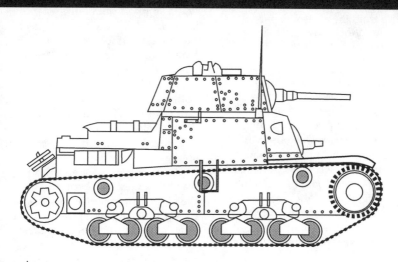

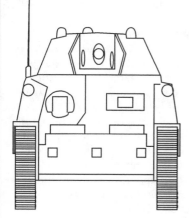

Three views of the M. 13/40 Italian Tank. The mainstay of Italy's armored force, it was under armed, under-powered, poorly armored and a high profile target.

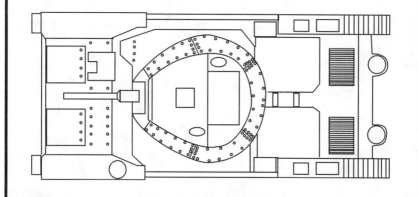

the desert sand in hard mirrors of spent metal. Then the rubber and oil would catch fire, and a spiral of funeral smoke would rise from the awesome pyre. Around the burned-out tank would lie the corpses of its crewmen....

There were a lot of antiquated vehicles in the desert in the early part of the war, so one has to look at the *evolution* of armored forces in the course of the war. One observer stated that, "generalization about the tanks themselves is apt to be misleading. The introduction of a new or modified model did not mean the immediate disappearance of the older tanks; consequently there were often several different models in use together."

It is interesting to note that the British always listed the L3 as a "tank" while the Germans, upon capturing Tobruk, listed all the Bren carriers as "tanks." The Germans started the war in the desert with the Panzer I which was nothing more then an efficient machine-gun carrier, and until 1942 some of the Allied infantry divisions were dependent in their Cavalry battalions on the Light Mk. VI which was also armed only with machine guns behind 14mm of armor. The reality of all this is that there is little to differentiate these vehicles and they should all be considered AFVs (armored fighting vehicles) and not tanks.

All belligerents in the war recognized that additional protection was necessary for their tanks. The Italians were especially noted for increasing protection by adding sandbags to their poorly armored medium tanks. The Germans did much to improve their armor too.

The diagram shows with the + symbols where additional armor was added, first in Africa, and later when shipped from Europe. The Germans also placed sandbags on horizontal surfaces and short lengths of tank track along the upper nose plate and other vulnerable areas. While authorities state that bolted armor is inferior to welded armor (and Italian bolted armor in particular held this reputation), welding does cause the armor to split at angles when hit.

It was common for all sides in the war to "laager" (a Boer term) up for the night. This entailed that the unit concentrate and set up camp, to provide mutual protection. It was not uncommon, especially for the Germans, to shoot off colored flares in the night to alert the enemy to stay away, and for straggling friends trying to find their way home.

Looking first at German doctrine we can see it as a refined rock, scissors, paper game. Infantry and soft targets—use tanks. If enemy artillery is hitting you—use Pz IV's with their 75mm gun and machine guns for counterbattery fire and infantry to knock out or go around the enemy. If enemy tanks advance, then you set up an AT gun line and use your tanks on their flanks. It was this element of flexibility combined with a quick reaction time, which was a trademark of Rommel. It was that push, that drive, which was so elemental in the German method, that brought success.

The Germans created a team of weapons and crews that acted together, which was usually led from the front by the divisional commander, a concept pioneered by General Guderian, German author of the Blitzkrieg, and certainly understood and emulated by Rommel. Reaction times were excellent, and when combined with the high level of quality training in the German army, was an excellent weapon. Plus, there are tricks which give an army the edge. For example, the Germans used throat microphones, that is, microphones that were flush on the throat (instead of in front of the mouth) of the commander so that his orders were a fraction quicker getting to the rest of the tank team. That edge might mean the difference between getting a shot off in time or not. The German armor trained heavily during the summer and fall of 1941. New tactics were developed and some of this also rubbed off on the Italian formations. The key change was that the AT guns and field artillery were no longer viewed as defensive weapons, but were employed as offensive weapons. Both types were pushed as far to the front as possible with the tanks and were to be used against enemy tanks and strong points. In a column of march the AT guns were interspersed with the armor so they could deploy quickly. The leading tanks were accompanied by 105mm guns and artillery staff officers, with the 150mm howitzers and remaining 105mm field guns directly behind and in support. It was also recognized that concentric fire from various angles at the enemy was important and was a tactic practiced for regular implementation. General Neumann-Silkow of the *15th Panzer* went so far as to state that "In many cases the tanks may leave the firing to the accompanying (AT) and artillery." When the tanks were employed in an attack,

the AT and field guns would open fire first and then the tanks would charge forward at full speed until they were in range of the enemy. The concept of engaging enemy tanks in the first clinch, and then withdrawing behind an AT line was finely tuned in 1941 and would give excellent results through the battle of Gazala, culminating in the destruction of the British tank strength at Gazala when they engaged the *Ariete* and *21st Panzer* at the Cauldron. By the time of El Alamein and Tunisia the Allied strength was too great and their quality had improved too much for the Axis to halt them.

Turning to Italian tactics, the 47mm was always the standard AT gun. It was comparable to a 2-pounder with less penetration ability. It had only one advantage: it had an HE (high explosive) shell and later an EP (*effetto pronto*) or round. But as the war continued, the 47mm gun remained Italy's main gun for tanks, which was a severely limiting factor. Italy could only make progress with self-propelled guns, or *Semoventi* (due to their 75mm and larger guns), or with the few truck-mounted AA weapons converted to AT roles. Colonel Arena made a report on armor warfare after the battle of El Alamein which stated, "To my mind, an armored mass which wants to effectively contest the English one should be formed with the *Semovente* with improved armor and armament. The artillery role of this mass should be performed by battalions of *Semoventi* armed with 88mm and 90mm guns."

The M series, or medium tanks, were mechanically unreliable. On one occasion Rommel planned a shoot-off between four German and four Italian tanks. Only one Italian tank arrived at the site due to mechanical breakdowns on the way to the shoot. The M series was called *Rollende Saerge*, or rolling coffin, by the Germans, due to the lack of armor and poor quality of the bolted plate. Dr. Monzel, a German interpreter in the Italian *XX Corps* said that "The chance of surviving an attack in such a tank, not to speak of success, lay beyond the realms of courage which can morally be demanded." It was underpowered as well, especially in comparison to the German tanks. It used a 125 horsepower engine on a 15 ton frame, while the German Pz III's and IV's had 320 horsepower to move almost 20 tons of tank. The Italians did increase horsepower on the later versions of the M series, but not significantly.

The Allies tended to discount Italian tank strength and worried most about German tanks, though, after Crusader, General Auchlinleck would say, "The Italian M13 tanks which, as a result of the previous campaign, we had inclined to dismiss as valueless, fought well, and had an appreciable effect on the battle." The Italians tried to compensate for their weak tanks by increasing the amount of artillery with their units, which did give them a bit more bite.

Italian doctrine envisioned the use of M tanks to punch holes in the enemy line with the L tanks acting as scouts, while the P tanks, which never appeared in Africa, and were essentially nonexistent, were to act as mobile artillery—the *Semovente* substituted in many ways for this lack. Their artillery doctrine, *fuoco*

da manovra (maneuvered fire), called for the employment of AT guns and field artillery forward close to the front and using massed fire, compensating in part for lack of range and older guns. This would be combined with *celere* (a light, partially mechanized division not sent to Africa) and infantry division support. The concept was close to the German *Blitzkrieg* and lacked only tactical airpower, which had been considered, but discarded by the *Regia Aeronautica* for the Douhet school of strategic bombing and a more independent role separate from the other two armed services. It was not so much in ideas and theory that Italy was deficient but in material and training. At the start of the war Italian tanks still relied on flags for signaling. Training was never as intensive at it was in the German army. There was always a lack of efficient tanks, of supplies, and war material which was never overcome. Italy had developed the concepts but lacked the materiel to implement them.

Italy produced a document on 12 June 1941 that considered producing German Pz III's in her factories, either for Germany, Italy or both. Part of this idea was that Germany would give 160% of the required material to build the tank, so the extra percentage would be the "profit" for Italy's war machine. The benefits of this proposed system was that it (1) made use of German war experience and their assistance, (2) could be done quickly, and (3) the tank was a successful design. Ultimately this course was not chosen, possibly due to the monopoly (duopoly) that Fiat and Ansaldo had on tank construction. (Other Italian companies were trying to break into this monopoly, or there may have been bribery, but in any event, Cavallero was given instructions on 4 February 1942 to refuse the German offer.) The de facto result was that business as usual would continue and the monopoly on Italian tank production would continue.

Early in the war Commonwealth tactics were wedded to the past. British command desired to separate tanks from the actions of the other arms and to view tanks as a form of cavalry. During Operation Crusader, the 7th Armored division fought with little in the way of artillery or infantry support. The commander even issued an order that read "This will be a tank commanders' battle. No tank commander will go far wrong if he places his gun within killing range of an enemy." It sounded as if tanks were ships at sea, and certainly not part of a totally integrated package ready to do battle with German methodology.

The I-tank concept was that it would be essentially an infantry support weapon used to punch a hole in the enemy line through which cruiser tanks would pass and exploit the breech. Rommel always wondered why the I-tank was considered an infantry support tank when it lacked an explosive shell. The British, when it was designed, felt that the heavy machine gun it carried would be sufficient to support infantry. Matilda was good but unreliable, hence the Valentine. The Valentine was quite similar but more dependable.

By the time of Operation Crusader, the Commonwealth still believed that the Germans used tanks to fight tanks, while the reality was

that the Germans believed that tanks destroyed troops, while AT guns destroyed enemy tanks. The Commonwealth continued to believe that their losses were due to enemy tanks, and not AT guns, until well into 1942. By the time of the second Axis advance in early 1942, the Commonwealth was concerned about the superiority of German tanks and AT guns, but Germany was sending still newer weapons, and Italy had begun to send some improved weapons of her own into the fray. It must be recalled that until October of 1941 "unqualified praise" for the Matilda and the 2-pounder was still rolling into London, based on O'Connor's campaign and the successful defense of Tobruk. The 6-pounder did not arrive in the Middle East until May 1942 and then there were only about one hundred. Design of the 17-pounder began in April 1941 and it appeared in the Middle East in January 1943.

The evolution of the anti-tank gun is also interesting. All AT guns at the start of the war were relatively weak—there was little difference between the German 37mm AT gun, the Italian 47mm gun, and the British 2-pounder. But as the war accelerated the weapons also evolved. In the case of the Germans their 88mm AA/AT gun was unmatched in the desert until the appearance of the Italian 90mm AT and the British 17-pounder. After the 37mm gun, the Germans also introduced a 50mm AT gun, and it was an effective weapon. It was a more powerful version than the one mounted on their early Pz III's. It was not until Alam Halfa that the British had the new 6-pounder AT gun widely distributed among various formations

237

of the 8th Army, and that was a weapon that could stop the Axis armor.

So what helped the Commonwealth was their numerical superiority as well as the steady improvement in tank and AT gun types. As the war moved on, it would be overall numbers combined with improved armor and better guns which would eventually nullify superior German tactics and the weakness of Italian technology and production.

German AFV Characteristics				
Name	Weight	Armament	Speed	Frontal Armor
Pz IB	5.7 tons	2 MGs	25 mph	15mm
Pz IIF	10 tons	one 20mm gun/1 MG	25 mph	35mm
Pz IIIG	20 tons	one 50mm (short) gun/2 MGs	24 mph	30mm
Pz IVD	19.7 tons	one 75mm (short) gun/2 MGs	26 mph	30mm
Pz 1B Stu	4.7 tons	one 47mm Czech	28 mph	14.5mm
Sd 222*	6.5 tons	one 20mm/1 MG	46 mph	14.5mm
Sd 231 6 wheel*	5.9 tons	one 20mm/1 MG	37 mph	14.5mm
Sd 231 8 wheel*	8.2 tons	one 20mm/1 MG	53 mph	14.5mm
Added in the course of the war:				
Pz IIIJ	22 tons	one 50mm (long) gun/2 MGs	25 mph	50mm
Pz IIIN	22 tons	one 75mm (short) gun/2 MGs	25 mph	57mm
Pz IVF	23.25 tons	one 75mm (long) gun/2 MGs	24 mph	50mm
Pz VI Tiger I	56 tons	one 88mm gun/2 MGs	24 mph	102mm
* = Armored Car				
Stu type = self-propelled gun. 27 of these arrived in early 1941.				
The German Pz IIIG and Pz IVD were given improved armor as soon as they arrived and later ones shipped over had already been uparmored by 30-35mm.				

Italian AFV Characteristics

Name	Weight	Armament	Speed	Frontal Armor
M11/39	11 tons	one 37mm gun/2 MGs	20 mph	30mm
M13/40	13.5 tons	one 47mm gun/3 MGs	20 mph	40mm
M13/40*	14 tons	one 47mm gun/3 MGs	20 mph	42mm
L6/40	6.8 tons	one 20mm gun/1 MG	26 mph	40mm
L3/35	3.2 tons	two MGs	26 mph	13.5mm
AB40**	6.5 tons	two MGs	46 mph	18mm
Added in the course of the war:				
M14	14.7 tons	one 47mm gun/4 MGs	20 mph	42mm
M15	15 tons	one 47mm gun/4 MGs	26 mph	45mm
S/47	6.8 tons	one 47mm gun/1MG	30 mph	30mm
S/75	15 tons	one 75mm gun/1 MG	25 mph	50mm
AB41**	7.5 tons	one 20mm gun/3 MGs	48 mph	18mm

* = Later edition with larger engine

** = Armored Car

S type = Semovente or self-propelled gun. The Semoventi armed with the 75mm/34 (earlier ones had the 75mm/18 howitzer or the 75mm/32 field gun) were considered to be good tank hunters.

Note that a speed of 25 mph on the road translates into open-country desert speed of 8-10 mph.

Commonwealth AFV Characteristics				
Name	Weight	Armament	Speed	Frontal Armor
MK VIB	5.2 tons	2 MGs	35 mph	14mm
MK I Cr. A9	12.7 tons	one 2 pdr gun/3 MGs	25 mph	14mm
MK II Cr. A10	14 tons	one 2 pdr gun/3 MGs	16 mph	30mm
MK IV Cr. A13	14.75 tons	one 2 pdr gun/1 MG	30 mph	30mm
MK II Matilda	26.5 tons	one 2 pdr gun/2 MGs	15 mph	78mm
Bren Carrier	4 tons	1 MG	46 mph	14.5mm
Rolls Royce**	4 tons	! MG	45 mph	8mm
Morris**	4.2 tons	one AT rifle/1 MG	45 mph	7mm
Added in the course of the war:				
S. Afr. MKII**	6 tons	one AT rifle/2 MGs	50 mph	12mm
MK I Cru. A15	19 tons	one 2 pdr gun/2MGs	27 mph	40mm
MK III Cru.	19.75 tons	one 6 pdr (short) gun/1MG	27 mph	51mm
MK II Valentine	16 tons	one 2 pdr gun/1 MG	15 mph	65mm
MK IX Valentine	16 tons	one 6 pdr gun/0-1 MG	15 mph	65mm
M3 Honey*	12.25 tons	one 37mm gun/2 MGs	36 mph	51mm
M3 Grant***	28.5 tons	one 37 mm & 75mm gun/1-3 MGs	35 mph	57mm
M4 Sherman*	30 tons	75mm gun/2 MGs	35 mph	76mm
M7 Priest#	22.6 tons	105mm/ 1 MG	25 mph	62mm
Bishop#	17.2tons	25 pdr	15 mph	60mm
MK III Churchill	38.5 tons	one 6 pdr (short) gun/2 MGs	15 mph	51mm
S. Afr. MKIV**	6.1 tons	one 2 pdr gun/1 MG	50 mph	12mm
Daimler MKI-II**	7.5 tons	one 2 pdr gun/1 MG	50 mph	16mm
* = USA built				
** = Armored Car				
***M3 Medium (37mm in turret, 75mm in sponson, USA built).				
# Self-propelled (SP) gun.				
Cr. = Cruiser Cru. = Crusader				

Artillery

While there are many examples of artillery used in North Africa in World War II, the accompanying chart lists the most common. The Allies tended to have a uniform type present, while the Axis, especially the Italians, would have a variety in North Africa. This would, in turn, cause supply problems, as ammunition had to match the gun type. Ranges are in meters, and shell weights in kilos.

ARTILLERY				
Year	Size	Type	Range	Shell Weight
German				
1933	75mm	field gun	12300	5.8
1941	105mm	field gun	20850	15.1
1935	105mm	howitzer	10675	14.8
1934	50mm	mortar	4800	0.2
1927	75mm 18	Infantry Gun	3550	6
1927	150mm 33	Infantry Gun	4700	38
1936	37mm	AT	4800	0.65
1940	50mm	AT	2700	2.25
1936	88mm	AT	20700	9.2
Commonwealth				
1904	18 pdr	field gun	10180	8.4
1940	25 pdr	field gun	14500	11.3
1939	4.5"	field gun	22200	25
1917	3.7"	howitzer	6500	9.1
1920s	3"Mk I	mortar	1730	4.5
1930s	2pdr	AT	2000	0.9
1940	6pdr	AT	6000	2.84
1942	17pdr	AT	10000	7.7
United States				
1934	75mm	field gun	11685	6.8
1939	105mm	howitzer	11200	14.9
1938	37mm	AT	11750	0.7
1941	57mm	AT	11585	2.9

(chart continues on next page)

Italian

1911	75/27	field gun	8380	6.3
1915	105/28	field gun	11425	15.5
1914	100/17	howitzer	8180	12.5
1914	149/13	howitzer	8400	40.33
1937	149/19	howitzer	14600	40
1935	81mm	mortar	4090	3.3
1913	65/17	infantry gun	6500	4.15
1935	47mm	AT	7000	1.45/2.35
1939/41	90mm	AT	11400	11.2

MC202/Me-109/Hurricane: A Comparison

Three important types of airplanes which fought in the desert war were the British Hawker Hurricane, the German Messerschmitt Me-109 and the Italian Macchi MC202 "Folgore" (Lightning). The Hurricanes appeared in late 1940 in the Desert and enjoyed air superiority over the Fiat CR42 and Macchi MC200 "Saetta" (Thunderbolt) until the arrival of the Me-109 which successfully contested the British aircraft. The Hurricane I especially suffered from the bulky tropical sandfilters which limited the maximum speed to just over 300 mph. More versions of this long-lived airplane, built in mass numbers, although not of a definitive design, reached the desert scene and fought there when better models were available elsewhere. In October 1941 the Hurricane IIB fighterbomber also joined the fight in the Western Desert. Just the next month, on 23 November 1941, the MC202 appeared for the first time in North Africa enjoying immediate success, and the crows of the Junkers 87 (Stuka) and Junkers 88 (twin engine

level bomber) often escorted by it felt better protected. This model mounted the Daimler-Benz DB601 German engine (produced in Italy and weighing 60 kilograms more) which allowed comparable performance to the aircraft in service in the RAF and *Luftwaffe*. The Macchi still remained outgunned because of its badly designed wings and had only two heavy 12.7 (0.50) machine guns.

Of course, these performances changed very often because new versions were sent to the front, especially for the Hurricane and Me-109, while the Macchi saw the new version, called MC205 Veltro with better wings, armament, and better engine (the DB605) during the invasion of Sicily. Moreover, the performances varied at different altitudes. Hurricanes were often confined after the appearance of the Spitfire to the fighter bomber role. According to one British airman, there were few differences between the Me-109 and MC202 in silhouette and speed and when the MC202 first appeared it was often mistaken.

Sometimes Italian and German pilots exchanged their planes, as veterans recalled, of course only when this exchange involved the Me-109 and MC202. It was difficult for the Germans, according to interviews with some pilots made by Hans Ring, to understand why the British still employed the Hurricanes in 1942 in the desert, since the plane was outmoded. Hurricanes could climb at 2,520 feet per minute while the Me-109F climbed at about 3,200 feet per minute. The MC202 could reach the level of about 10,000 feet in 2 minutes and 47 seconds, and 19,685 feet in 5 minutes and 55 seconds.

According to battle reports of Italian pilots, the MC202 was superior to the Hurricane for speed/maneuverability and speed of climbing, while it was inferior in armament. It is generally accepted that the MC202 was slightly inferior to the contemporary Me-109 versions. But while training and quality of aircraft was vital in the war in the desert, it also saw the Allies build up a numerical superiority that could not be defeated by the Axis in the long run.

Plane Data			
	Hurricane IIA	Me-109F	MC202
Armament	8x.303 MGs	1x15 cannon, 2x7.9 MGs	2x12.7 MGs
Max speed	325 mph	373 mph	373 mph
Ceiling	32000 feet	37700 feet	37700 feet
MGs = machine guns			

Selected Bibliography

Unpublished Sources
National Archives, Washington
Microfilm Series T78, Rolls: 324, 325, 344
Series T84, Rolls: 273, 276, 279
Series T313 Rolls: 417, 430, 469, 477, 478
Series T821 Rolls: 9, 23, 31, 125, 200, 250, 489
Bundesarchiv-Militärarchiv, Freiburg (Germany)
RH VIII/252, 322
RM7/235, 934, 945
Italian Army Archives, Rome (Archivio Ufficio storico SME)
Cavallero Diary
Comando Supremo Diary
Life and Campaigns of Fieldmarshall Erwin Rommel (David
Irving microfilm collection) Rolls 1, 3, 9, 11.

Published Sources
Agar-Hamilton and Turner, L.F.C., *The Sidi Rezegh Battles: 1941,*
(Oxford, Oxford U.Press, 1957) Very good South African Offi-
cial History, with his companion *Crisis in the Desert May-July
1942,* (Cape Town-Oxford, 1952).
Arena, Nino, *La Regia Aeronautica 1939-1943,* four volumes (Rome,
1981-86). Lots of data, and great picture history.
Barlozzetti, Ugo and Pirella, Alberto, *Mezzi dell'esercito Italiano
1935-1945.* (Editoriale Olimpia, 1986). Good technical data.
Barnett, Correlli, *The Desert Generals,* (Ballantine Books, 1972 ed.).
Classic discussion of British leadership.
Behrendt, Hans-Otto, *Rommel's Intelligence in the Desert Campaign
1941-1943,* (William Kimber, 1985). Excellent book on the intelli-
gence war from the German perspective.
Carell, Paul, *Die Wüstenfüchse,* Ullstein, 1958 (Engl. edition: *The
Foxes of the Desert,* New York, Bantam Books, 1972). Popular

German point of view of the war, a bit dated and contains errors.

Carver, Michael, *Tobruk*, (London, 1964). Excellent study by one who served there, though lacks insight into Italy's war effort. Carver also wrote *El Alamein* and *Dilemmas of the Desert War*, the latter being a view of General Ritchie's problems.

Cavallero, Ugo, *Comando Supremo. Diario del Capo di*, (SMG 1940-1943, Bologna, 1948). Incomplete (i.e., selective memory) edition of the diaries of Cavallero.

Ceva, Lucio, *Africa settentrionale 1940-1943*, (Rome, Bonacci, 1982). Very good survey of the Italian literature on the war in North Africa, but also examines the Allied side.

Ceva, Lucio and Andrea Curami, *La meccanizzazione dell'esercito italiano fino al 1943*, 2 vols. (Rome, Ufficio storico Stato maggiore esercito, 1989). A milestone in the Italian language AFV historiography. Using various archives authors arrived at unexpected conclusions to explain why the Italian weapons were so unequal to the situation.

Das Deutsche Reich und der Zweite Weltkrieg, vol.3: Gerhard Schreiber, Bernd Stegemann, Detlef Vogel, *Der Mittelmeerraum und Südosteuropa*, (Stuttgart, DVA, 1984); vol.6: Horst Boog, Werner Rahn, Reinhard Stumpf, Bernd Wegner, Der Globale Krieg, (Stuttgart, DVA, 1990). Semi-official history of the Second World War in ten volumes being translated into English. Well researched and balanced, though some contributions are uneven.

Diario storico del Comando Supremo, ed. by Antonello Biagini and Fernando Frattolillo, (Rome 1986-1993) War Diary of the Italian High Command. First four volumes of a long series; some documents left out.

Falessi, Cesare and Pafi, Benedetto, *Veicoli de combattimento dell'ercito Italiano dal 1939-1945*. (Interconair Media Group, 1976). Good vehicle technical data.

Forty, George, *General O'Connor's Desert Triumph: The First Victory*, (Tunbridge Wells, 1990). Great photographs; in error on Italian details.

Greene, Jack, *Mare Nostrum*, (Watsonville, 1990). Many details on the various Italian formations, with essays on the three services.

Hinsley, Frederick H., *British Intelligence in the Second World War, vol.I and vol.II*. (London, HMSO, 1979 and 1981).

Keegan, John, editor, *Churchill's Generals*, (New York, 1991). Uneven new volume, though with some insights on individual generals.

Knox, Macgregor, *Mussolini Unleashed*, (Cambridge, 1982). Excellent work on the war until German intervention.

Kuhn, Volkmar, *Rommel in the Desert*, (1991, West Chester). New work repeating many old errors. Nice pictures.

Lundari, Giuseppe, *Italian Parachutist Units 1937/45*, (1989, Milano). Number 9 of the "de Bello" Series, the Italian equivalent of the "Osprey" Series, it includes English text. Discusses history of the Italian paratroops.

Maughan, Barton, *Tobruk and El Alamein*, (Canberra, 1966). Quite good Official History and detailed, companion to Gavin Long's *To Benghazi*.

McKee, Alexander, *El Alamein ULTRA and the Three Battles*, (London, 1991). Surprisingly good ex-journalist's study, but the title is only about one-third of the book and has some holes.

Millett, Allan R., and Murray, Williamson, *Military Effectiveness, The Second World War*, (Boston, 1988). Uneven but for the most part excellent study of the major powers.

Montanari, Mario, *Le Operazioni in Africa Settrionale*, four volumes, (Rome 1985-1993). New Official History, which uses source material from all languages. Very detailed and addresses many unsettled questions.

Pignacca, Brizio, *Ruote in Divisa, I Veicoli Militari Italiani 1900-1987*. (Giorgio Nada Editore, 1989) Good technical information on Italian vehicles in both world wars.

Pitt, Barrie, *The Crucible of War* (London 1980/1986) Three volume general history with some personal anecdotes thrown in; competent.

Reuth, Ralf Georg, *Entscheidung im Mittelmeer. Die südliche Peripherie Europas in der deutschen Strategie des Zweiten Weltkrieges 1940-1942*, (Bernard & Graefe, Koblenz, 1985). A study on the 1942 decisions in the Mediterranean from the German point of view. The same author also wrote a Rommel biography: *Erwin Rommel. Des Führers General*, München, 1987.

Sadkovich, James, J. "Of Myths and Men: Rommel and the Italians in North Africa 1940-1942," *The International History Review*, Volume XIII, 2, May 1991. A revisionist view of Rommel by a bountiful writer on Italy's war effort.

Santoro, Giuseppe, *L'aeronautica italiane nella seconda guerra mondiale*, Two volumes, (Rome, 1950). Dated but good.

Schmidt, Heinz Werner, *With Rommel in the Desert*, (Costa Mesa, 1991 reprint). Well written and well used account of being with Rommel with inaccuracies common with many "popular" German accounts.

Shores, Christopher and Ring, Hans, *Fighters Over the Desert*, (London, 1969). Like most of Shores' works, very detailed day-to-day combat history, using German and some limited Italian sources.

Stumpf Reinhard, "Probleme der Logistik im Afrikafeldzug 1941-1943," in: *Die Bedeutung der Logistik für die militarische Führung von der Antike bis in die neueste Zeit*, Herford, Bonn, 1986 (Vorträge zur Militärgeschichte, 7, pp. 211-239). Important German study on the logistical problems in the Mediterranean.

Sullivan, Brian R., *A Thirst for Glory*, (University Microfilm International, 1984—thesis) and "The Impatient Cat: Assessments in Military Power in Fascist Italy, 1936-1940" from Murray, Williamson, *Calculations*, (New York, 1992). Both are very insightful on the prewar view of Italy, while *Thirst* has great insights on the war in Ethiopia and the Italian military.

Van Creveld, Martin, "Sirte to Alamein," 6th chapter of *Supplying War: from Wallenstein to Patton*, (Cambridge, Cambridge U.Pr., 1977). An essay on the influence of facilities in the supply failure of the Axis in Africa.

Verney, G.L., *The Desert Rats. The History of the 7th Armoured Division 1938 to 1945*, (London, 1954).

Vicini, Diego, *L'8° Bersaglieri e la guerra in Africa Settentrionale (1941-1943)*, (Bologna, Tamari, 1977). Privately printed, one of the scarcest and most valuable pieces of research on the story of the *Ariete*.

Walker, R., *Alam Halfa and Alamein*, (Wellington, New Zealand, Department of Internal Affairs, 1962) - one volume in an excellent series.

Orders of Battle

ORDER OF BATTLE ON 17 NOVEMBER, 1941

Army Headquarters
General Erwin Rommel

German Afrika Korps
General Ludwig Cruewell
- 15th Panzer Division
  - 8th panzer regiment
  - 115th motorized infantry regiment(-)
  - 200th motorized infantry regiment
  - 33rd recce battalion
  - 33rd motorized artillery regiment
  - 33rd panzer jaeger (AT) battalion
  - support troops
- 21st Panzer Division
  - 5th panzer regiment
  - 104th motorized infantry regiment
  - 3rd recce battalion
  - 155th motorized artillery regiment(-)
  - 605th panzer jaeger battalion
  - 39th panzer jaeger battalion
  - support troops
- Afrika Infantry Division
  - 361st "Africa" infantry regiment (two battalions of ex French Foreign Legion)
  - 155th infantry regiment (three battalions)
  - 300th Oasis battalion (a company?)
  - 900th z.b.V. engineer battalion
  - 2nd celere motorized artillery regiment (Italian - one battalion of 100/17mm guns of three batteries and two batteries of 75/27mm guns of two batteries each)
  - support troops
  - (attached to the division):
    - 2nd battalion/255th infantry from 110th Infantry Division
    - 3rd battalion/347th infantry from 197th Infantry Division
    - (The above two battalions had many older men and young recruits)
    - 2nd battalion of the 115th motorized infantry regiment
- 55th Savona Infantry Division
  - 15th infantry regiment
  - 16th infantry regiment
  - 12th artillery regiment (one battalion of 75/27mm and one battalion of 100/71mm guns)
  - (attached):
    - 155th machine gun battalion
    - 4th battalion (gruppo squadroni) Genova Cavalleria armored cars

one company of Arditi
major elements of the German 300th Oasis battalion (five companies total-not all present)

XXI Army Corps
General Enea Navarini

3rd celere artillery regiment (one battalion of 100/17mm guns and two battalions of 75/27mm guns)

16th raggruppamento Corps artillery (three battalions of 105/28mm guns)

24th raggruppamento Corps artillery (two battalions of 105/28mm guns and one of 100/17mm guns) (-)

5th raggruppamento army artillery (four battalions of 149/35mm guns)

8th raggrupamento army artillery (this was a recent arrival and in October of 1942 would consist of one battalion of 149/40mm, one battalion of 152/37mm, and one battalion of 149/28mm guns. At the time of Crusader's start it did have a specific duty, but reported towards the end of the battle as being low on ammunition, so we are unsure of its status and change in its status)

304th raggruppmento frontier guard artillery (four battalions of 77/28mm guns)

340th engineer battalion

service troops

17th Pavia Infantry Division

27th infantry regiment

28th infantry regiment

26th artillery regiment (one battalions of 75/27mm and one battalion of 100/17mm guns)

(attached to the division):

5th battalion of light tanks

6th battalion Lancieri Aosta armored cars

25th Bologna Infantry Division

39th infantry regiment

40th infantry regiment

205th artillery regiment (two battalions of 75/27mm and one battalion of 100/17mm guns)

27th Brescia Infantry Division

19th infantry regiment

20th infantry regiment

1st celere artillery regiment (two battalions of 75/27mm guns)

(attached):

27th machine gun battalion

102nd Trento Motorized Infantry Division (motorized in name only)

61st motorized infantry regiment

62nd motorized infantry regiment

7th motorized Bersaglieri regiment

46th motorized artillery regiment (two battalions of 75/27mm and one battalion of 100/17mm guns)

(attached):
 551st AT battalion

Army Corps of Manuever
General Gastone Gambara
 Milmart - three batteries of 102/35mm guns (naval guns mounted on
  trucks and attached to the Ariete)
 one battalion of motorized engineers
 1st Carabinieri paratroop battalion in rear
 132nd Ariete Armored Division
  132nd medium armor regiment
  32nd light armor regiment
  8th motorized Bersaglieri regiment
  132nd motorized artillery regiment (two battalions of 75/27mm)
  (attached):
   one battalion of 75/27mm guns detached from the Pavia
   one battalion of 105/28mm guns from the 24th raggruppamento
    corps artillery
 101st Trieste Motorized Infantry Division (forming)
  65th motorized infantry regiment
  66th motorized infantry regiment
  9th motorized Bersaglieri regiment
  21st motorized artillery regiment
  (attached):
   508th battalion was mixed 47mm AT guns and 20mm AA/AT guns
 Raggruppamento Esplorante (RECAM) (much of this unit was in the rear)
  two battalions of Giovani Fascisti infantry
  one battalion of police units (one armored car company and two
   motorcycle companies)
  52nd medium armor battalion (forming)
  3rd/32nd light armor battalion
  experimental company of L6's and armored cars
  one machine gun company
  Flying Batteries:
   1st and 3rd battalions of 65/17mm guns
   one independent battery of 65/17mm guns
   one battery of 100/17mm guns
   one battery of 20mm AA guns

8th Army
Alan Cunningham

XIII Army Corps
Lt. General Alfred Godwin-Austen
 Corp Troops
  7th Medium Regiment Royal Artillery
  68th Medium Regiment Royal Artillery (6" howitzer and 4.5" howitzer)
  73rd regiment AT guns
  one regiment heavy AA

three regiments of light AA
(2nd South African division in rear: three brigades, and divisional troops)
4th Indian Division (mountain capable)
    5th Indian Infantry brigade (three infantry battalions)
    7th Indian Infantry brigade (three infantry battalions)
    11th Infantry brigade (three infantry battalions)
    Central India Horse (motorized)
    1st Field Regiment Royal Artillery (total of 56 25 pdrs in all three regiments)
    25th Field Regiment Royal Artillery
    31st Field Regiment Royal Artillery
    65th AT regiment
    57th Light AA regiment
2nd New Zealand Division
    4th Infantry brigade (three infantry battalions)
    5th Infantry brigade (three infantry battalions)
    6th Infantry brigade (three infantry battalions)
    28th Maori battalion
    2nd New Zealand Divisional Cavalry (Mark VIB light tanks and Bren carriers - assigned to 4th Indian Division at start of the battle)
    27th New Zealand machine gun battalion
    4th New Zealand Field Regiment Artillery (24 25 pdrs)
    5th New Zealand Field Regiment Artillery (24 25 pdrs)
    6th New Zealand Field Regiment Artillery (24 25 pdrs)
    7th New Zealand AT regiment (2pdrs and 75mm guns on portees)
    14th New Zealand Light AA regiment
    Mixed engineer (three field companies)
1st Army Tank Brigade (132 total tanks, including a small recce group built around 3 cruiser tanks)
    8th Royal Tank Regiment (Valentine tanks)
    42nd Royal Tank Regiment (Matilda tanks)
    44th Royal Tank Regiment (Matilda tanks)

XXX Army Corps
Lt. General Willoughby M. Norrie
    Corps Troops
    7th Armored Division
    General W.H.E. "Strafer" Gott
        Divisional troops
            1st King's Dragoon Guards (armored cars—one sqd in Tobruk)
            11th Hussars (armored cars)
            1st Light AA regiment
        7th Armored brigade
            7th Hussars, 2nd and 6th Royal Tanks (168 tanks, with 71 A15's, 71 A13's, and 26 old A10's)
            71 A13's and 26 old A10's
        22nd Armored brigade

3rd and 4th County of London Yeomanry, and 2nd Royal
Gloucestershire Hussars (158 Crusader tanks)
4th Armored Brigade
8th Hussars, 3rd and 5th Royal Tanks (165 Stuart tanks)
7th Support Group (three motorized infantry battalions)
3rd Royal Horse Artillery Regiment (24 25 pdrs)
4th Royal Horse Artillery Regiment (24 25 pdrs)
60th Field Regiment Royal Artillery
Mixed engineer (one squadron)
(attached)
4th South African armored car regiment
1st South African Division
1st motorized infantry brigade (three infantry battalions)
5th motorized infantry brigade (three infantry battalions)
1st South African armored car regiment (three squadrons)
President Steyn machine gun regiment (four companies)
one company of Die Middlandse machine gun regiment
3rd South African Field Regiment Artillery (25 pdrs)
7th South African Field Regiment Artillery (25 pdrs)
1st South African AT regiment
1st South African Light AA regiment

Tobruk Garrison
Lt. Gen. Ronald Scobie (C.O. of the 70th)
70th Infantry Division
14th infantry brigade (three infantry battalions)
16th infantry brigade (three infantry battalions)
23rd infantry brigade (three infantry battalions)
1st Royal Horse Artillery
104th Royal Horse Artillery
107th Royal Horse Artillery
1st Royal Northumberland Fusiliers machine gun battalion
(attached)
two companies of Australian infantry
Czech Battalion
Carpathian Brigade
three infantry battalions
Polish cavalry regiment
1st Polish artillery regiment (25 pdrs)
two companies of AT guns
one company of engineers
32nd Army Tank Brigade
C Sqd. King's Dragoon Guards
1st Royal Tank Regiment (32 old cruisers and 25 light tanks)
4th Royal Tank Regiment (Matilda tanks - total with unit below of 69)
D Sqd. 7th Royal Tank Regiment (Matilda tanks)

ORDER OF BATTLE ON 24 MAY, 1942

Superior Command Armed Forces in North Africa
(Comando Superiore Forze Armate Africa Settentrionale)
General Ettore Bastico Chief of Staff: General Curio Barbasetti de Prun

Units Directly Under Superior Command
133rd Littorio Armor Division
> 133rd medium armor regiment (two battalions of M tanks)
> 12th motorized Bersaglieri regiment (three battalions)
> 133rd motorized artillery regiment (one battalion of 75/27mm)
> 33rd mixed engineer battalion

25th Bologna Infantry Division
> 39th infantry regiment (two battalions)
> 40th infantry regiment (two battalions)
> 205th artillery regiment with one battalion of 100/17mm howitzers
> and three of 75/27mm guns
> 25th mixed engineer battalion

Various attached units
> Raggruppamento Giovani Fascisti of two battalions and IV Granatieri
> AT battalion. The Granatieri was detached from the "Granatieri
> (Grenadier) di Sardegna," or Guards which was also the only
> three-regiment infantry division in the army. Later assigned to the
> Trento.
> Raggruppamento North African celere
> 9th infantry battalion
> 291st battalion of g.a.f. artillery (border/fortress troops) (77/27mm
> guns)
> 332nd battalion of g.a.f. artillery (100/17mm howitzers)
> battalion of San Marco marines (part employed in the Hecker Group)

Armata Corazzata "Africa" (Panzerarmee Afrika)
General Erwin Rommel

"Kampfstaffel" group. Known as Kampf Gruppe Kiehl, it had one AT company, one AA company, a few tanks, and two companies of 88mm guns. General Cruewell acted as commander along the Axis Gazala line and was captured within the first few days of the operation when his plane was forced down behind enemy lines. General Kesselring filled in for him after that loss.

Italian Artillery Command
General Salvatore Nicolini
> 8th raggruppamento of army artillery
> > 33rd battalion (three batteries of 149/40 guns with a range of 17,500
> > yards)
> > 131st battalion (two batteries of 149/28 Krupp guns)
> > 192nd battalion (two batteries of 149/28 Krupp guns)
> > 52nd 152mm/37 artillery (four guns - WWI piece with a range of
> > 21,800 meters with a r.o.f. of one round every two minutes)

556th rear area commando
service troops

X Army Corps
General Benvenuto Gioda

Corps Troops
9th Bersaglieri regiment (two battalions)
16th artillery raggruppameto (two battalions of 100/17mm howitzers
and two of 75/27mm guns)
31st Guastatori Engineers (Demolition) (assigned from army HQ)
10th Engineer Battalion
Service troops
17th Pavia Infantry Division (two battalions were detached to the Hecker
Group in the course of the battle for the attack on Bir Hacheim)
27th infantry regiment (three battalions)
28th infantry regiment (three battalions)
26th artillery regiment (two battalions of 105/28mm)
18th mixed engineer regiment
27th Brescia Infantry Division
19th infantry regiment (three battalions)
20th infantry regiment (three battalions)
1st celere artillery regiment (two battalions of 75/27mm and two
battalions of 100/17mm howitzers, and one of 88/56mm AT/AA
guns)
27th mixed engineer battalion

XXI Army Corps
General Enea Navarini

7th Bersaglieri regiment (two battalions)
33rd demolition engineer battalion
service troops
102nd Trento Motorized Infantry Division (motorized in name only)
61st motorized infantry regiment (three battalions)
62nd motorized infantry regiment (three battalions)
46th motorized artillery regiment (two battalions of 75/27mm guns
and two battalions of 100/17mm howitzers)
51st mixed engineer battalion
60th Sabratha Infantry Division
85th infantry regiment (two battalions)
86th infantry regiment (two battalions
3rd celere artillery regiment (two battalions of 75/27mm guns and one
battalion of 100/17mm howitzers
60th mixed engineer battalion
15th Schutzen brigade (German)
Colonel Erwin Menny
200th infantry regiment (two battalions)
361st infantry regiment (two battalions)(detached from 90th)
528th artillery battalion (one battery)
533rd artillery battalion

612th AA battalion of 20mm (four batteries + two platoons of smoke generators)

XX Army Corps
General Ettore Baldassarre
191st/8th regiment of artillery of 149/28mm guns
(German gun sold to the Italians. 14 pieces in Africa as of September 1942 with a maximum range of 13,300 meters)
34th special engineer battalion
132nd Ariete Armored Division
General Giuseppe De Stefanis
132nd medium armor regiment (three battalions)
8th motorized Bersaglieri regiment (three battalions)
132nd motorized artillery regiment (two battalions of 75/27mm, one of 105/28mm guns, and one of 90/53 AA/AT)
3rd battalion "Lancieri di Novara" with L6's
3rd battalion of "Nizza Cavalleria" with armored cars
2nd/24th regiment of AA artillery (105/28mm guns)
551st battalion of semoventi (self-propelled) 75/18mm howitzers
552nd battalion of semoventi 75/18mm howitzers
6th artillery AA/AT of 88/56mm guns
32nd mixed motorized engineer battalion
101st Trieste Motorized Infantry Division
65th motorized infantry regiment (two battalions)
66th motorized infantry regiment (two battalions)
21st motorized artillery regiment (two battalions of 100/17mm howitzers, two 75/27mm guns, and one 75/50mm guns)
11th medium tank battalion
8th Bersaglieri armored car battalion
32nd mixed motorized engineer battalion

German Afrika Korps
General Walther Nehring

135th Flak regiment HQ (Luftwaffe)
1st battalion of 18th Flak regiment (Luftwaffe) (three batteries of four 88mm AA/AT and five batteries of 12 20mm AA guns)
1st battalion of 33rd Flak regiment (Luftwaffe)
617th light AA battalion Army (three batteries each of 12 20mm self-propelled AA guns)
605th AT battalion
15th Panzer Division
General Gustav von Vaerst
8th panzer regiment (two battalions)
115th panzer grenadier regiment (three battalions)
33rd recce battalion
33rd motorized artillery regiment
1st art. battalion (1-3 art. batteries each with four 105mm howitzers)
2nd battalion (4-6 art. batteries each with four 105mm howitzers)

3rd art. battalion (7-9 art. batteries; 7 with four 105mm guns; 8 and 9 each with four 150mm howitzers)

33rd panzer jaeger battalion

33rd engineer battalion

support troops

21st Panzer Division
General Georg von Bismarck

5th panzer regiment (two battalions)

104th panzer grenadier regiment (two battalions)

3rd recce battalion

115th motorized artillery regiment (three battalions as above)

39th panzer jaeger battalion

200th engineer battalion

support troops

90th Light Afrika Motorized Infantry Division

288th "Sonderverband" panzer grenadier regiment

155th motorized infantry regiment

580th recon company (increases to battalion in July, 1942)

190th AT battalion

900th engineer battalion

606th army light AA battalion

361st Afrika artillery battalion

  three batteries of four 105mm field howitzers

  one battery of 12/120mm AA guns

  (may be 190th artillery regiment of two battalions with 16 105mm howitzers and eight 100mm guns)

support troops

(attached)

Fallschirmjaeger Lehr (Parachute) Battalion

  Approximately 1100-1200 men stationed at Martuba

(attached)

Hecker Amphibious unit

  Approximately 650 men or just over 800 if third San Marco company arrives

  3rd San Marco Battalion was in Africa. 373 men of two companies and possibly a third company (168 men) would have been used in the proposed operation

  778th Pioneer Landing Company (A German Amphibious Assault Engineer company numbering 73 men)

  13th company of the 800th Brandenburger Regiment (100 men, 60 of whom had lived in Palestine and spoke some Arabic)

  Vehicles: Three British tanks, either light Mk VI's, or medium Mk IV's. Also three armored car, and two SP guns

  Artillery included 13 47mm AT guns, three 50mm, six 37mm, and 4 2pdrs

Army Artillery

221st artillery regiment (Artillerie-Regiment 221 z.b.V.)

408th motorized heavy artillery battalion (three batteries of four 105mm guns (range of 16,200 yards)

2nd battalion of the 115th motorized heavy artillery regiment (two batteries of three 210mm howitzers; one battery of four 105mm Italian guns)

902nd motorized heavy artillery battery (three 170mm guns mounted on howitzer carriages)

8th Army
General Neil Ritchie

5th Indian Division

Divisional troops

10th Indian brigade group

2nd Highland Light Infantry

4th battalion 10th Baluch regiment

2nd battalion 4th Gurkha

28th Field Regiment Royal Artillery

11th Indian Brigade (arrived during the battle-from 4th Indian division)

2nd Cameron Highlanders

2nd 7th Gurkha

2nd 5th Mahratta Light Infantry

25th Field Regiment Royal Artillery (two batteries)

20th Indian Brigade (arrived during the battle - from 10th Indian division - 21st and 25th Indian brigades arrived later, also from 10th Indian division)

1st South Wales Borderers

1st 6th Raiputana Rifles

3rd Royal Garhwal

97th Field Regiment Royal Artillery

1st Free French brigade (five Free French infantry battalions, 1st Free French Field Artillery regiment, 22nd North African AT battery, 1st Fusiliers Marines AA battalon, and an attached Jewish unit)

2nd Free French brigade group (two battalions)

4th Hussars (a tank transfer unit at this point, joined 2nd Armor brigade in course of the fighting - from 1st Armored brigade along with 1st and 6th Royal Tank Regiments also arrived and used as replacements)

1st Duke of Cornwall's Light infantry (arrived June 5 during battle from Baghdad)

157th Field Regiment Royal Artillery

95th Royal Artillery AT regiment (-)?

149th Royal Artillery AT regiment?

Stationed at Tobruk were some miscellaneous troops and artillery.

Dencol, made up of South African, Free French, Middle East Commando, and Libyan Arab Force troops

XIII Army Corps
Lt. General "Stafer" Gott

Corps Troops
11th Hussars
7th Medium Regiment Royal Artillery
67th Medium Regiment, Royal Artillery (eight 4.5" field guns and eight 155mm howitzers) (assigned to 1st South Africa)
68th Medium Regiment, Royal Artillery (assigned to 1st South Africa)
73rd Regiment AT guns
one regiment heavy AA
three regiments of light AA

50th (Northumbrian) Infantry Division
69th Infantry brigade (three infantry battalions)
150th Indian Infantry brigade (three infantry battalions)
151st Infantry brigade (three infantry battalions)
74th Field Regiment Royal Artillery
72nd Field Regiment Royal Artillery
124th Field Regiment Royal Artillery
2nd Cheshire Machine gun battalion
(attached)
6th South African armored car

1st South African Division
Major General D. H. Pienaar
1st motorized infantry brigade (three infantry battalions)
2nd motorized infantry brigade (three infantry battalions)
3rd motorized infantry brigade (three infantry battalions)
3rd South African armored car battalion
2nd battalion regiment Botha
President Steyn machine gun regiment
B company of Die Middlandse machine gun regiment
1st South African Field Regiment artillery
4th South African Field Regiment artillery
5th South African Field Regiment artillery
7th South African Field Regiment artillery
1st South African AT regiment
2nd South African Light AA regiment
1st South African Light AA regiment

2nd South African Division
Major General D.B. Klopper
4th motorized infantry brigade (three infantry battalions)
6th motorized infantry brigade (three infantry battalions)
7th South African armored cars battalion
Die Middlandse machine gun regiment (-)
2nd South African Field Regiment artillery
3rd South African Field Regiment artillery
6th South African AT regiment
2nd South Afican Light AA regiment
(Attached)

9th Indian brigade group (from 5th Indian division)
   3rd Royal Frontier Force Rifles
   3rd 9th Jats
   2nd West Yorkshire
   4th Field Regiment Royal Artillery
   95th Royal Artillery AT battery
1st Army Tank Brigade
   8th Royal Tank Regiment (Valentine tanks)
   42nd Royal Tank Regiment (Matilda tanks)
   44th Royal Tank Regiment (Matilda tanks)
32nd Army Tank Brigade (arrived just as battle started)
   4th Royal Tank Regiment (Valentine tanks)
   7th Royal Tank Regiment (Valentine and Matilda tanks)

XXX Army Corps
Lt. General Willoughby M. Norrie

Corps Troops
1st Armored Division (Major-General H. Lumsden)
   Divisional troops
      2nd Royal Dragoons (armored cars) (assigned to 2nd Armored)
      12th Royal Lancers (armored cars) (assigned to 22nd Armored)
      divisional artillery
   2nd Armored brigade
      10th Hussars, 9th Lancers, Queen's Bays, (1/3rd Grant, 2/3rds
         Crusader tanks)
      1st Rifle Brigade
      11th Royal Horse Artillery regiment
   22nd Armored brigade
      3rd and 4th County of London Yeomanry, and 2nd Royal
         Gloucestershire Hussars, (1/3rd Grant, 2/3rds Stuart tanks)
      107th Royal Horse Artillery regiment
      50th Reconnaissance Battalion
   201st Guards Motor brigade (old 200th) (2nd Scots Guards, 3rd
      Coldstream Guards, and 9th Rifle Brigade. The 1st Sherwood
      Foresters and 1st Worcestshire reinforced them during the battle as
      did 2nd Royal Field Artillery)
7th Armored Division
General F. W. Messervy
Divisional troops
   102nd Royal Horse AT artillery
   1st King's Dragoon Guards
   15th light AA regiment
   61st AT regiment
(attached)
   4th South African armored car regiment
4th Armored Brigade
   8th Hussars, 3rd and 5th Royal Tanks (2/3rds Grant, 1/3rd Stuart
      tanks)

1st Royal Horse Artillery
1st Battalion King's Royal Rifle Corps
7th Motor brigade group
2nd Battalion King's Royal Rifle Corps
9th Battalion King's Royal Rifle Corps
2nd Battalion Rifle Brigade
4th Royal Horse Artillery (from Corps command)
3rd Indian Motor brigade group
1st Frontier Force, Prince Albert Victor's Own
2nd Royal Lancers (Gardner's House)
18th King Edward VII's Own
2nd Royal Indian Field artillery
29th Indian Motor brigade group (from 5th Indian division)
1st Worcestershire (later to 201st Guards)
1st Mahratta regiment
3rd of the 2nd Punjab
62nd Royal Field Artillery
3rd Field Regiment Royal Artillery
Mixed engineer (one squadron)

ORDER OF BATTLE ON 23 October, 1942

Armata Corazzata "Africa"
(Panzerarmee Afrika)
General Georg Stumme (temporary)

X Army Corps
General Enrico Frattini
Corps Troops
9th Bersaglieri regiment (two battalions)
49th/16th artillery battalion of 105/28mm guns
147th /816th artillery battalion of 149/28mm guns
31st demolition engineers battalion
Service troops
17th Pavia Infantry Division
27th infantry regiment (two battalions)
28th infantry regiment (two battalions)
26th artillery regiment
2nd battalion of 75/27mm
3rd battalion of 75/27mm
4th battalion of 75/27mm
401st and 404th batteries of 20mm AA
17th engineer regiment
27th Brescia Infantry Division
19th infantry regiment (two battalions)
20th infantry regiment (three battalions)
1st celere artillery regiment
1st battalion of 100/17 model 14

3rd battalion of 75/27mm
4th battalion of 75/27mm
5th battalion of 88/55 AA/AT
401st and 404th batteries of 20mm AA
27th engineer battalion
185th Folgore Parachute Division
186th infantry regiment (three battalions)
187th infantry regiment (three battalions)
185th artillery regiment
1st battalion of 47/32
2nd battalion of 47/32
8th demolition engineer battalion

XXIst Army Corps
General Alessandro Gloria (temporary)
7th Bersaglieri regiment (two battalions)
8th raggruppamento army artillery
33rd battalion of 149/40mm guns
52nd battalion of 152/37mm howitzers
131st battalion of 149/28mm guns
support troops
102nd Trento Motorized Infantry Division
61st motorized infantry regiment (three battalions)
62nd motorized infantry regiment (three battalions)
46th motorized artillery regiment
1st battalion of 100/17 model 14
2nd battalion of 100/17 model 14
3rd battalion of 75/27mm
4th battalion of 75/27mm
412th and 414th batteries of 20mm AA
51st engineer battalion
(attached)
4th battalion of Granatieri di Sardegna AT
355th battalion of 77/28mm guns
254th battalion of 77/27mm guns
25th Bologna Infantry Division
39th infantry regiment (three battalions (maybe two)
40th infantry regiment (three battalions)
205th artillery regiment
1st battalion of 100/17 model 14
2nd battalion of 100/17 model 14
3rd battalion of 75/27mm
4th battalion of 75/27mm
4th and 437th batteries of 20mm AA
25th engineer battalion

XX Army Corps
General Giuseppe De Stefanis
two companies of Bersaglieri
24th engineer battalion
one battery of 20mm AA from the 132nd artillery regiment
132nd Ariete Armored Division
132nd medium armor regiment (three battalions)
8th motorized Bersaglieri regiment (three battalions)
132nd motorized artillery regiment
1st battalion of 75/27mm guns
2nd battalion of 75/27mm guns
3rd of 105/28 of 105/28mm guns
31st battalion of 88/55mm AA/AT guns
15th of 105/28mm guns
501 battalion of 90/53mm and 20mm AA
5th battalion of semoventi (SP) 75/18mm howitzers
6th battalion of semoventi (SP) 75/18mm howitzers
3rd battalion of Nizza Cavalleria with armored cars
32nd motorized engineer battalion
133rd Littorio Armored Division
133rd medium armor regiment (three battalions of M tanks)
4th battalion
12th battalion
51st battalion
12th motorized Bersaglieri regiment (two battalions)
3rd celere artillery regiment
332nd of two battalion of 100/17mm howitzers
2nd/133rd of 75/27mm guns
29th battalion of 88/55mm AA/AT guns
5th battery of the 133rd regiment and 406th battery of 20mm AA
554th battalion of semoventi (SP) 75/18mm howitzers
556th battalion of semoventi (SP) 75/18mm howitzers
3rd battalion of Lancierie Novara with L6's
33rd engineer battalion
101st Trieste Motorized Infantry Division
65th motorized infantry regiment (two battalions)
66th motorized infantry regiment (three battalions)
21st motorized artillery regiment
1st battalion of 100/17mm howitzers
2nd battalion of 100/17mm howitzers
3rd 75/27mm guns
146th and 411th batteries of 20mm AA
8th Bersaglieri armored car battalion
11th battalion of M13 tanks
52nd engineer battalion

German Afrika Korps
General Wilhelm von Thoma
    19th Flak division HQ (Luftwaffe)
    288th "Sonderverband" panzer grenadier regiment HQ (two
      battalions) (Menton group)
    104th Artillery Command
    605th AT battalion (panzer jaeger)
(attached)
Giovani Fascisti Infantry Division
  two battalions
136th artillery regiment
    14th battalion of three batteries with 65/17mm guns
    15th battalion of three batteries with 65/17mm guns
    16th battalion of three batteries with 65/17mm guns
    17th battalion of two batteries with 100/17mm howitzers
    88th battery of 20mm AA
  9th independent infantry battalion
  15th engineer battalion
  3rd battalion of Monferrato armored cars
  (by December this unit was reinforced by the 8th Bersaglieri and three
    additional batteries of various calibers)
  support troops
15th Panzer Division
  8th panzer regiment (two battalions)
  115th panzer grenadier regiment (three battalions)
  33rd recce battalion
  33rd motorized artillery regiment (three battalions)
  33rd panzer jaeger battalion
  33rd engineer battalion
  support troops
21st Panzer Division
  5th panzer regiment (two battalions)
  104th panzer grenadier regiment (three battalions)
  3rd recce battalion
  155th motorized artillery regiment (three battalions)
  39th panzer jaeger battalion
  200th engineer battalion
  support troops
90th Light Afrika Motorized Infantry Division
  155th motorized infantry regiment (two battalions)
    Regimental HQ and HQ company
      motorized signal platoon
      motorized engineer platoon with three light MG's
      motorcycle platoon with six light MG's
    13th motorized infantry gun company (six 150mm guns and four
      75mm guns)
    14th engineer comapany (nine light MG's, three AT rifles, and six

75mm or 76.2mm AT guns
1st motorized infantry battalion
  battalion HQ
  four motorized infantry companies (each with 18 light MG's, two
    81mm mortars, one AT rifle, and six 75mm or 76.2mm AT guns
  2nd motorized infantry battalion (same as above)
200th motorized infantry regiment (two battalions same as above)
361st motorized infantry regiment (two battalions same as above
  except 13th infantry gun company has no 75mm infantry guns)
580th recon battalion
  Heavy armored car platoon (six AC with 75mm guns)
  Armored car company (24 armored cars)
  Armored Recon company (two heavy MG's, 18 light MG's, three AT
    rifles, and four AT 75mm or 76.2mm guns)
  Heavy Recon company
    Engineer platoon
    AT platoon with three self-propelled 75 of 76.2mm guns and three
      light MG's)
    Signal platoon
  Motorized artillery battery (four 105mm howitzers and two light
    MG's)
190th artillery regiment
  190th light AA company (12 motorized 20mm guns)
  1st motorized artillery battalion
    two motorized 105mm howitzer batteries and two light MGs
    one motorized 105mm gun battery and two light MGs
  2nd motorized artillery battalion (same)
190th armored battalion
  three light tank companies
  one medium tank company
900th motorized engineer battalion (two companies each with nine
  light MG's, three AT rifles, and three 50mm AT guns and one
  "Sturm" engineer company-no details)
190th AT battalion (two AT companies, each with nine 37mm AT guns
  and six light MG's)
190th armored signal battalion
support troops
164th Light Afrika Motorized Infantry Division
  125th motorized infantry regiment (two battalions)
    Regimental HQ and HQ company
      motorized signal platoon
      motorized engineer platoon with three light MG's
      motorcycle platoon with six light MG's
    13th motorized infantry gun company (six 150mm guns)
    14th engineer company (nine light MG's, three AT rifles, and six
      50mm AT guns)
    1st motorized infantry battalion

battalion HQ
four motorized infantry companies (each with 18 light MG's, two
    81mm mortars, three AT rifles, and six 75mm or 76.2mm AT guns
2nd motorized infantry battalion (same as above)
382nd motorized infantry regiment (two battalions same as above)
433rd motorized infantry regiment (two battalions same as above)
220th recon battalion
    Heavy Armored Car platoon (six AC with 75mm guns)
    Armored Car company (24 armored cars)
    Armored Recon company (two heavy MGs, 18 light MGs, three AT
        rifles, and four AT 75mm or 76.2mm guns)
    Heavy Recon company
        Engineer platoon
        AT platoon with three self-propelled 75 or 76.2mm guns and three
        light MG's
        Signal platoon
    Motorized artillery battery (four 105mm howitzers and two light
        MGs)
220th artillery regiment
    1st artillery battalion of three motorized batteries (each with four
        105mm field howitzers)
    2nd artillery battalion of two mountain batteries (each with four
        75mm pack guns)
220th engineer battalion (three companies each with nine light MGs,
    three AT rifles, and three 50mm AT guns)
220th AT battalion (two AT companies, each with nine 50mm AT guns
    and six light MGs)
220th armored signal battalion
Support troops
Ramcke Parachute Brigade
    4 battalions
    2nd Fallschirmjaeger Artillery Battalion 12 75mm Mountain guns
    AT company of 12 37mm guns

Commonwealth Order of Battle on 23 October, 1942

This is from Joslen's *Orders of Battle Second World War, 1939-1945* and from
Le Operazioni in Africa Settentrionale volume III

8th Army
General Bernard L. Montgomery

1st Army Tank brigade (Scorpion tanks)
12th AA brigade
2nd AA brigade
HQ protection included six armored cars and six tanks

X Army Corps
General Herbert Lumsden

Corps Troops
    Repair and service troops

1st Armored Division
    2nd Armored brigade (three battalions of armor and one motorized infantry)
    7th Motorized brigade (three battalions)
    12th Lancers (55 armored cars)
    2nd Royal Horse Artillery Regiment (24 25 pdrs)
    4th Royal Horse Artillery Regiment (24 25 pdrs)
    11th Royal Horse Artillery Regiment (24 105mm SP guns)
    78th Field Regiment Royal Artillery (24 25 pdrs)
    76th AT regiment (64 6 pdrs)
    42nd Light AA regiment (48 Bofors)
    Mixed engineer ad hoc (three Sqds, one company) (attached)
        Hammerforce:
            4/6 South Africa Armored Car regiment (55 armored cars)
            146th Field Regiment Royal artillery (24 25 pdrs)
            73rd AT regiment (48 6 pdrs)
            56th Light AA regiment

10th Armored Division
    8th Armored brigade (three battalions of tanks and one motorized infantry)
    24th Armored brigade (three battalions of tanks and one motorized infantry)
    133rd Lorried Infantry brigade (three battalions)
    Royal Dragoons (46 armored cars)
    1st Royal Horse Artillery Regiment (24 25 pdrs)
    104th Royal Horse Artillery Regiment (24 25 pdrs)
    84th Field Regiment Royal Artillery (24 25 pdrs)
    76th AT regiment (64 6 pdrs)
    42nd Light AA regiment (48 Bofors)
    Mixed engineer group (three squadrons and two companies) (attached)
        5th Royal Horse Artillery Regiment (24 25 pdrs)

XIII Army Corps
General Brian Horrocks

Corps Troops
    two Grants, 13 armored cars, 1 company engineers, 118th and 124th Royal Tank Regiments (dummy tanks), troop of 4/6th South African armored cars, repair, and service troops

7th Armored Division
    4th Light Armored brigade (two armor battalions and one motorized infantry)

22nd Motorized brigade (three armor battalions and one motorized infantry)
Household Cavalry (53 armored cars)
11th Hussars (61 armored cars)
2nd Derbyshire Yeomanry (50 armored cars)
3rd Royal Horse Artillery Regiment (24 25 pdrs)
4th Field Regiment Royal Artillery (16 25 pdrs)
97th Field Regiment Royal Artillery (16 25 pdrs)
65th AT Regiment (64 6 pdrs)
15th Light AA Regiment (48 Bofors)
Mixed engineer (two squadrons)
(attached)
    44th Recce Regiment from 44th Infantry
    two troops of Scorpion tanks
(under command of)
    1st Free French brigade group (three infantry battalions, 1st Free French (FF) artillery regiment (16 25 pdrs and 4 5.5" guns), 2nd AA company (12 Bofors), 2nd FF AT company (16 6 pdrs), 22nd North African AT company (2 75mm guns), 1 company engineers
(attached)
    3rd Field Regiment Royal Artillery (16 25 pdrs)
    1 FF Flying Column of a sqd of armored cars (Morocco Spahis), 1FF AT company (4 75mm guns, 1 50mm gun - portee troop 1 Morocco Spahis)
50th Infantry Division
    69th Infantry brigade (three infantry battalions)
    151st Infantry brigade (three infantry battalions)
    1st Greek infantry brigade group (three infantry battalions, 1st Greek Field regiment artillery (24 25 pdrs), 1 Greek machine gun company and one company of field engineers)
    74th Field Regiment Royal Artillery (16 25 pdrs)
    111th Field Regiment Royal Artillery (24 25 pdrs)
    124th Field Regiment Royal Artillery (16 25 pdrs)
    102nd AT Regiment (64 6 pdrs)
    34th Light AA Regiment (48 Bofors)
    Mixed engineer (two field companies)
(attached)
    154th Field Regiment Royal artillery (24 25 pdrs)
(under command of)
    2nd Free French brigade group (two infantry battalions, 21st North African AT company (12 75mm guns), 23rd North African AT company (4 75mm guns), 1 company engineers
44th Infantry Division
    131st Infantry brigade (three infantry battalions)
    132nd Infantry brigade (three infantry battalions)
    133rd detached to 10th Armored
    6th Cheshire machine gun battalion

57th Field Regiment Royal Artillery (24 25 pdrs)
58th Field Regiment Royal Artillery (24 25 pdrs)
65th Field Regiment Royal Artillery (24 25 pdrs)
57th AT Regiment (48 6 pdrs and 16 2 pdrs)
30th Light AA Regiment (48 Bofors)
Mixed engineer (three field companies)
(attached)
    53rd Field Regiment Royal Artillery (24 25 pdrs)
    one company of field engineers

XXX Army Corps
General Oliver Leese

Corps Troops
3 troops of 4/6 South African armored car regiment
7th Medium Regiment (8 4.5" and 8 5.5" guns)
64th Medium Regiment (8 4.5" and 8 5.5" guns)
69th Medium Regiment (16 4.5" guns)
(Corps Reserve) 46th Royal Tanks (49 Valentines)
121st Field Regiment Royal Artillery (16 25 pdrs SP), one battery light
  AA,
one company engineers
4th Indian Division (mountain capable)
5th Infantry brigade (three infantry battalions) (in Corps reserve)
7th Infantry brigade (three infantry battalions)
161st Infantry brigade (three infantry battalions)
1st Field Regiment Royal Artillery (16 25 pdrs)
11th Field Regiment Royal Artillery (16 25 pdrs)
32nd Field Regiment Royal Artillery (16 25 pdrs)
149th AT Regiment (54 6 pdrs and 10 2 pdrs)
57th Light AA Regiment (48 Bofors)
Mixed engineer (three field companies)
51st Highland Infantry Division
151st Infantry brigade (three infantry battalions)
152nd Infantry brigade (three infantry battalions)
153rd Infantry brigade (three infantry battalions)
126th Field Regiment Royal Artillery (24 25 pdrs)
127th Field Regiment Royal Artillery (24 25 pdrs)
128th Field Regiment Royal Artillery (24 25 pdrs)
61st AT Regiment (48 6 pdrs and 16 2 pdrs)
40th Light AA Regiment (48 Bofors)
Mixed engineer (three field companies)
(attached)
    50th Royal Tanks of 23rd Armored Brigade (44 Valentines)
    one company of field engineers
9th Australian Division
20th Infantry Brigade (three infantry battalions)
24th Infantry Brigade (three infantry battalions)
26th Infantry Brigade (three infantry battalions)

9th Australian Divisional Cavalry (28 Crusader tanks)
2/2 Australian machine gun battalion
2/7th Australian Field regiment artillery (24 25 pdrs)
2/8th Australian Field regiment artillery (24 25 pdrs)
2/12th Australian Field regiment artillery (24 25 pdrs)
3rd Australian AT regiment (64 4 pdrs)
4th Australian Light AA regiment (48 Bofors)
Mixed engineer (three field companies and one pioneer battalion)
(attached)
    40th Royal Tanks of 23rd Armored brigade (42 Valentines)
2nd New Zealand Division
    5th Infantry brigade (four infantry battalions)
    6th Infantry brigade (three infantry battalions)
    9th Armored brigade (three armor battalions and one motorized
        infantry battalion)
    2nd New Zealand Divisional Cavalry (29 Stuart tanks)
    27th New Zealand machine gun battalion
    4th New Zealand Field regiment artillery (24 25 pdrs
    5th New Zealand Field regiment artillery (24 25 pdrs)
    6th New Zealand Field regiment artillery (24 25 pdrs)
    7th New Zealand AT regiment (59 6 pdrs)
    14th New Zealand Light AA regiment (48 Bofors)
    Mixed engineer (three field companies)
1st South African Division
    1st Infantry brigade (three infantry battalions)
    2nd Infantry brigade (three infantry battalions)
    3rd Infantry brigade (three infantry battalions)
    3rd South African armored car regiment (55 cars)
    President Steyn machine gun regiment
    one company of Die Middlandse machine gun regiment
    1st South African Field regiment artillery (24 25 pdrs)
    4th South African Field regiment artillery (24 25 pdrs)
    7th South African Field regiment artillery (24 25 pdrs)
    1st South African AT regiment (48 6 pdrs, 16 2 pdrs, 3 18 pdrs, 6 50mm)
    1st South African Light AA regiment (48 Bofors)
    Mixed engineer (four field companies)
    (attached)
        8th Royal Tanks of 23rd Armored brigade (51 Valentines)

Index